Sir Thomas ELYOT
and Roger ASCHAM

a reference guide

A
Reference
Guide
to
Literature

Jim Harner
Editor

Sir Thomas ELYOT
and Roger ASCHAM

a reference guide

JEROME STEELE DEES

G.K.HALL&CO.

70 LINCOLN STREET, BOSTON, MASS.

Library of Congress Cataloging in Publication Data

Dees, Jerome Steele.
  Sir Thomas Elyot and Roger Ascham, a reference guide.

  (A Reference guide to literature)
  Includes indexes.
  1. English prose literature—Early modern, 1500-
1700—History and criticism—Bibliography. 2. Elyot,
Thomas, Sir, 1490?-1546—Bibliography. 3. Ascham,
Roger, 1515-1568—Bibliography. I. Title. II. Series:
Reference guides to literature.
Z2014.P795D43   [PR767]   016.94205'2'0922   80-26951
ISBN 0-8161-8353-8   AACR1

This publication is printed on permanent/durable acid-free paper
MANUFACTURED IN THE UNITED STATES OF AMERICA

Contents

Preface vii

Acknowledgments ix

Introduction. xi

Abbreviations xv

Writings About Sir Thomas Elyot (ca. 1490-1546) 1

Writings About Roger Ascham (1515?-1568) 67

Addendum 157

Index to Elyot 159

Index to Ascham 171

THE AUTHOR: Jerome S. Dees received his B.A. from Catawba College,
his M.A. from Florida State University, and his Ph.D. from the University of Illinois at Urbana-Champaign. He has taught at Clemson
University, The University of New Hampshire, and Virginia Commonwealth University. He is currently Associate Professor of English
and Director of Graduate Studies at Kansas State University. His
publications include articles on Spenser, Milton, Sir Thomas Elyot,
Roger Ascham, Thomas Traherne, and Giles Fletcher, appearing in
Studies in Philology, Anglia, English Literary Renaissance, and
Texas Studies in Literature and Language.

Preface

In these two bibliographies I have sought to keep in mind the needs
of two different readers: the specialist who wishes to know handily
what has been written about Elyot or Ascham, and the more general
student or the cultural historian, who might be interested in either
man's later reputation or in such questions as "Who was writing
about Elyot or Ascham in the late nineteenth century, for what purpose, and for whom?" Mindful of the first reader, I have tried not
to burden either list with very brief general discussions; I have,
for example, examined and excluded over sixty items from Tannenbaum's bibliography (Ascham 1946.1). Mindful of the second reader,
however, I have included brief general discussions when in my esti-
mation they express the judgments of important critics or historians
(men of the stature of Johnson, Henry Hallam, W. C. Hazlitt,
Jusserand, or Saintsbury) or when they have appeared in books,
journals, or dictionaries of a sort to mold public taste (e.g.,
Dictionary of National Biography, Cambridge and Oxford histories of
literature, The American Journal of Education, or Times Literary
Supplement). I have tried to make the annotations indicate which
items are suitable for which reader.

My aim has been to make both lists inclusive through 1979 (with
the single exception of my own "Recent Studies in Ascham" [1980.1]),
and as complete as possible consistent with the principles of the
preceding paragraph. Although this is a bibliography of writings
about Elyot and Ascham, I have included all editions which contain
introductory matter and, in a few instances (e.g., Ascham 1904.1),
important editions lacking an introduction. (See "Editions" in
the Index.) I omit several recent photo-reproductions of early
editions lacking apparatus. I have also included all bibliographies
I am aware of, even when they have been superseded by National Union
Catalog or Tannenbaum. (See "Bibliographies" in the Index.)

In the case of oft-reprinted eighteenth- and nineteenth-century
studies, I have annotated the edition that I was able to obtain by
inter-library loan, indicating at the end of the annotation the date
of the first publication and providing a separate entry at the

original date. For photo-reproductions I give reprint information at the date of first publication, without a separate entry. I have included Ph.D. dissertations and Master's theses, as well as some reviews of editions and major scholarly works. Works not seen are marked by an asterisk, with sources of reference in the annotation.

Ascham has frequently appeared as a character in fictional treatments of Lady Jane Grey. I have included all of these save one (1946.1, no. 160; merely a two-line allusion) on the grounds of their potential interest to cultural historians. For a few items that I found difficult to obtain I provide location information.

Acknowledgments

Most of my reading for this work was done in the Farrell Library at
Kansas State University and the Watson Memorial and Spencer Research
Libraries at the University of Kansas. Although many of the librar-
ians who assisted me remain unknown, I wish in particular to thank
Ellyn Taylor, Inter-Library Loan Librarian at Kansas State, and her
assistants Ginger Rogers and Linda Tanner. Without their patience,
good will, resourcefulness, and at times ingenuity, this work would
have floundered in a sea of "not seen's." I am grateful also to
Alexandra Mason, Special Collections Librarian at the Spencer Research Library, and to her assistants, for giving much time to
tracing down incomplete citations. I have received invaluable
assistance from Louise Sherby of the Columbia University Library;
John Gabel and Edwin Robbins, former colleagues at Ohio State,
located obscure works in the library there; and Leland and Ann
Warren gave up part of a trip to London to secure otherwise
impossible-to-get items.

My research assistant, Kathleen Oberle, spent numberless hours
tracing and retracing the aisles of library stacks to retrieve and
return books; patiently filling out inter-library loan request
forms; and capably checking and double-checking bibliographies and
catalogues. Without Brian Graul's assistance in translating
nineteenth-century German dissertations and articles, this work
would be appearing some months later than it is. And through the
sharpsightedness and bibliographical expertise of my field editor,
James L. Harner, not only was I spared some embarrassing omissions,
but I have been able to give the work a consistency of format that
it otherwise would have lacked.

I wish to acknowledge receipt of a research grant from the
Graduate College at Kansas State University, which allowed me to
hire a research assistant and paid for travel and supplies.

To Sandra Worcester I owe a particular debt of gratitude, not
only for producing the final typescript, but for patiently, and with

Acknowledgments

good humor, retyping page after page to correct my oversights—and
all this under the pressure of a deadline. My final thanks go to
my wife, Diann, for performing that most thankless of the book-
maker's tasks—proofreading.

Introduction

That Elyot and Ascham should have been almost as inseparably linked
in the minds of students of the Renaissance as Wyatt and Surrey is
in part the fault of history. The two men probably knew one another
(Ascham records having once asked Elyot a question about archery);
each served in important governmental capacities throughout most of
his adult life, including embassies to the court of the Emperor
Charles V (Elyot as ambassador, Ascham only as the ambassador's
private secretary); each weathered, not without taint to his personal integrity, periods of political and religious upheaval; each,
considered by his peers both wise and learned, contributed significantly to the dissemination of Greek and Roman thought in England
in the sixteenth century; and each added materially to the budding
of an English prose style that was to flower in Sidney, Hooker,
Bacon, and Browne. That they should continue to be so linked will
probably be an unfortunate side-effect of this Reference Guide.
Each deserves to stand on his own merits and to be recognized for
his distinctiveness as a writer and as an important--even if minor--
figure in the history of English letters.

Except perhaps in his own century and in the past twenty-five
years, Ascham's reputation, both critical and popular, has always
been more secure than Elyot's, despite the fact that he published
considerably fewer works on a considerably narrower range of subjects. One test of this security is the number and quality of
editions of the two men's works and of substantial biographies. To
take the most important work of each, whereas Ascham's Scholemaster
has been reprinted on an average of once a generation since 1711
(1711, 1743, 1761, 1815, 1863, 1864, 1870, 1895, 1900, 1904, 1934,
1966, 1967), Elyot's Governour did not see its first modern edition,
and that a bad one, until 1834, to be followed by only Croft's edition of 1880 and "Everyman" editions of 1907 and 1962. Similarly,
whereas Ascham's biography in standard eighteenth- and nineteenth-
century biographical dictionaries (oft-repeated and oft-plagiarized)
typically ran to between four and eight thousand words and was
relatively accurate (see 1747.1 and 1812.1), Elyot's was normally
about one-fourth that length, with a high degree of error in both

biographical fact and the attribution of works (see 1750.1, 1814.1).
Much of this disparity, of course, comes from the fact that Ascham
left a wealth of biographical material in nearly two hundred letters, as opposed to twelve of Elyot's which survive. Aside from
the availability of information, however, the fact remains that
fewer people knew about or were interested in Elyot. Nothing perhaps illustrates this better than the entries for the two men from
the 1850s. While the pages of Notes and Queries and other journals
reflected the scholarly ferment preceding Mayor's and Giles's great
editions of the sixties (Ascham 1863.4 and 1864.1), C. H. Cooper was
responding in Notes and Queries to a reader requesting, in effect,
"anything you can tell me about Elyot" (1853.1).

Standard histories of English literature and of education provide not only another index of the relative reputation of the two
men but also some insight into how they were perceived. While
Ascham nearly always merits some treatment in both kinds of history,
even the most general, Elyot often goes unnoticed or appears merely
by name. Hallam is virtually alone before the present generation in
claiming that Elyot is "worthy to hold a higher place than Ascham"
(Elyot 1855.2). From the mid-eighteenth century until the early
twentieth, historians of education tended to view the two men differently. While customarily judging Ascham's pedagogical theory in
terms of its current applicability or value, they saw Elyot exclusively from a historical or antiquarian perspective; pedagogically,
one was a live writer, the other dead. A notable exception is
Foster Watson (1907.1). Elyot fares somewhat better in histories of
literature, and when the discussion touches on prose style, as it
occasionally does, he might stand his own ground. But more common
is the view either that he is a "connecting link" between More and
Ascham (see 1893.1) or that Governour (often the only one of his
works discussed as literature) "must now be condemned to the soli-
tary imprisonment of the antiquary's cell" (1881.1). In general,
those historians or critics who know works other than Governour,
Dictionary, and Castel have given him higher marks (e.g., Brink,
1896.1).

Still another mark of the relative reputation of the two men is
in the number of studies by foreign scholars. Elyot shows nothing
comparable to what seems at times a German industry in Ascham mono-
graphs. Again, this difference can be partly explained by Ascham's
having written Report; but only partly, for there are notably fewer
critical studies of Elyot in French or Italian. Only of Ascham can
we say that until 1963 the most authoritative biography was in German and that still today the most complete book-length study is in
Italian. Elyot has no bibliography comparable to Tannenbaum's for
Ascham (1946.1).

The standard editions of Ascham and Elyot date respectively
from 1864 and 1880, and though Wright's edition of Ascham's English
Works (1904.1) accurately transcribes the texts of the first editions,

we do not have a published critical edition of any work of either
man that will meet the exacting demands of today's textual scholars;
however, critical editions of several of Elyot's works have been
recently produced as doctoral dissertations (1964.3, 1970.5,
1971.4-5) as has one of Ascham's Toxophilus (1974.3).

Both men have been well served by sympathetic and competent
biographers from Giles (Ascham 1864.1) and Croft (Elyot 1880.1)
down to Ryan (Ascham 1963.3) and Lehmberg (Elyot 1960.2; supplemented by 1967.3). They have fared less well at the hands of literary critics. Although much attention has been given to the two
men's prose style, it has been for the most part piece-meal,
sketchy, and derivative. Apart from two unpublished doctoral
dissertations on Ascham (1970.2 and 1971.3), no one has looked
systematically at all of the prose of either man.

Historically, critical interest in both men has exhibited similar patterns, although they are more pronounced in the case of
Ascham. From the time of Johnson to the mid-nineteenth century,
discussion is dominated by what might be called "soft" biography, a
concern to see the man's personality in the context of sweeping
generalizations about the Renaissance or about human nature. This
impulse gives way after about 1850 to "hard" biography, a concern to
recover documents and establish facts with greater accuracy. From
the 1860s, until about 1940, criticism of Ascham was dominated by
educational historians, abetted by literary historians whose major
interest was in the vigor of his prose. During the same period
Elyot was seen as the author of either Governour or Dictionary; in
the first guise he brought knowledge and Italian culture to a still
"primitive" nation, while in the second he enriched an impoverished
language. Criticism of both men since the 1940s has turned more
exclusively to such literary matters as style, structure, sources,
and influence. Much remains to be done.

For Elyot there is yet no satisfactory account of the structural
principles of Governour. Critics seem to assume that such principles must reside in Elyot's sources rather than come from a creative
mind acting upon traditions. Despite a large quantity of research
in this century, our knowledge of Elyot's contributions to the
vocabulary of sixteenth-century English is still imprecise and contradictory. A thorough assessment of his place among the great
sixteenth-century translators is overdue. Elyot's contribution to
the development of early legal theory is virtually unbroken ground;
nor are we much farther along in understanding his place in the
history of naturalism and medicine. The immense popularity of
Castel has prompted no full study of its aims and accomplishments.
The most pressing need, however, remains reliable critical editions
of his works.

Ascham is somewhat better off. Within the last ten years major
reassessments have begun on several fronts. The articles of Salamon

(1973.3-4), Strozier (1973.5), Vos (1974.5; 1976.3, 5), and Wilson (1976.6) address fundamental questions about his style, his literary relationships, and the structure of his major works. In the civic applications of his erudition, Ascham stands comparison with the great philologists of the Italian Renaissance; his connections with Italy need further study. He is yet to be appreciated adequately as a theoretician and practitioner of the writing of history. We understand imperfectly the dynamics of and the implicit literary theory behind such "unfinished" works as Scholemaster and Report; understanding their unfinished state will have implications for the great unfinished "histories" of Sidney and Spenser. The nature and extent of Ascham's influence on Sidney and Hooker is still not known. Much work remains to be done on the Ascham manuscripts. We need perhaps more than all else a complete and accurate critical edition of the letters, with translations. Such an edition would not only enable us to gauge Ascham's accomplishment as a letter-writer, but would help us assess more satisfactorily his prose style.

Abbreviations

ADD   American Doctoral Dissertations. Compiled for the Association of Research Libraries. Ann Arbor: University Microfilms International, 1967-

BM   British Museum General Catalogue of Printed Books. Photolithographic Edition to 1955. London: Trustees of The British Museum, 1965.

CL   Comparative Literature

DDAU   Doctoral Dissertations Accepted by American Universities. New York: H. W. Wilson Co., 1934-55

EA   Études Anglaises

ELH   Journal of English Literary History

ELN   English Language Notes

ELR   English Literary Renaissance

ES   English Studies

HLQ   Huntington Library Quarterly

Index   Index to Theses Accepted for Higher Degrees in the Universities of Great Britain and Ireland. London: Aslib, 1953-

JEGP   Journal of English and Germanic Philology

JHI   Journal of the History of Ideas

MLN   Modern Language Notes

MLQ   Modern Language Quarterly

MLR   Modern Language Review

MP   Modern Philology

N&Q   Notes and Queries

NM   Neuphilologische Mitteilungen

NUC   National Union Catalog: Pre-1956 Imprints. Chicago and
            London: Mansell, 1969-

PBSA   Papers of the Bibliographical Society of America

PMLA   PMLA: Publications of the Modern Language Association
            of America

PQ   Philological Quarterly

RenQ   Renaissance Quarterly

RES   Review of English Studies

SP   Studies in Philology

SQ   Shakespeare Quarterly

TLS   Times Literary Supplement (London)

UTSE   University of Texas Studies in English (title appears
            variously as Texas University Studies in English and
            Texas Studies in English)

UTQ   University of Toronto Quarterly

Throughout I use the following abbreviated titles for Elyot's and
Ascham's works.

Elyot:

Bankette   The Bankette of Sapience. 1534? 1539

Bibliotheca   Bibliotheca Eliotae. 1542

Castel   The Castel of Helth. 1534? 1539

Defence   The Defence of Good Women. 1540

Dialogue   A Dialogue betweene Luciane and Diogenes. 1528?
                  (attributed to Elyot)

Dictionary   The Dictionary of Syr Thomas Elyot. 1538

Doctrinal   The Doctrinal of Princes. 1533

Education   The Education or Bringinge Up of Children. 1533

Governour   The Boke Named the Governour. 1531

Hermathena   P. Gemini Eleatis Hermathena. 1522 (attributed
                to Elyot)

Image   The Image of Governance. 1541

Knowledge   Of the Knowledeg [sic] Which Maketh a Wise Man.
                1533

Pasquil   Pasquil the Playne. 1533

Preservative   A Preservative agaynste Deth. 1545

Profit   Howe One May Take Profit of His Enemyes. 1533?

Rule   The Rule of a Christen Life Made by Picus Erle of
                Mirandula. 1534 (published with Sermon)

Sermon   A Swete and Devoute Sermon of Sayngt Ciprian. 1534
                (published with Rule)

Ascham:

Apologia   Apologia . . . pro Caena Domenica. 1577

Epistolarum   Dissertissimi Viri Rogeri Aschami Angli . . .
                Familiarum Epistolarum Libri Tres. 1576

Oecumenius   "Oecumenius's Commentaries on Paul's Epistles to
                Philemon and Titus." 1543 (manuscript transla-
                tions)

Report   A Report and Discourse Written by Roger Ascham of
                the Affaires and State of Germany and the Em-
                peror Charles His Court. 1570?

Scholemaster   The Scholemaster, or Plaine and Perfite Way of
                Teachying Children, to Understand, Write and
                Speake, the Latine Tong. 1570

Themata   Themata Theologica. 1577

Toxophilus   Toxophilus, the Schoole of Shootinge Conteyned in
                Two Bookes. 1545

Sir Thomas Elyot
(ca. 1490-1546)

Writings About Sir Thomas Elyot

1662

*1   FULLER, THOMAS. The History of the Worthies of England.
      Endeavored by Thomas Fuller. London: Printed by
      J. G. W. L. and W. G.
         See 1840.1.

1684

1   [FULLER, THOMAS.] Anglorum Speculum: Or the Worthies of
      England in Church and State. Alphabetically Digested into
      the Several Shires and Counties Therein Contained; Wherein
      Are Illustrated the Lives and Characters of the Most Emi-
      nent Persons since the Conquest to This Present Age.
      London: John Wright, Thomas Passinger, and William
      Thackery, p. 96.
         "Preface" signed "G. S." [George Sandys]; so cited in
      Wing and catalogued in some libraries. Categorizes Elyot
      as a "noted sheriff" and lists only Defence and Dictionary
      among his works. Essentially the same as 1840.1.

1691

*1   WOOD, ANTHONY à. Athenae Oxonienses: An Exact History of All
      the Writers and Bishops Who Have Had Their Education in the
      Most Ancient and Famous University of Oxford. Printed for
      Tho. Bennett.
         See 1813.1.

1721

*1   STRYPE, JOHN. Ecclesiastical Memorials, Relating Chiefly to
      Religion, and the Reformation of It. London: Printed for
      J. Wyat.
         See 1822.1.

1750

1   Biographia Britannica: Or, the Lives of the Most Eminent
    Persons Who Have Flourished in Great Britain and Ireland,
    from the Earliest Ages, Down to the Present Times . . .
    Digested in the Manner of Mr. Bayle's Historical and
    Critical Dictionary. Vol. 3. London: W. Innys et al.,
    pp. 1840–41.
       A brief life, with emphasis on Elyot's university
    education, and calling him "an excellent Grammarian, Poet,
    Rhetorician, Philosopher, Physician, Cosmographer, and
    Historian." Footnotes list his works and quote Leland's
    commendatory verses in De Rebus Britannia Collectanea
    (Oxford, 1715).

1784

1   A New and General Biographical Dictionary; Containing an
    Historical and Critical Account of the Lives and Writings
    of the Most Eminent Persons in Every Nation; Particularly
    the British and Irish. Vol. 5. New Edition . . . Greatly
    Enlarged and Improved. London: Printed for W. Strahan et
    al., pp. 86–87.
       Routine brief life and list of works.

1811

*1 Biographie universelle ancienne et moderne, ou histoire, par
    ordre alphabétique. Paris: Michaud.
       See 1855.1.

1813

1   WOOD, ANTHONY à. Athenae Oxonienses. An Exact History of All
    the Writers and Bishops Who Have Had Their Education in the
    University of Oxford. To Which Are Added the Fasti, or
    Annals of the Said University. Vol. 1. New Edition, with
    Additions, and a Continuation by Philip Bliss. London:
    F. C. and J. Rivington, et al., cols. 150–53.
       Claims to "find one Tho. Elyot to be admitted . . . to
    the degree of bach. of arts, and in the time of Lent the
    same year, 1518, he did compleat that degree by determina-
    tion in school-street." Thus important for the controversy
    over whether Elyot had a university education. See
    Lehmberg (1960.2) pp. 12–14. First edition, 1691.1.

1814

1   CHALMERS, ALEXANDER. The General Biographical Dictionary:
    Containing an Historical and Critical Account of the Lives
    and Writings of the Most Eminent Persons in Every Nation.
    Vol. 13. New Edition, Revised and Enlarged. London:
    Printed for J. Nichols & Son, et al., pp. 175-78. Reprint.
    New York: AMS Press, Inc.; Kraus Reprint Co., 1969.
        In contrast to the relative accuracy of the Ascham
    biography (see Ascham, 1812.1), contains a high incidence
    of error and legend (e.g., the 1535 second embassy to
    Charles V). Quotes 1536 letter to Cromwell, but omits the
    infamous statement about More. Of Governour, says that
    it "consisted of several chapters, treating concerning
    affability, benevolence, beneficence, the diversity of
    flatterers, and other similar subjects." Discussion of
    Castel limited to its effect on college of Physicians.
    Characterizes Elyot as "excellent grammarian, rhetorician,
    philosopher, physician, cosmographer, and historian."

1815

1   BRYDGES, SIR [SAMUEL] EGERTON, ed. Censura Literaria: Con-
    taining Titles, Abstracts, and Opinions of Old English
    Books, with Original Disquisitions, Articles of Biography,
    and Other Literary Antiquities, Vol. 5. 2d ed. London:
    Longman, Hurst, Rees, Orme & Brown, pp. 414-28.
        Summary accounts of Castel and Preservative, with quo-
    tations to illustrate Elyot's "manner and reasoning."
    First edition, 1805-9.

1822

1   STRYPE, JOHN. Ecclesiastical Memorials, Relating Chiefly to
    Religion, and the Reformation of It, and the Emergencies
    of the Church of England under King Henry VIII, King Edward
    VI, and Queen Mary I. Vol. 1, part 1. Oxford: Clarendon
    Press, pp. 341-46.
        An appreciative digression from the main business of
    chronicling the religious history of the reign of Henry
    VIII; calls Elyot "one of the learnedest and wisest men of
    this time," and comments on Governour, Knowledge, and
    Castel, closing with quotations illustrative of Elyot's
    "wisdom." This is Vol. 13 of Strype's Collected Works,
    1820-40. First edition, 1721.1.

1824

1 DIBDIN, THOMAS FROGNALL. The Library Companion: Or, the
Young Man's Guide, and the Old Man's Comfort, in the Choice
of a Library. London: Printed for Harding, Triphook &
Leophard, pp. 585-86.
In enumerating the works of Elyot, generalizes in a
phrase or sentence the merit of each, and indicates a location; gives for some the probable cost of a "good copy."

2 WATT, ROBERT. Bibliotheca Britannica; or a General Index to
British and Foreign Literature. Vol. 1. Edinburgh:
Archibald Constable & Co.; London: Longman, Hurst, Rees,
Brown & Green, pp. 335-36.
Printing history of Governour, Pasquil, Doctrinal,
Sermon, Rule, Castel, Dictionary, Image, Defense, Biblio-
theca, Bankette, Preservative, Education, De Rebus, and a
work which Watt titles An Introduction to Wisedom (London,
1540), almost certainly Knowledge.

1832

1 VARRO [Isaac Disraeli]. "Of the Three Earliest Authors in
our Vernacular Literature," The New Monthly Magazine and
Literary Journal 35 (August): 114-24.
The other two authors are More and Ascham. Emphasizes
the difficulties of being a writer in Elyot's time, that
is, the hard reception which Governour and Castel got.
Claims for him a "confidential" embassy to Rome to nego-
tiate the divorce of Catherine. Discusses at some length
Elyot's letters to Cromwell seeking monastic lands and
sees his famous reference to More as "Peter denying his
Master." Essentially the same as 1841.1 and 1881.1.

1834

*1 LOWNDES, WILLIAM THOMAS. The Bibliographer's Manual of Eng-
lish Literature, Containing an Account of Rare, Curious,
and Useful Books. London: W. Pickering.
See 1871.1.

1837

*1   HALLAM, HENRY.   Introduction to the Literature of Europe, in
      the Fifteenth, Sixteenth, and Seventeenth Centuries.
      London: J. Murray.
        See 1855.2.

1840

1   FULLER, THOMAS.   The History of the Worthies of England.
      Vol. 1.   New ed.   Edited by P. Austin Nuttall.   London:
      Printed for Thomas Tegg, p. 257.   Reprint.   New York: AMS
      Press, 1965.
        Brief biography, noteworthy for omitting Governour,
      naming only Defense and Dictionary among Elyot's "many
      excellent works."   Claims Elyot "skilled" in Greek.   First
      edition, 1662.1.   See also 1684.1.

1841

*1   DISRAELI, ISAAC.   "The Difficulties Experienced by a Primitive
      Author."   In Amenities of Literature, Consisting of
      Sketches and Characters of English Literature.   London:
      E. Moxon.
        See 1881.1.

1843

*1   ANON.   "Sir Thomas Elyot."   In Cyclopaedia of English Litera-
      ture: Consisting of a Series of Specimens of British
      Writers in Prose and Verse.   Edinburgh: W. and R. Chambers.
        See 1901.2.

1853

1   COOPER, C[HARLES] H[ENRY].   "Sir Thomas Elyot."   N&Q 8
      (17 September): 276.
        Responding to a query (p. 220), cites fourteen works
      giving "particulars respecting this once celebrated dip-
      lomat and scholar."   Claims that Sir Richard Elyot was of
      Wiltshire, not Suffolk, and cites documents.

1855

1 Biographie universelle (Michaud) ancienne et moderne, ou
    histoire, par ordre alphabétique, de la vie publique et
    privée de tous les hommes qui se sont fait remarquer par
    leurs écrits, leurs actions, leurs vertus ou leurs crimes.
    Vol. 13. New ed. Paris: Chez Madame C. Desplaces et
    Chez M. Michaud, p. 426.
      Intriguing for the volume of misinformation it conveys
    in some 320 words. Of all Elyot's works, Dictionary is
    "le seul qui soit connu aujourd'hui." First edition,
    1811.1.

2 HALLAM, HENRY. Introduction to the Literature of Europe, in
    the Fifteenth, Sixteenth, and Seventeenth Centuries.
    Vol. 1. 5th ed. London: John Murray, pp. 406-8.
      Treats Elyot in a chapter on "Moral and Political
    Philosophy," calling him "equal perhaps in learning and
    sagacity to any scholar of the age of Henry VIII" and
    "worthy . . . to hold a higher place than Ascham," to whom
    he bears resemblance. Earliest dated edition, 1837.1.

1858

1 COOPER, CHARLES HENRY, and COOPER, THOMPSON. "Thomas Elyot."
    In Athenae Cantabrigienses. Vol. 1. 1500-1585. Cambridge:
    Deighton, Bell & Co.; London: Bell & Daldy, pp. 89-90.
      Claims "good evidence" that Elyot was educated at Jesus
    College, Cambridge and not St. Mary's Hall, Oxford (com-
    pare 1813.1). Emphasizes Elyot's monetary problems
    caused by service to the King and sees him as a "time
    server" in his relations to More, Tyndale, and Wolsey.
    Closes with a list of Elyot's works, including disputed
    ones, and a description of his arms.

1859

*1 GRAESSE, JEAN GEORGE THÉODORE [Graesse, Johann Georg Theodor].
    Trésor des livres rares et précieux, ou nouveau diction-
    naire bibliographique. Dresden: R. Kuntze, et al.
      See 1950.1.

1866

1   ANON.   "Sir Thomas Elyot."   The American Journal of Education
16 [n.s. 6], no. 44 (September): 483-96.
An eclectic introduction, consisting of a brief biography; a list of publications taken from Biographia
Brittanica (1750.1), with that work's commentary on Castel;
an analytical account of Book I of Governour, indicating
its general aim and plan, and containing sections on music,
painting, carving, poetry, oratory, and muscular exercises;
and, finally, brief paragraphs sketching the contents of
Books II and III.   Watson (1907.1) claims that this is a
translation from Karl Georg von Raumer's Geschichte der
Pädagogik (4 vols. Stuttgart: S. G. Liesching, 1846-54),
but this is nowhere indicated in Journal, nor do I find
any extended passage on Elyot in Raumer.

1871

1   LOWNDES, WILLIAM THOMAS, and BOHN, HENRY G.   The Bibliographer's Manual of English Literature, Containing an Account
of Rare, Curious, and Useful Books, Published in or Relating to Great Britain and Ireland.   Vol. 1.   New Edition,
Revised, Corrected and Enlarged.   London: Bell and Daldy,
p. 736.
Lists Dictionary, Governour, Pasquil, Knowledge, Castel,
Image, Bankette, Preservative, Defence, with publishing
history where applicable.   First edition, 1834.1.

1878

1   ANON.   "Elyot, Sir Thomas.   In The Encyclopaedia Britannica:
A Dictionary of Arts, Sciences, and General Literature.
Vol. 8.   9th ed.   New York: Samuel L. Hall, p. 156.
Surveys evidence for Elyot's having "evidently received
a university education."   Contains misspellings of names
(e.g. Tynderne for Fynderne), and dating errors, both for
events in Elyot's life and publications of his works.
Elyot's fame rests on Governour and Dictionary.   Compare
1929.1 and 1975.1.

2   MORLEY, HENRY. "Elyot's Governour." In Sketches of Longer
    Works in English Verse and Prose, Selected, Edited and
    Arranged. Cassell's Library of English Literature.
    London, Paris & New York: Cassell, Petter, Galpin & Co.,
    pp. 278-81.
        Abstract of the contents of Governour, introduced by
    brief commentary on Elyot's life and works.

1880

1   CROFT, HENRY HERBERT STEPHEN. "Life of Elyot," in his edition
    of The Boke Named the Governour. Vol. 1. London: Kegan
    Paul, Trench & Co., pp. xix-clxxxix.
        The first modern scholarly biography of Elyot. Supplies
    new evidence regarding Elyot's birthplace and connections
    between Elyot, Fyndern, and Fetiplace families, and cor-
    rects several errors in previous "lives." Spends consid-
    erable time defending Elyot against various charges by
    previous biographers: for example, that he was a time-
    server, that he denied his friendship with More, that he
    plagiarized Image. Perpetuates other errors, however, by
    providing "evidence" to prove that Elyot was on the conti-
    nent in July 1535, and by constructing a lengthy argument
    showing Richard Puttenham the author of Arte of English
    Poesie. Sees Governour as primarily a treatise on moral
    philosophy and notes the "remarkable similarity in plan"
    between it and Patrizi's De Regno (see 1938.3-4 and 1950.4.)
    Quotes liberally from Elyot's letters throughout.

1881

1   DISRAELI, ISAAC. "The Difficulties Experienced by a Primitive
    Author." In Amenities of Literature, Consisting of Sketches
    and Characters of English Literature. Vol. 1. New ed.,
    edited by the Earl of Beaconsfield. London and New York:
    Frederick Warne & Co., pp. 268-75.
        A mild depreciation of a man in whom "we detect the
    aberrations of a mind intent on a great popular design,
    but still vague and uncertain, often opposed by contempo-
    raries, yet cheered by the little world of his readers."
    The Governour "must now be condemned to the solitary im-
    prisonment of the antiquary's cell." Essentially the same
    as 1832.1. First dated edition, 1841.1.

1884

1   [BULLEN, GEORGE], ed. Catalogue of Books in the Library of
    the British Museum, Printed in England, Scotland, and
    Ireland, and of Books in English Printed Abroad, to the
    Year 1640. Vol. 1. London: Trustees of the British
    Museum, pp. 526–27.
        Cites twenty-nine copies, including early editions of
    Bibliotheca, Governour, Castel, Defence, Dictionary,
    Doctrinal, Education, Image, Knowledge, Pasquil, Preserva-
    tive, and Rule.

1885

1   SINKER, ROBERT. A Catalogue of the English Books Printed
    before MDCI Now in the Library of Trinity College Cambridge.
    Cambridge: Deighton, Bell & Co.; London: George Bell &
    Sons, pp. 31, 32, 78, 112.
        Provides bibliographical description of copies owned of
    Image (items 65, 187), Governour (item 312), and Biblio
    theca (item 68).

See Addendum for 1889.1

1891

1   MORLEY, HENRY. English Writers: An Attempt towards a History
    of English Literature. Vol. 7. From Caxton to Coverdale.
    London, Paris, and Melbourne: Cassell & Company, pp. 286–
    95.
        Gives a summary analysis of the contents of Governour,
    preceded by the claim that it "well represents the energy
    of thought concerning education in the reign of Henry
    VIII"; speculates that the book was a direct influence on
    Spenser's Faerie Queene. Summarizes Castel more briefly.
    The few biographical statements perpetuate several errors.

1893

1   AINGER, ALFRED. "Sir Thomas Elyot." In English Prose:
    Selections with Critical Introductions by Various Writers.
    Vol. 1. Fourteenth to Sixteenth Century. Edited by Henry
    Craik. New York and London: Macmillan & Co., pp. 191–93.
        Discusses Elyot as "a kind of connecting link" between
    More and Ascham, "less archaic than the former, and less
    modern than the latter," and notes "a certain resemblance"

1893

between Governour and Utopia, claiming that the "aim" of
the two men "is one." Sees Governour as the only one of
Elyot's works "necessary to consider."

2   Catalogue of Original and Early Editions of Some of the
    Poetical and Prose Works of English Writers from Langland
    to Wither, with Collations & Notes, & Eighty-seven Facsim-
    iles of Titlepages and Frontispieces. New York: Grolier
    Club, pp. 74-76. Reprint. New York: Cooper Square Pub-
    lishers, 1963.
        Bibliographical descriptions of Castel, third and fourth
    editions, both 1541; and of 1553 edition of Governour; all
    with collation.

1894

1   S., C. "Sir Thomas Elyot's Armorial Quarterings." N&Q,
    8th ser. 6 (4 August): 88.
        Describes Elyot's coat of arms and laments that since no
    tinctures are given it is impossible to determine which
    family they belong to.

1896

1   BRINK, BERNHARD [AEGIDIUS KONRAD] TEN. History of English
    Literature (from the Fourteenth Century to the Death of
    Surrey). Vol. 2, part 2. Edited by Alois Brandl.
    Translated by L. Dora Schmitz. New York: Henry Holt &
    Co., pp. 192-201.
        A concise evaluative survey of Elyot's writings and
    assessment of his importance for English letters in the
    first half of the sixteenth century. A "character alto-
    gether typical of the period," who wrote a "middle kind of
    literature . . . in an eminently practical sense for the
    educated world," Elyot is remarkable for his "manysided-
    ness." More than a "mere compilation," Governour "shows us
    individuality." Its object is political, its methods
    ethical and pedagogical; Image is a "supplement" to it and
    is "superior" to Guevara's Marcus Aurelius in "genuine
    richness of subject." Dates are not always accurate,
    especially those of first or subsequent editions, and Brink
    accepts attributions which have since been called into
    question.

1901

2 LEPZIEN, A[UGUST MARTIN JOHANN]. Ist Thomas Elyot ein
Vorgänger John Locke's in der Erziehungslehre? Leipzig:
Oswald Schmidt, 52 pp.
Chapters on Elyot's life, educational theory, and
sources precede a comparison of Elyot and Locke, chiefly
by means of parallel passages. Lepzien concludes that
Elyot is "indeed a predecessor of Locke as an educational
theorist. Both strive toward the same educational ideal—
the virtuous gentleman who is also diligent in practical
manners—and the path by which they attempt to reach this
goal, broadly outlined by Elyot, is more sharply formulated
and more clearly delineated by Locke, with the aid of his
pragmatic philosophy."

3 PARMENTIER, JACQUES. Histoire de l'éducation en Angleterre;
Les doctrines et les écoles depuis les origines jusqu'au
commencement du XIXe siècle. Paris: Perrin et Cie,
Libraires-Éditeurs, pp. 24-38.
Chapter 2, "Sir Thomas Elyot," provides a selective
survey of some key ideas in Book I of Governour, preceded
by a brief account of its influence on later writers, Budé,
Sturm, Ascham, Mulcaster, and Locke. Observes some cor-
respondences between Elyot and Rousseau. Notes that Elyot
treats questions which are still pressing to educators in
the nineteenth century and laments that German historians
of education have ignored him.

1898

1 SAINTSBURY, GEORGE. A Short History of English Literature.
London: Macmillan & Co., pp. 234-35. Reprint. London:
Macmillan & Co.; New York: St. Martin's Press, 1966.
Finds it "difficult to give any reason" for the position
held by Governour. As a prose stylist, Elyot is "com-
mendable rather than distinguished; free from obvious and
glaring defects rather than possessed of distinct merits."

1901

1 MOULTON, CHARLES WELLS, ed. "Sir Thomas Elyot." In The
Library of Literary Criticism of English and American
Authors. Vol. 1. Buffalo, N.Y.: Moulton Publishing Co.,
pp. 253-54.
Appreciative quotations by eight biographers and histori-
ans, from Fuller (1840.1) to Saintsbury (1898.1).

1901

2   P[ATRICK], D[AVID], ed. "Sir Thomas Elyot." In <u>Chambers's</u>
     <u>Cyclopaedia of English Literature</u>. Vol. 1. New ed.
     London and Edinburgh: W. & R. Chambers, pp. 127–28.
         Recounts main facts of Elyot's life and lists his works,
     but, interestingly, quotes entirely the passage from
     <u>Governour</u> which influenced Shakespeare's account of Prince
     Hal and the Judge in <u>II Henry IV</u>, suggesting that it may be
     a displacement of an episode occurring to Edward II.
     First edition, 1843.1.

1903

1   GARNETT, RICHARD. <u>English Literature: An Illustrated Record</u>.
     Vol. 1. <u>From the Beginnings to the Age of Henry VIII</u>.
     London: William Heinemann; New York: Macmillan Co.,
     pp. 327–29.
         <u>See</u> 1906.1.

2   HALE, EDWARD E., JR. "Ideas on Rhetoric in the Sixteenth
     Century." <u>PMLA</u> 18, no. 3 (July): 424–44.
         Presents Elyot's ideas on the need to enrich the English
     vocabulary through foreign borrowings and argues that over
     the course of Elyot's writings, these ideas became less
     exaggerated. Sees Cheke's views as opposing those of Elyot
     and examines those of Wilson, Puttenham, and Nashe. The
     period was "a time of no fixed principles," but was "a time
     of ideas; men were thinking."

3   LAURIE, S[IMON] S[OMERVILLE]. "<u>The Governour</u>, by Sir Thomas
     Elyot: d. 1546." In <u>Studies in the History of Educational</u>
     <u>Opinion from the Renaissance</u>. Cambridge: Cambridge
     University Press, pp. 38–45.
         <u>See</u> 1905.2.

1904

1   EMKES, MAX ADOLF. <u>Das Erziehungsideal bei Sir Thomas More,</u>
     <u>Sir Thomas Elyot, Roger Ascham und John Lyly</u>. Marburg:
     R. Friedrich's Universitätsbuchdruckerei.
         Compares the thinking of each man under the headings of
     "physical," "intellectual," and "moral" education, with
     the second section subdivided into 1) the qualifications
     of a tutor, the proper relations between pupil and tutor
     and parents and tutor and 2) "Particular Disciplines,"
     including such topics as Latin and Greek authors, rhetoric,
     logic, geography, history, moral philosophy, music,
     painting, and sculpture.

1905

1   BENNDORF, CORNELIE. Die englische Pädagogik im 16. Jahrhundert, wie sie dargestellt wird im Wirken und in den Werken
von Elyot, Ascham, und Mulcaster. Vienna and Leipzig:
Wilhelm Braumüller.
     Chapter 3 gives an account of Elyot's life and of the
publication history of his works. Chapter 4 compares the
pedagogical views of the three men, with special reference
to the impact of humanism on their thought and to their
views on such matters as physical exercise, the teaching
of languages, the education of women, etc. Chapter 5 compares the literary qualities and "philosophies" of the
three.

2   LAURIE, S[IMON] S[OMERVILLE]. "The Governour, by Sir Thomas
Elyot: d. 1546." In Studies in the History of Educational
Opinion from the Renaissance. Cambridge: Cambridge
University Press, pp. 38-45.
     Elyot's book is important for two reasons: it is the
first treatise in English written in the spirit of earlier
Italian humanism, and it directly influenced Ascham. Laurie
attempts to give the reader a "fair acquaintance" with
the spirit of the book by "stringing together its leading
precepts." Quotes passages on importance of early training; on the way to begin teaching Latin; on what authors
to read; on deficiencies in schoolmasters; and on the true
method of teaching literature, advice in Laurie's view,
"beyond all question the best ever written in so far as my
knowledge extends." First edition 1903.3.

1906

1   GARNETT, RICHARD. English Literature: An Illustrated Record.
Vol. 1. From the Beginnings to the Age of Henry VIII.
London: William Heinemann; New York: Macmillan Co.,
pp. 327-29.
     General introduction to Elyot and Governour, character-
ized as "a work of great good sense, though sometimes
amusingly pedantic." First edition, 1903.1.

2   WOODWARD, WILLIAM HARRISON. "Thomas Elyot and The Boke Named
the Governour, 1531." In Studies in Education during the
Age of the Renaissance, 1400-1600. Cambridge: Cambridge
University Press, pp. 268-94. Reprint. New York: Russell
& Russell, 1965.

A concise topical survey of the educational principles contained in Governour, written from the premise that it was produced in response to a realization that "England had entered upon a higher stage of development, that a new governing class, a lay, professional class, was being called into existence, and that for it a freshly devised equipment was essential." Emphasis on Elyot's adaptation of his sources, mainly Italian and Erasmus, whom Elyot "interpreted" for England. For Elyot, "the educational process . . . was continuous, insistent, and rested on the principle of imitation, example, and personal stimulus and not on the imparting of knowledge."

In surveying Elyot's views on such matters as physical exercise, recreation, the content of the curriculum of instruction, Woodward both quotes at length and succinctly analyzes the import of the quotation, for example, concerning the value of the study of history: "Four points here are disclosed: the style of the historian, the lessons of the military events described, the cause of growth and decline in states, the political skill and moral worth of rulers, with the effects of these upon national well-being."

1907

1   WATSON, FOSTER. Introduction to his edition of The Boke Named the Governour Devised by Sir Thomas Elyot, Knight. Everyman's Library. London: J. M. Dent & Co.; New York: E. P. Dutton & Co., pp. xi-xxxvi.

Presents Elyot as a "Humanist-Democrat," with emphasis on his "modernness" and his "nearness" to the educational problems of Watson's own day. "He was in himself, and within his limits, a 'Society for the Diffusion of Useful Knowledge' nearly four hundred years ago." Stresses Elyot's understanding of "the importance of the realistic side of education." Briefly surveys Governour in light of these assumptions.

1908

1   L[EE], [SIR] S[IDNEY]. "Elyot, Sir Thomas." In Dictionary of National Biography. Vol. 6. Edited by Leslie Stephen and Sidney Lee. New York: Macmillan Co.; London: Smith, Elder & Co., pp. 765-68.

A reissue of the 1885 edition with errors corrected and bibliographies revised. In roughly two halves, the first biographical, with emphasis on Elyot's public life; the

second a listing, with some commentary, of Elyot's works.
Among controversial claims are these: that in 1532 Elyot
was "no doubt" sympathetic to Catherine; that he served a
second embassy to the court of Charles V (see 1930.4);
that he was an "intimate friend" of Ascham; that there is
no evidence that Elyot plagiarized Image from Guevara and
others. The dating of many of Elyot's works is in error.
See 1889.1.

2   WATSON, FOSTER. The English Grammar Schools to 1660: Their
    Curriculum and Practice. Cambridge: Cambridge University
    Press, pp. 262-63, 305-6, 388-89, 469-70, 489. Reprint.
    London: Frank Cass & Co., 1968.
        Summarizes Elyot on the proper age to begin grammar
    study; the importance and publishing history of Dictionary;
    whether school boys should write verses; the importance of
    their knowing Greek.

1   LINDSAY, T. M. "Englishmen and the Classical Renascence." In
    The Cambridge History of English Literature. Vol. 3.
    Renascence and Reformation. Edited by A[dolphus] W[illiam]
    Ward and A[lfred] R[ayney] Waller. Cambridge: Cambridge
    University Press, pp. 21-24.
        A brief introduction to Governour as an "attempt to
    introduce into English life an ideal of the many-sided
    culture which the classical renascence had disclosed,"
    followed by a listing of Elyot's other writings. By means
    of his dictionary, Elyot rendered the classical renascence
    "accessible to the mass of people who had no acquaintance
    with the languages of antiquity."

1   JUSSERAND, [ADRIEN ANTOINE] J[EAN] J[ULES]. A Literary His-
    tory of the English People. Vol. 2. From the Renaissance
    to the Civil War. 2d ed. New York and London: G. P.
    Putnam's Sons, pp. 66-70, 104-5.
        Summarizes the main tenets of Elyot's educational theory
    in Governour, which presents "a remarkable picture of all
    that a young English nobleman . . . ought to know." Sees
    in Elyot's emphasis on the arts "indeed the spirit of the
    Renaissance."

1910

2   MOORE, J[OHN] L[OWRY]. <u>Tudor-Stuart Views on the Growth,
     Status, and Destiny of the English Language</u>. Studien zur
     englischen Philologie, no. 41. Halle a.S.: Max Niemeyer,
     pp. 10-12, 14-24, 33-34, 38-41, 44-50 passim.
         Cites Elyot frequently in chronicling the views among
     users of early modern English as to "the powers, capacity
     and relative worth of the mother-tongue, what was surmised
     of its past, what hoped for its future." The "Appendix,"
     pp. 82-89, adds additional quotations from Elyot, including
     examples of his method of glossing new words in <u>Governour</u>.

3   VERNON HARCOURT, L[EVENSON] W[ILLIAM]. "The Two Sir John
     Fastolfs." <u>Transactions of the Royal Historical Society</u>,
     3rd ser. 4: 47-62.
         Argues that previous historians had incorrectly identi-
     fied the Sir John Fastolf, prototype of Shakespeare's
     Falstaff, as Fastolf of Caister; he is rather Fastolf of
     Nacton and was engaged in a lawsuit against Sir Hugh Old-
     castle, father of Sir John. In demonstrating the thesis,
     suggests that Elyot's account of the arraignment of Prince
     Hal by Judge Gascoign is "in all probability" true.

                              1911

1   <u>Catalogue général des livres imprimés de la Bibliothèque
     Nationale</u>. Vol. 47. Paris: Imprimerie Nationale, col.
     258.
         Cites only five imprints, two each of <u>Bibliotheca</u> and
     <u>Governour</u>, one of <u>Castel</u>.

                              1912

1   WATSON, FOSTER, ed. <u>Vives and the Renascence Education of
     Women</u>. London: Edward Arnold, pp. 18-19 and 211-13.
         The general introduction to this collection of treatises
     claims that between the publication of <u>Governour</u> and
     <u>Defence</u>, Elyot changed his attitude concerning the pro-
     priety of women engaging in government. Claims in the
     introduction to <u>Defence</u> (text on pp. 213-39), that in
     Zenobia Elyot intended his readers to think of Catherine
     of Aragon and that the book's lack of dedication is con-
     firmation of Elyot's attachment to Catherine.

1915

1   BRANDL, ALOIS. "Thomas Elyot's 'Verteidigung guter Frauen'
    (1545) und die Frauenfrage in England bis Shakespeare.
    Anhang: Thomas Elyot's 'Schutzmittel gegen den Tod'
    (1545)." Jahrbuch der deutschen Shakespeare-Gesellschaft
    51: 111-70.
        An edition of the 1545 Defence, preceded by a survey of
    major treatments of the subject between Chaucer and Elyot,
    and followed by a brief account of Elyot's influence on
    writers between his time and Shakespeare. To this is
    appended, for reasons hard to see, Elyot's Preservative.

1919

1   MILLET, FRED B. "English Courtesy Literature before 1557."
    Bulletin of the Departments of History and Political and
    Economic Science in Queen's University, Kingston, Ontario,
    Canada, no. 30 (January), pp. 1-16.
        Distinguishing manners from morals as "that portion of
    conduct, the neglect of which is . . . an error but not a
    disgrace," and defining courtesy as "manners raised to the
    dignity of a system," surveys four classes of courtesy
    literature: that addressed to boys, girls, serving men,
    and gentlemen. Concludes: the largest quantity of books
    of manners is addressed to the first three (with Governour
    being the only clear example of a courtesy book addressed
    to gentlemen); contents, style, and method are constant
    from 1430-1557; the bulk of writing "constitutes a litera-
    ture of manners, not a system of courtesy"; Italian
    influence is "negligible." Compare 1935.2.

1920

1   BERDAN, JOHN M. Early Tudor Poetry, 1485-1547. New York:
    Macmillan Co., pp. 304-33 passim. Reprint. [Hamden,
    Conn.]: Shoestring Press, 1961.
        On Elyot's importance in the transmission of humanistic
    ideas from 1530-50. Elyot is frequently compared to Vives
    and to Ascham, generally by means of lengthy quotations
    from his works set beside familiar passages from the other
    two men. Sees humanism as a "movement," and Elyot as a
    transition between a second and third "stage" in which it
    becomes identified with the "true religion," and in which
    classical "authorities" change from Latin ones to Greek.

1920

2 SCHROEDER, KURT. <u>Platonismus in der englischen Renaissance</u>
   <u>vor und bei Thomas Eliot, nebst Neudruck von Eliots "Dis-</u>
   <u>putacion Platonike," 1533.</u> Palaestra, 83. Berlin: Mayer
   und Müller, pp. 85-115.
       Chapter 6, "Thomas Elyot," identifies quotations from
   and references to Plato in both <u>Governour</u> and <u>Knowledge</u>.
   For the latter gives an extended analysis of the contents
   and discusses Elyot's assimilation of Platonic notions of
   God and the world, of man and the soul, and of Plato's
   ethics and theodicy. Elyot knew a great number of Plato's
   works and set many of them on the same level as the Bible.
   He also knew commentary on Plato. However, Elyot does not
   offer a "pure" Platonic system but rather one influenced by
   Stoic, Neoplatonic, and Christian points of view. Some
   of the Platonic influence is through Pico.

1921

1 WATSON, FOSTER, ed. <u>The Encyclopaedia and Dictionary of</u>
   <u>Education</u>. Vol. 2. London, Bath, Melbourne, Toronto, and
   New York: Sir Isaac Pitman & Sons, pp. 542-43.
       Brief biography and introduction to the educational
   theory in <u>Governour</u>, with short bibliography.

1922

1 GOODE, CLEMENT TYSON. "Sir Thomas Elyot's <u>Titus and Gysippus</u>."
   <u>MLN</u> 37, no. 1 (January): 1-11.
       Citing thirty-four differences between Elyot's story and
   the versions of Boccaccio and Beroaldo, argues that we must
   abandon the idea that Elyot's version is a "translation."
   In addition to these two versions, Elyot probably used the
   <u>Disciplina Cerlicalis</u> of Petrus Alphonsus. Rebuts S. L.
   Wolff's argument (in "A Source of <u>Euphues: The Anatomy of</u>
   <u>Wyt</u>," <u>MP</u> 7 [1910], 577-85) that Lyly did not draw upon
   Elyot for <u>Euphues</u>: Lyly "deliberately planned to maintain
   the same moral idea as Elyot."

1924

1 LILJEGREN, S[TEN] B[ODVAR]. <u>The Fall of the Monasteries and</u>
   <u>the Social Changes in England Leading up to the Great</u>
   <u>Revolution</u>. Lunds Universitets Årsskrift, n.s. 19, no. 10.
   Lund: C. W. K. Gleerup; Leipzig: Otto Harrassowitz,
   150 pp.

Has no direct reference to Elyot, but documents the
transfer of vast amounts of land into the middle class,
April 1536-February 1547, and the consequent socio-
political effects which this had. Background only. <u>See</u>
1959.2.

2   THOMPSON, ELBERT N[EVIUS] S[EBRING]. <u>Literary Bypaths of the
Renaissance</u>. New Haven: Yale University Press; London:
Humphrey Milford, Oxford University Press, pp. 141-43.
Assesses <u>Governour</u> as the "first" and "finest" courtesy
book in English. Though lacking the "ease and spontaneity,
even gayety of Castiglione's <u>Courtier</u>," Elyot's book is
nevertheless "saved from dullness and frigidity by its
author's fineness of temper."

1926

*1   JOYCE, HEWLETT E. "Sir Thomas Elyot's <u>The Image of Gover-
nance</u>." Ph.D. dissertation, Yale University.
Rotograph copy of the first edition, with introduction,
notes, glossary, and literary history of <u>Image</u>. <u>See</u>
1964.3.

2   POLLARD, A[LFRED] W[ILLIAM], and REDGRAVE, G[ILBERT] R[ICHARD].
<u>A Short-Title Catalogue of Books Printed in England,
Scotland, and Ireland and of English Books Printed Abroad,
1475-1640</u>. London: Bibliographical Society, pp. 170-71.
Reprint. 1946.
Cites forty-four editions, distributed as follows:
Bankette, 5 (1539, 1542, 1545, 1557, 1564); <u>Governour</u>, 8
(1531, 1537, 1544, 1546, 1553, 1557, 1565, 1580); <u>Castel</u>,
15 (1539-1610); Defence, 1 (1545); <u>Dictionary-Bibliotheca</u>,
4 (1538, 1548, 1552, 1559); <u>Image</u>, 4 (1540, 1544, 1549,
1556); <u>Knowledge</u>, 3 (1533, 1534, [after 1548]); <u>Pasquil</u>, 3
(1532, 1533, 1540); <u>Preservative</u>, 1 (1545). Supplemented
by 1933.1.

3   STENBERG, THEODORE. "Sir Thomas Elyot and the <u>Ars Poetica</u>."
<u>N&Q</u> 151, no. 15 (9 October): 259.
<u>Encyclopedia Britannica</u> and <u>DNB</u> err in attributing to
Elyot the translation of eight lines from Horace's <u>Ars
Poetica</u>; the lines in question are from the Epistle to
Augustus.

4   _____. "Sir Thomas Elyot's Defense of the Poets." <u>UTSE</u> 6:
121-45.

1927

Argues the five-fold thesis that Elyot is the first
English writer to attempt a distinction between the function of rhetoric and that of poetry; that unlike the
typical humanist Elyot gives a "basic" place in his system
of education to poetry rather than rhetoric or style; that
Elyot is the first English poet to attempt a defense of
poetry; that in doing so he anticipates Sidney, Webbe, and
Puttenham by half a century; that Sidney's Defense "certainly owes something" to Elyot, while Webbe's Discourse
"is heavily indebted" to him. To make the last point,
quotes at length ten parallel passages.

1927

1   CONLEY, C[AREY] H[ERBERT]. The First English Translators of
    the Classics. New Haven: Yale University Press; London:
    Humphrey Milford, Oxford University Press, pp. 5, 6, 12,
    13, 16, 47, 57, 59, 60-61, 76, 77, 100, 109, 110.
       Cites Elyot in support of various generalizations con-
    cerning what Conley calls the "translation movement"--
    particularly regarding the function of history; the use
    of translation to influence national consciousness, to
    support the Reformation, or to condemn medieval literature;
    and the reception of or opposition to translations.

2   STARNES, D[EWITT] T[ALMAGE]. "Elyot's Governour and Peacham's
    Compleat Gentleman." MLR 22, no. 3 (July): 319-22.
       Shows by means of parallel passages that the sixth,
    seventh, and sixteenth chapters of Peacham's book have
    "quite demonstrable" correspondences to Governour.

3   _____. "Notes on Elyot's The Governour (1531)." RES 3, no. 9
    (January): 37-46.
       Illustrates by means of parallel passages the influence
    of Governour on Mirror for Magistrates, on John North-
    brooke's An Invective against Diceplaying, on William
    Webbe's Discourse of English Poetry, and on Puttenham's
    Arte of English Poesie.

4   _____. "Shakespeare and Elyot's Governour." UTSE 7: 112-32.
       Argues that many of Shakespeare's plays contain "thought,
    imagery, political theory, implied or expressed," which are
    analogous to those in Governour. In some cases inter-
    mediary sources would account for the similarities, but
    when such sources are considered, "there are still some
    agreements that deserve further study," especially in

2 Henry IV, Henry V, Troilus and Cressida, and Coriolanus
(see 1930.1). Provides parallel passages from each of
these plays and Governour. Concludes that Shakespeare knew
Governour first hand.

1928

1   DRESSLER, BRUNO. Geschichte der englischen Erziehung: Versuch
einer kritischen Gesamtdarstellung der Entwicklung der
englischen Erziehung. Leipzig: B. G. Teubner, pp. 25-28.
Calling Elyot "the first great theoretician of English
education," discusses briefly his "Ansichten," his emphasis
on physical education, his conception of virtue, and his
influence on later English educational theory.

2   McKNIGHT, GEORGE H., with the assistance of EMSLEY, BERT.
Modern English in the Making. New York and London: D.
Appleton-Century Co., pp. 99-103.
Summary of Elyot's contributions to the enrichment of
the English language in the sixteenth century: "Perhaps
no other man set out as deliberately . . . to enrich the
vocabulary by foreign borrowing."

1929

1   ANON. "Elyot, Sir Thomas." In The Encyclopaedia Britannica.
Vol. 8. 14th ed. London and New York: Encyclopaedia
Britannica Co., p. 282.
Biographical survey about half the length of ninth edition's, though with most dating and spelling errors corrected, and with a more reliable list of works, some with
characterizing phrases or brief discussions. Sees Elyot as
a collector of quotations. Compare 1878.1, 1975.1.

2   KELSO, RUTH. The Doctrine of the English Gentleman in the
Sixteenth Century, with a Bibliographical List of Treatises
on the Gentleman and Related Subjects Published in Europe
to 1625. Urbana: University of Illinois Press, 288 pp.
Reprint. Gloucester, Mass.: Peter Smith, 1964.
Elyot is referred to on an average of every four pages.
The most extended discussion is in Chapter V, "The Moral
Code of the Gentleman," pp. 70-110, which analyzes in detail Elyot's contribution to the theory of what constitutes
gentlemanly virtue, distinguishing his ideas from those of
other English and Italian writers on the subject. Elyot's
was "by far the most detailed and original discussion of

the virtues of the gentleman." Also sees Elyot, pp. 117-
29, passim, as signally important for the theory of the
gentleman's education: "none so urbanely, even lovingly,
strove to make studies attractive to the gentleman."

3   ROBERTSON, W. G. AITCHISON. "The Castel of Helth and Its
    Author, Sir Thomas Elyot." Annals of Medical History n.s.
    1 (May): 270-83.
        A general survey of Elyot's career (in which dates are
    often incorrect) followed by a series of extracts illus-
    trating the contents, organization, and style of Castel,
    the extracts generally, though not exclusively, conforming
    to the arrangement of the work.

1930

1   CONKLIN, WILLET TITUS. "Two Further Notes on Shakespeare's
    Use of Elyot's Governour." UTSE 10: 66-69.
        Suggests influence of Governour II, vi on Henry V, IV.
    vii. 36-42; Starnes' contention (see 1927.4) that Elyot
    influenced Coriolanus III.i.106-17 is not convincing; rather
    the influence is directly from Plutarch (Elyot's source).

2   HOGREFE, PEAL. "Elyot and the 'Boke Called Cortigiano in
    Ytalion.'" MP 27, no. 3 (February): 303-9.
        Investigates evidence to indicate that Governour was
    "possibly" influenced by Courtier: Bonner's 1530 letter to
    Cromwell mentioning the book; Elyot's familiarity with
    Cromwell at the time; and some characteristic passages in
    which Elyot differs from other humanists like More,
    Erasmus, and Vives, but agrees with Castiglione.

3   MILLER, FLORENCE GRAVES. "The Humanistic Theory of Education."
    Master's thesis, University of Oklahoma, pp. 108-36.
        Chapter 4, "The Educational Theories of Thomas Elyot,"
    summarizes and comments briefly on the contents of Gover-
    nour.

4   POLLARD, A[LBERT] F[REDERICK]. "Sir Thomas More and Sir Thomas
    Elyot." TLS, 17 July, p. 592.
        Shows that the supposed embassy to court of Charles V in
    1535 is a "fiction," as Elyot was in England at the time.
    Furthermore, since Elyot's 1531-32 embassy was terminated
    in March of April 1532, it is unlikely that the Emperor
    made his famous statement to Elyot on the occasion of More's
    retirement. See 1932.1 and 1951.2.

1931

1   FULTON, JOHN F. "Early Medical Humanists: Leonicenus, Lin-
     acre and Thomas Elyot." The New England Journal of Medicine
     205, no. 3 (July 16): 141-46.
         The text of an address to the New Haven, Conn. "Eliza-
     bethan Club," 28 April 1931, on the impact of Nicolaus
     Leonicenus of Ferrara on medical humanism in England, par-
     ticularly on Linacre. The section on Elyot, to all pur-
     poses "tacked on," presents Elyot as champion of the
     vernacular in medicine, and quotes from the "Proheme" to
     the 1541 Castel. The last third of the talk is given to
     remarks on Governour and the state of education in America,
     whose "methods are in a state of flux."

2   STARNES, DEWITT T[ALMAGE]. "The Picture of a Perfit Common
     Wealth (1600)." UTSE 11: 32-41.
         Indicates by means of parallel passages the nature and
     extent of Thomas Floyd's indebtedness to Governour: he
     generally paraphrases the thought and he may in some in-
     stances be said to have improved Elyot's organization,
     though in the main the work is "undistinguished."

3   STUDNICZKA, HANS. Introduction to his abridged translation,
     Das Buch vom Führer. Der Philosophischen Bibliothek, vol.
     106. Leipzig: Felix Meiner, pp. v-xxx.
         A general introduction to Elyot and his work; reviews
     educational, historical, and political trends of the period;
     discusses at some length Elyot's influence on later writers
     (including Montaigne and Budaeus, Shaftesbury and Chester-
     field), and, more briefly, his influence on the British
     concept of the gentleman and on education in the twentieth
     century.

1932

1   HITCHCOCK, ELSIE VAUGHAN, and CHAMBERS, R[AYMOND] W[ILSON], eds.
     The Life and Death of Sir Thomas More, Knight, Sometymes
     Lord High Chancellor of England, Written in the Tyme of
     Queene Marie by Nicholas Harpsfield. London, New York,
     and Toronto: Oxford University Press, pp. 205-6 and note
     on pp. 353-55.
         Analyzes the circumstances surrounding the transmission
     of the anecdote of the Emperor's remarks at More's death to
     point out that it would have been "impolitic" of Elyot to
     have recounted the episode after More's imprisonment, as it

1932

would have been perceived as an affront to the King. Elyot
told the story in context of More's resignation and Roper's
memory failed him. See 1930.4, 1951.2.

2   NUGENT, JOHN RICHARD. "The Utopian Ideals in English Prose
     of the Renaissance." Master's thesis, University of Okla-
     homa, pp. 44-46, 57-62, 77-78, 90-91, 102-4, 110.
          Governed by the assumption that Governour "shows . . .
     the Utopian ideal," surveys Elyot's contributions to Uto-
     pian thought under the categories, respectively, of
     "Domestic Life," "Education," "Religion," "Morals, Public
     and Private," "Politics," and "Science."

                              1933

1   EDMONDS, C[ECIL] K[AY]. "Supplement to the Short Title Cata-
     logue." Huntington Library Bulletin, no. 4 (October): p. 45.
          Supplements numbers 7643, 7648, and 7658 of 1926.2.

2   HOYLER, AUGUST. "Elyots Governour-Ideal," in Gentleman-Ideal
     und Gentleman-Erziehung: Mit besonderer Berücksichtigung
     der Renaissance. Erziehungsgeschichtliche Untersuchungen:
     Studien zur Problemgeschichte der Pädagogik. Leipzig:
     Felix Meiner, pp. 207-21.
          Comparing Elyot to Ascham and Castiglione, considers the
     place of Elyot's concept of the governor in the larger con-
     text of the notion of the ideal gentleman in the Renaissance.
     Both concepts are based on class distinctions; both stress
     "inner formation" and self-discipline; both require obliga-
     tion to the people; both subordinate theoretical learning
     to practice; both are grounded in virtue rather than in
     power or wealth.

3   LATHROP, HENRY BURROWES. Translations from the Classics into
     English from Caxton to Chapman, 1477-1620. University of
     Wisconsin Studies in Language and Literature, no. 35.
     Madison: University of Wisconsin Press, pp. 31, 40-42, 44,
     67, 71, 72, 78, 79, 106, 153, 183, 189, 301, 305, 309.
          As a translator, Elyot is "unaffectedly vigorous, his
     sentences are firmly constructed, and his syntax is not
     incorrect." There is "no evidence" that Elyot was transla-
     tor of Plutarch's essay on deriving profit from one's
     enemies. Isocrates' letter to Nicocles (Elyot's Doctrinal)
     was his first translation directly from Greek. Elyot, not
     Ascham, should be given credit for inaugurating the Iso-
     cratean influence into England. Elyot's Bankette is im-
     portant in the tradition of translations of aphorisms.

4   McCOY, SAMUEL JESSE. "The Language and Linguistic Interests
of Sir Thomas Elyot." Ph.D. dissertation, University of
North Carolina, xviii, 412 pp.
    Contains chapters on Elyot's life and his "linguistic
world," (i.e., language developments in Italy, France, and
Germany, as well as England), on Elyot's "linguistic interests and activities," on his vocabulary, on his syntax and
style, and, finally, on "linguistic science in the late
sixteenth century," largely a survey of comments by writers
of the fourth quarter of the century on the state of the
language. Deliberately excludes discussion of phonology
and morphology. Three appendices. The first transcribes,
in chronological order, the title pages and colophons of
each of Elyot's works; each work's preface or proheme and,
in some cases, extracts from the body; the dates of subse-
quent editions. The second reviews "the most significant
orthographical phenomena found in Elyot." The third lists
Elyot's neologisms, classified into six subsections, e.g.,
words introduced between 1500 and the date of Elyot's use,
words introduced by Elyot, meanings introduced by Elyot,
etc.

5   MOHL, RUTH. The Three Estates in Medieval and Renaissance
Literature. New York: Columbia University Press, pp. 156-
61. Reprint. New York: Frederick Ungar Press, 1962.
    Analyzes Elyot's theory of the origin of government. He
"is neither the political idealist that More is, nor simply
a religious dogmatist, though he is finally satisfied with
the explanation of the divine origin of government and of
classes of society." Notes a contradiction between Elyot's
notion of divine origin of estates and his claim in Book II
that in the beginning people had all in common but bestowed
private possessions and dignities on the virtuous and in-
dustrious. This is the only extended discussion, though
Elyot is cited frequently as evidence in the Chapter entitled "The Philosophy of the Estates of the World,"
pp. 276-340; see especially pp. 301-8.

6   STARNES, D[EWITT] T[ALMAGE]. "Sir Thomas Elyot and the 'Sayings of the Philosophers.'" UTSE 13: 5-35.
    Traces through the sixteenth century the history of the
genre "lives and sayings of the philosophers" (originating
in the third century with Diogenes Laertius and including
such notable sixteenth-century examples as Erasmus's
Apophthegmes); establishes the connections between Elyot's
writings (Governour, Image, and Dictionary) and later books
in this tradition: Thomas Palfreyman's A Treatise of Morall

1935

Philosophy (many editions), Wits Commonwealth (1597-98),
Wits Theater of the Little World (1599), Belvedere, the
Garden of the Muses (1600), A Perfit Commonwealth (1600),
and Vertues Commonwealth (1603).

1935

1   CHAMBERS, R[AYMOND] W[ILSON]. Thomas More. London and Toron-
      to: Jonathan Cape, [1935?], pp. 287-90.
         Presents the evidence that the Emperor Charles V's
      famous statement in praise of More occurred at the occasion
      of his retirement, not death. See 1930.4 and 1932.1.

2   MASON, JOHN E. Gentlefolk in the Making: Studies in the
      History of English Courtesy Literature and Related Topics
      from 1531 to 1774. Philadelphia: University of Pennsyl-
      vania Press, pp. 23-57 passim.
         Although only the first section contains extended dis-
      cussion of Governour, the entire chapter, "from the Gover-
      nour of Sir Thomas Elyot to the Basilikon Doron of King
      James I," is valuable as the most succinct account of the
      different types of courtesy literature produced in England
      in the sixteenth century. Distinguishes four main types of
      courtesy literature: the book of parental advice, the
      treatise on the position and upbringing of a gentleman or
      lady, the book of statecraft, and the manual of civility.
      Uses Elyot consistently as a touchstone for demonstrating
      relationships and differences. He is indebted more strongly
      to classical sources and ideals than to contemporary Italian
      ones, and Governour is "not a manual of civility," but a
      work designed to create "an ideal impersonal figure, in
      whose behavior, we may assume, the more intimate niceties
      of conduct are to be taken for granted." Elyot is a be-
      liever in "liberty and in rectitude . . . solid worth and
      solid learning," but he is "happily indifferent to esthetic
      considerations." Compare 1919.1.

See Addendum for 1936.1

1936

2   STARNES, D[EWITT] T[ALMAGE]. "More about the Prince Hal
      Legend." PQ 15, no. 4 (October): 358-66.
         Examines connections between Elyot's account of the
      legend and those of Angel Day (1586), John Case (1584),
      and Barnabe Barnes (1606).

1937

1   BUSH, DOUGLAS. "Julius Caesar and Elyot's Governour." MLN
52, no. 6 (June): 407-8.
Caesar's rejection of Artemidorus's warning (III.i.6-10)
is indebted to Governour II, v.

*2   SCHIRMER, WALTER F[RANZ]. Geschichte der englischen und
amerikanischen Literatur von der Anfängen bis zur Gegenwart.
Halle: Max Niemeyer.
See 1954.5.

3   SORIERI, LOUIS. Boccaccio's Story of "Tito e Gisippo" in
European Literature. Comparative Literature Series. New
York: Institute of French Studies, pp. 152-57.
Analyzes the "many and fundamental" changes that Elyot
introduces into Boccaccio's story; in particular, the scene
in the barn and the conclusion seem Elyot's own inventions.
Elyot is "not a slavish imitator."

4   TANNENBAUM, SAMUEL A. Introduction to "The Castel of Helthe"
(1541) by Sir Thomas Elyot, Together with the Title Page
and Preface of the Edition of 1539. New York: Scholars'
Faccimiles & Reprints, pp. iii-xi.
Discusses dating and the number of editions in the six
teenth and seventeenth centuries; contents; interesting
features of style and subject matter; its reception and
popularity.

1938

1   GRETHER, EMIL. Das Verhältnis von Shakespeares "Heinrich V"
zu Sir Thomas Elyots "Governour." Marburg-Lahn: Hermann
Bauer, 46 pp.
Indicates by means of parallel passages the extent of
Elyot's influence on Henry V, which is "great" and extends
beyond thematic influence to choice of words.

2   HELTZEL, VIRGIL B. "Breton, Elyot, and The Court of Honour."
MLN 53, no. 8 (December): 587-90.
Though the rare 1679 "character book" is based largely
on Breton's The Good and the Badde, it also contains a
lengthy extract from Elyot's Governour (the analogy between
bees and monarchy).

1938

3 SCHLOTTER, JOSEF. Thomas Elyots "Governour" in seinem
   Verhältnis zu Francesco Patrici [sic]. Endingen-Keiser-
   stuhl: Emil Wild, 119 pp.
      Disputes Croft's contention (see 1880.1, pp. lxv ff.)
   that Elyot was heavily dependent on Patrizi in Governour.
   Similarities are more often than not due to the two men's
   knowledge of Plato, and differences far outweigh the similarities, both in their considerations of the state and of
   justice and in their programs of education. See p. 99 for
   a succinct concluding statement of contrasts between the
   two. See 1950.4.

*4 WARREN, LESLIE C. "Humanistic Doctrines of the Prince from
   Petrarch to Sir Thomas Elyot." Ph.D. dissertation, University of Chicago.
      See 1950.4.

                              1939

1 EXNER, HELMUTH. Der Einfluss des Erasmus auf die englische
   Bildungsidee. Neue deutsche Forschungen, Abteilung
   englische Philologie, vol. 13. Berlin: Junker und
   Dunnhappt, pp. 117-20, 144-46.
      Discusses Erasmus's influence on the educational and
   political theory in Governour. The two men's concepts of the
   virtuous Christian leader are very similar; they differ in
   Elyot's more utilitarian goals, which are absent in Erasmus.
   Elyot wants to help create a national "Führeradel."

2 REBORA, PIERO. "Aspetti dell'Umanesimo in Inghilterra."
   Rinascimento 1, no. 4: 387-95 passim.
      A brief evaluation of Elyot's importance within human-
   istic education as influenced by Italian theory, and in
   particular Castiglione.

3 SCHRINNER, WALTER. Castiglione und die englische Renaissance.
   Neue deutsche Forschungen, Abteilung englische Philologie,
   vol. 14. Berlin: Junker und Dunnhaupt, pp. 41-45.
      "Castiglione's influence on Elyot is not to be understood
   in the sense of an inner permeation of Castiglione's ideas
   in Elyot's works, but in the sense of an outer inspiration
   which led to the formation of a national idea." Castiglione
   was more interested in individual perfection of character;
   Elyot was a more pragmatic "Realpolitiker."

1940

1   BAUMER, FRANKLIN LE VAN. The Early Tudor Theory of Kingship.
    New Haven: Yale University Press, pp. 200-6. Reprint.
    New York: Russell & Russell, 1966.
        Discusses Elyot briefly, among others, as representing
    the second of three distinct classes of writers who treated
    the king's moral responsibility: radical Protestants,
    secular writers in the speculum principis tradition, and a
    miscellaneous group of government servants, loyal to the
    king. Although "not one whit original," Elyot's works are
    nevertheless "more constructive" than many of his con-
    temporaries'.

2   HOWARD, EDWIN JOHNSTON. Introduction to his edition of Sir
    Thomas Elyot's "The Defence of Good Women." Oxford, Ohio:
    Anchor Press, pp. v-ix.
        Limited almost entirely to textual matters. The edi-
    tion, based on the Huntington Library copy of the 1540
    edition, contains textual notes, a glossary, and index.

3   KAHIN, HELEN ANDREWS. Review of Sir Thomas Elyot's The Defence
    of Good Women, edited by Edwin Johnston Howard. MLQ 2,
    no. 2 (June), 310-19.
        Points out that Howard (1940.2) did not know of Watson's
    edition of Defence in Vives and the Renaissance Education
    of Women (1912.1) and that his claim that Defence was
    written between 1531 and 1538 implies, though without
    stating explicitly, that 1540 was not the first edition.

4   PHILLIPS, JAMES EMERSON. The State in Shakespeare's Greek and
    Roman Plays. Columbia University Studies in English and
    Comparative Literature, no. 149. New York: Columbia Uni-
    versity Press, pp. 76-83 passim, 106-8, 185-86, 199-200.
        Cites Elyot as the chief spokesman for a theory of
    political structure in which "the vocations to which men
    are naturally adapted are maintained in the proper order of
    their degrees of merit and contribution." Without claiming
    direct influence, points to "exact" correspondences between
    Elyot's thought and that in Shakespeare's Julius Caesar and
    Antony and Cleopatra.

5   SWEETING, ELIZABETH J. Early Tudor Criticism: Linguistic and
    Literary. Oxford: Basil Blackwell, pp. 48-57 passim and
    59-77 passim. Reprint. New York: Russell & Russell,
    1964.
        Calling Elyot's critical sense "developed to a degree
    remarkable for the time," notes his importance as a

1941

translator: since translation "fostered linguistic and
literary judgment, had an ordered system of style and
method, explored the resources of the English language and
augmented them where necessary," it "made an invaluable
contribution to the training of critical habit." Likewise,
Elyot's theories concerning grammar and the study of language reveal an uncommon alertness to "the possibilities
of the critical activity."

1941

1 PACE, GEORGE B. "Sir Thomas Elyot against Poetry." MLN 56,
   no. 8 (December): 597-99.
       The contradiction between Elyot's defence of poets in
   Governour and his attack on them in Defence may be explained
   by the fact that Elyot follows two different traditions.
   See 1970.3.

2 R[EED], A. W., comp. "Sir Thomas Elyot (1499?-1546." In The
   Cambridge Bibliography of English Literature. Vol. 1. 600-
   1660. Edited by F[rederick] W[ilse] Bateson. New York: Macmillan Co., Cambridge: Cambridge University Press, p. 670.
       In two sections, "Works" and "Biography and Criticism."
   The first does not include Brandl's 1915 editions of
   Defence of Good Women and Preservative. The second lists
   only three works: Benndorf (1905.1), Pollard (1930.4) and
   a single Starnes article (1933.6). See 1974.2.

1942

1 HOWARD, EDWIN J[OHNSTON]. "Sir Thomas Elyot on the Turning
   of the Earth." PQ 22, no. 4 (October): 441-43.
       Notes opposing statements by Elyot regarding whether
   the earth turned or was stable and speculates on whether
   Elyot had read Copernicus' Commentariolus, circulated in
   MS as early as 1530.

1943

1 HOWARD, EDWIN J[OHNSTON]. "Some Words in Sir Thomas Elyot's
   Of the Knowledge Which Maketh a Wise Man." MLN 55, no. 5
   (May): 396-97.
       Records eleven words used by Elyot "in ways not recorded
   by NED" or used earlier than instances noted by NED.

1945

1   RICHARDS, GERTRUDE R. B. "The Castle of Health." More Books:
     The Bulletin of the Boston Public Library 20 (February):
     47-50.
        Announces the library's acquisition of a 1541 edition of
     Castel, with a brief description, and a general account of
     its publishing history. Notes other Elyot works owned by
     the library.

*2   WILSON, KNOX. "Xenophon in the English Renaissance from Elyot
     to Holland." Ph.D. dissertation, New York University.
        Cited in DDAAU, 1945, p. 57.

1946

1   HOWARD, EDWIN JOHNSTON. Introduction to his edition of Of the
     Knowledge Which Maketh a Wise Man Oxford, Ohio: Anchor
     Press, pp. vii-xxxii.
        Discusses publication history (showing that two editions
     listed as STC 7669 and 7670 are in fact one); the theme of
     the work; its sources; differences between the Platonic
     dialogue and its sixteenth century imitations, including
     Elyot's; Elyot's skill in handling the dialogue form.
     Argues that the work is an allegory intended to warn Henry
     VIII against the dangers of tyranny, the immediate cause of
     this warning being Henry's treatment of More in context of
     the divorce issue.
        The edition, a "page-for-page reprint of the first ex-
     tant edition (1533)," has textual notes and index.

1947

1   ATKINS, J[OHN] W[ILLIAM] H[EY]. English Literary Criticism:
     The Renascence. London: Methuen & Co., pp. 70-71, 99-101.
        The first passage is an exposition of Elyot's attitudes
     toward rhetorical study; the second analyzes his importance
     as one of the earliest defenders of poetry in England.
     Elyot's defense against the charge of poetry's immorality
     is primarily that of Plutarch: that reading poetry needs
     discrimination and a wise selection. In Elyot's criticism
     ethical considerations remain "uppermost," but "the
     medieval line of defense, that of allegorical interpreta-
     tion, is to some extent being modified."

1947

*2   BAKER, HERSCHEL. The Dignity of Man: Studies in the Persist-
      ence of an Idea. Cambridge, Mass.: Harvard University
      Press.
        Reprinted as 1961.2.

3   BUTT, JOHN. Review of Sir Thomas Elyot's Of the Knowledge
      Which Maketh a Wise Man, edited by Edwin Johnston Howard.
      RES 23, no. 9 (July): 273-75.
        Observes that those who know only Governour miss two
      important marks of Elyot's humanism: his Christianity and
      his concern for interpreting the classics for his country-
      men. Regrets that Howard did not provide a glossary or
      indicate sources; in particular, a glossary would have
      supplemented OED "in a period where that work is not
      strong." See 1946.1.

4   RAVEN, CHARLES E. English Naturalists from Neckam to Ray: A
      Study of the Making of the Modern World. Cambridge:
      Cambridge University Press, pp. 42-44, 72-74, 197, 198.
      Reprint. New York: Kraus Reprint Co., 1968.
        Concludes that the English renderings of the names of
      flora and fauna in Dictionary show Elyot to be a naturalist
      of minor importance and some originality. As a botanist,
      he "often shows considerable research," and though he "cer-
      tainly" knew William Turner's Libellus de Re Herbaria, he
      is "a real and independent student." Dictionary indicates
      that Elyot was mainly concerned with finding in the English
      tongue and country equivalents for the plants and animals
      of classical antiquity. Argues that Turner and Elyot knew
      one another and that Turner probably stayed with Elyot at
      Long Combe while Elyot was working on Dictionary between
      1536 and 1538.

1948

1   BARKER, SIR ERNEST. Traditions of Civility: Eight Essays.
      Cambridge: Cambridge University Press, pp. 124-58 passim.
        Although only pp. 133-36 deal directly with Elyot, the
      entire chapter, "The Education of the English Gentleman in
      the Sixteenth Century," succinctly compares Governour,
      Starkey's Pole and Lupset, Hoby's Courtier, and Ascham's
      Scholemaster as statements of the educational ideal in
      sixteenth-century England.

1948

2   BROOKE, [C. F.] TUCKER. "The Renaissance." In <u>A Literary</u>
    <u>History of England</u>. Edited by Albert C. Baugh. New York
    and London: Appleton-Century-Crofts, pp. 329-32.
        Calling Elyot "the great organizer of the learning that
    the English humanists had gathered," evaluates briefly each
    of his major works.   Claims that "no English writer of this
    time was more imbued with the spirit of Platonic philoso-
    phy," and says of <u>Knowledge</u> that "the arguments are handled
    neatly, and with a certain dramatic vividness." Elyot's
    primary achievement in <u>Governour</u> is "the creation of a
    prose style," one "compendious, sententious, and delect-
    able." <u>Castel</u> contains "priceless details of sixteenth-
    century dietary and hygiene." Revised as 1967.1.

3   PARKS, GEORGE B. "Before <u>Euphues</u>." In <u>Joseph Quincy Adams</u>
    <u>Memorial Studies</u>. Edited by James G. McManaway, Giles E.
    Dawson, and Edwin E. Willoughby. Washington: Folger
    Shakespeare Library, pp. 475-93.
        Pages 482-87 treat Elyot's tale of Titus and Gysippus
    as "the first psychological novella in English" and commend
    Elyot's "amplification" of the psychological analysis in
    the original. The overall argument is that as a "psycho-
    logical novel" <u>Euphues</u> comes "near the end of a tradition
    of prose fiction."

4   PEERY, WILLIAM. "The Three Souls Again." <u>PQ</u> 27, no. 1
    (January): 92-94.
        Rebuts Crofts' suggestion that Elyot is indebted to <u>Le</u>
    <u>Livre du Trésor</u> for his ideas concerning the three souls;
    the notion is too commonplace to ascribe direct influence.

5   WORTHAM, JAMES. "Sir Thomas Elyot and the Translation of
    Prose." <u>HLQ</u> 11, no. 3 (May): 219-240.
        A seminal article. Elyot believed that a translation
    should translate sentences, not words or phrases and should
    take account of "idiom," differences in the two languages
    of syntax, accidence, sentence length, etc. Elyot supplied
    three needs for English translation: fidelity to the orig-
    inal, a more analytic style, a greater clarity of syntax.
    His translation of Isocrates' <u>Ad Nicoclem</u> shows his most
    important innovations as a translator; it "goes beyond
    craftsmanship and becomes art by virtue of his own control in
    English of diction, rhythm, and melody." Examination of
    all the prose translations of classical works before 1580
    reveals "no other which seems to fulfill all the principles
    recognized by Elyot, that is, reproduction of figures of
    sound or <u>schemata verborum</u>; a consideration of rhythm;

compendiousness, or a dislike of inflated language; the
idea that style is substance; a desire to render sense, as
opposed to complete literal accuracy." Accepts the attribution of Dialogue between Lucian and Diogenes to Elyot.

1949

1   PHILLIPS, ELIAS H. "Humanitas in Tudor Literature." Ph.D.
dissertation, University of Pennsylvania, 184 pp.
     Argues that Governour (one of eight works or groups of
works considered, among them Utopia, Courtier, and Scholemaster) was "written and read" under the influence of
Ciceronian humanitas, embodying the ideas that the political order in the commonwealth coincides with the physical
and moral order of the universe and that through paideia
man is capable of perfection.

2   SLEDD, JAMES. "A Footnote on the Inkhorn Controversy," UTSE
28: 49-56.
     Cites fifty examples of words which appear in Elyot's
Bibliotheca and Cooper's Thesaurus which are earlier than
OED attribution. Concludes: "What matters is that so
many of the words are compounds, derivatives, words already
established in other senses, technical or 'low' words
which might exist for a long time in speech before they
made their way into general literature. . . . Careful
sampling, then, of the English columns in the dictionaries
does not show that the lexicographers had an undue predi-
lection for inkhorn terms or a real aversion to them.
Rather they appear to be in the main stream of Elizabethan
English."

3   STARNES, DEWITT T[ALMAGE]. "Thomas Cooper's Thesaurus: A
Chapter in Renaissance Lexicography." UTSE 28: 15-48.
     In two parts. The first surveys Cooper's sources by
way of asking whether Cooper plagiarized. In untangling
Cooper's indebtedness to Elyot, Stephanus, and Frisius,
shows that by the standards of the day he does not plagia-
rize. The second part demonstrates Cooper's contribution
to lexicography and is not concerned with Elyot. Revised
slightly as 1954.9.

1950

1   GRAESSE, JEAN GEORGE THÉODORE [Graesse, Johann George Theodor].
    Trésor des livres rares et précieux, ou nouveau diction-
    naire bibliographique. Vol. 2. Milan: G. G. Gorlich,
    p. 470.
       Cites nine imprints, with brief bibliographical commen-
    tary on Bankette, Image, Castel, and Dictionary. First
    edition, 1859.1.

2   HEXTER, J. H. "The Education of the Aristocracy in the Ren-
    aissance." The Journal of Modern History 22, no. 1 (March):
    1-20.
       A seminal article which asks "What . . . was the educa-
    tion of the aristocrats during the Renaissance, how many of
    them received it, and what did they want with it?" and
    provides answers which apply to England, France, and the
    Netherlands. The evidence of attendance at schools, of
    theoretical treatises on education, and of public documents
    by and relating to governmental servants indicates that far
    from acquiescing in ignorance, as is so often the charge,
    members of the Renaissance aristocracy pursued vigorously
    the learning that would enable them to "perform well their
    duty of service to their prince in council, in embassies,
    and in the governance of the commonwealth." This ideal of
    the end of learning remains generally constant from mid-
    fifteenth century to the late sixteenth; the means and
    methods become better understood. Although there is no
    extended discussion of Elyot, provides a concise general
    background for placing his educational theories in the
    larger European socio-political context.

3   SARGENT, RALPH M. "Sir Thomas Elyot and the Integrity of the
    Two Gentlemen of Verona." PMLA 65, no. 6 (December):
    1166-80.
       Shows that the tale of Titus and Gissypus in Governour
    II.xii is Shakespeare's "second major source" for Two Gen-
    tlemen and calls Governour II.xi "the locus classicus for
    the exposition of friendship in the English Renaissance."
    In Two Gentlemen, Shakespeare "stresses exactly the ele-
    ments of friendship that Elyot does."

4   WARREN, LESLIE. "Patrizi's De Regno et Regis Institutione and
    the Plan of Elyot's The Boke Named the Governour." JEGP
    49, no. 1 (January): 67-77.
       "Clarifies" Croft's contention (1880.1) that Patrizi's
    De Regno is the main source for Governour; Book I and part
    of III follow Patrizi, but where Elyot differs significantly,

in II, he shows a clearer conception of plan. Elyot limits
his work in three ways which differentiate it from De Regno:
his emphases on England rather than on kingship; on the in-
ferior governor and not the king; on private and moral
matters rather than on public and political. Only within
the limits of these differences can Governour be said to be
modelled on De Regno. Condensation of 1938.4. See also
1938.3.

1951

1 BUTT, JOHN. "A Plea for More English Dictionaries." Durham
University Journal n.s. 12 (June): 96–102.
Points out examples of foreign words introduced into
English by Elyot but which are not recorded by OED until
much later and argues for the necessity for period dictionaries to supplement OED. "In attempting to do so much,"
OED "presents us with a false record of the language as it
has been written and spoken at any one time. . . ."
Asserts also the need for more knowledge of the vocabulary
of Elyot's contemporaries like More and Wyatt; how did
they address the deficiencies of English for rendering the
moral-social-ethical ideas of the classics?

2 DONNER, H. W. "The Emperor and Sir Thomas Elyot." RES n.s.
2, no. 5 (January): 55–59.
Examines the famous statement attributed to Charles V
on hearing of the death of More. Noting a parallel to a
statement placed in the mouth of Aristippus in Elyot's
Knowledge, and assuming that Elyot wrote Knowledge in part
to help More, argues that the Emperor probably said "We
would rather lose the six best cities in our dominions,
than part with such a chancellour" on the occasion of
More's resignation. See 1930.4 and 1932.1.

3 LASCELLES, MARY. "Sir Thomas Elyot and the Legend of Alexander Severus." RES n.s. 2, no. 8 (October): 305–18.
Poses alternative, although "not mutually exclusive,"
answers to the question of whether Elyot intended to de-
ceive by claiming Image to be a translation. Suggests
1531–32 as the date of composition and says that Elyot was
either writing for a "circle" familiar with Guevara's work
at the Emperor's court or he actually had access to a work
composed under the influence of Guevara's circle. Also
discusses those elements in Elyot's work which influenced
later writers and shows that Alexander Severus materials
could be used for opposite purposes: to support king or
Parliament.

1952

4   STARNES, D[EWITT] T[ALMAGE]. "Some Sources of Wits Theatre of
    the Little World (1599) and Bodenham's Belvedere (1600)."
    PQ 30, no. 4 (October): 411-18.
        Wits Theatre is indebted in at least twenty passages to
    Governour; quotes seven in parallel format.

5   ____. "Thomas Cooper and the Bibliotheca Eliotae." UTSE 30:
    40-60.
        Discusses Cooper's augmentations to Elyot's Dictionary
    and their sources: Stephanus' Dictionarium Latino-Gallicum
    (1548) and Nicholas Udall's Floures for Latine Speakynge
    (1533). "Practically all of Udall's book is incorporated."
    Further augmentations in the 1552 edition are mainly in the
    area of herbs and birds and these make heavy use of William
    Turner's books. Cooper's main contributions to the devel-
    opment of English lexicography are an improved arrangement
    of entries; greater attention to the inflection and gender
    of nouns; addition of proper names of men, deities, cities;
    and "an incredible number of corrections in orthography
    and in other respects." Revised slightly as 1954.7.

1952

1   BENNETT, H[ENRY] S[TANLEY]. English Books and Readers, 1457
    to 1557: Being a Study in the History of the Book Trade
    from Caxton to the Incorporation of the Stationers' Company.
    Cambridge: Cambridge University Press, pp. 50, 51, 56, 61,
    90, 101, 102, 156, 157, 158, 164, 208.
        Although none of the references or citations is lengthy,
    valuable for the context in which Elyot's books are dis-
    cussed, their relationship to similar kinds of books,
    original or in translation, their illustration of shared
    attitudes or problems in book-publishing in the sixteenth
    century.

2   HEBEL, J[OHN] WILLIAM, HUDSON, HOYT H., JOHNSON, FRANCIS R.,
    and GREEN, A. WIGFALL, eds. Prose of the English Renais-
    sance: Selected from Early Editions and Manuscripts. New
    York: Appleton-Century-Crofts, pp. 795-99.
        Introduction and notes to selections from Governour.
    "To Elyot belongs the primary credit for establishing among
    the English scholars of the sixteenth century a vigorous
    tradition that they had an obligation to make their supe-
    rior knowledge available to others by opening the rich
    storehouse of wisdom enclosed in the writings of the an-
    cients."

1952

3   MEISSNER, PAUL. England im Zeitalter von Humanismus, Renais-
     sance, und Reformation. Heidelberg: F. H. Kerle, pp. 97–
     103 passim.
         Although Elyot is cited or referred to scores of times,
     Meissner's chief extended discussion is in these pages.
     In tracing the evolution of the English gentleman to
     Elyot's time, notes that Elyot for the first time adds a
     "political reality" to the concept. In contrast to the
     Italian notion that knowledge is a means to nurture the
     aesthetic personality, for Elyot it serves first the
     practical needs and political demands of leadership.

4   SIEGEL, PAUL N. "English Humanism and the New Tudor Aristo-
     cracy." JHI 13, no. 4 (October): 450–68.
         Analyzes the character of the "New Tudor Aristocracy"
     (that is, "the top-most reaches of the commercial gentry")
     and shows how it found in the humanist picture of man "a
     satisfyingly idealized image of itself and its society."
     Valuable background study.

                               1953

1   JONES, RICHARD FOSTER. The Triumph of the English Language:
     A Survey of Opinions Concerning the Vernacular from the
     Introduction of Printing to the Restoration. Stanford:
     Stanford University Press, pp. 13–14, 48–49, 78–93 passim.
         Sees Elyot as "the most deliberate and conscientious
     neologizer of the period," and gives examples of his
     method of clearly defining new terms. Concludes that Elyot
     was "interested both in improving the tongue and in trying
     it out to see what its good points were" and that "he was
     a linguistic experimenter testing and observing the verna-
     cular, pointing out its strength, and remedying its weak-
     ness."

2   MORRIS, CHRISTOPHER. Political Thought in England: Tyndale
     to Hooker. London, New York, and Toronto: Geoffrey Cum-
     berlage, Oxford University Press, pp. 23–25.
         Claims that Governour "might be called the political
     testament of English humanism," though it has an "element
     of escapism" at a time when "sweetness and light were dis-
     appearing fast." Sees significance in the way Elyot draws
     "eclectically" from all traditional sources but puts all
     on an equal footing.

1954

3   SCHOECK, R[ICHARD] J.   "Rhetoric and Law in Sixteenth-Century
    England."   SP 50, no. 2 (April): 110–27.
        In the course of sketching the broad outlines of the
    relations between rhetoric and law in the sixteenth cen-
    tury, contends that the "first important synthesis" of the
    two is in Elyot, "where law is treated not so much as
    adjunct to rhetoric but as the final study for the forming
    of perfect orators."   See 1957.1.

1954

1   BÜHLER, CURT F.   "Diogenes and The Boke Named the Governour."
    MLN 69, no. 7 (November): 481–84.
        Shows that an aphorism misattributed to Diogenes by
    Croft is in fact probably from Walter Burley's De vita et
    moribus philosophorum.

2   CASPARI, FRITZ.   Humanism and the Social Order in Tudor Eng-
    land.   Chicago: University of Chicago Press, pp. 76–109.
    Reprint.   New York: Teacher's College Press, Columbia
    University Press, 1968.
        Chapter 4, "Sir Thomas Elyot," provides the best con-
    cise introduction to Elyot's educational and social thought.
    Argues that unlike Erasmus, whose vision of society was too
    vague in its cosmopolitanism, and unlike More, whose com-
    munism was too radical for English implementation, Elyot
    produced in Governour a more practical social and educa-
    tional treatise which reflects the reality of the social
    order of Tudor England and which aims in relatively con-
    crete ways at improving the existing structure.   Although
    a "crude" counterpart to Castiglione's Courtier, "without
    the Italian's superb mastery of form," Governour is still
    "a genuine creation of Elyot's mind," and "the two writers
    are truly representative of their respective civilizations."
        In analyzing Governour, Caspari is particularly inter-
    ested in the prominent place which the study of poetry
    plays in Elyot's educational theory and in the relation
    between earlier broad, humanistic education and later,
    more technical training in jurisprudence.   He discusses the
    importance of Plato's influence on Elyot's notions of love
    and friendship, of wisdom and contemplation, and of hier-
    archy in the universe and state.   In explicating the last,
    ne gives attention to Elyot's economic theories, to his
    notion of Justice as the highest virtue, to his beliefs
    regarding freedom of the will, and to his views on the
    relative merits of virtue and good lineage in the determi-
    nation of a good "Governour."

41

1954

3   LEWIS C[LIVE] S[TAPLES]. English Literature in the Sixteenth
    Century, Excluding Drama. The Oxford History of English
    Literature, vol. 3. Oxford: Clarendon Press, pp. 273-76.
        Dictionary is probably the most useful thing that Elyot
    did. Governour is representative of a "new type" of work,
    less philosophical and universal than Erasmus's Institutio
    Regis Christiani, "more rooted in the realities of a par-
    ticular time and place." Elyot is probably most interest-
    ing for what we would today call aesthetic education. He
    is "a well informed man, not a scholar; a sensible man .
    . . not a deep thinker." Elyot's sentences "do not simply
    happen, they are built"; his prose is "more literary than
    More's," and "the ear of man must sometimes prefer him."

*4   MAJOR, JOHN M. "Sir Thomas Elyot: Studies in Early Tudor
    Humanism." Ph.D. dissertation, Harvard University.
        See 1964.2.

5   SCHIRMER, WALTER F[RANZ]. Geschichte der englischen und
    amerikanischen Literatur von der Anfängen bis zur Gegenwart.
    2d ed., rev. Vol. 1. Tubingen: Max Niemeyer, pp. 209-10.
        Brief general introduction to Elyot as representative
    humanist. First edition, 1937.2.

6   SLEDD, JAMES. "Nowell's Vocabularium Saxonicum and the Elyot-
    Cooper Tradition." SP 51, no. 2 (April): 143-48.
        Examines Nowell's work in relation to Cooper's 1565
    Thesaurus to correct statements of A. H. Marckwardt about
    the relation of Nowell to William Somner's Dictionarium
    Saxonico-Latino-Anglicum; both works are independently
    indebted to Cooper-Elyot.

7   STARNES, DEWITT, T[ALMAGE]. "Bibliotheca Eliotae: Eliotis
    Librarie (1548)." In Renaissance Dictionaries: English-
    Latin and Latin-English. Austin: University of Texas
    Press, 68-84.
        Revision of 1951.5, with some examples transposed and a
    few transitions altered.

8   _____. "The Dictionary of Syr Thomas Eliot (1538)." In
    Renaissance Dictionaries: English-Latin and Latin-English.
    Austin: University of Texas Press, pp. 45-67.
        Contains a bibliographical description, including "The
    Addicion of Syr Thomas Eliot knight"; an account of the
    principal sources (chiefly Ambrosius Calepinus' Dictionari-
    um, 1520); a detailing of the changes in the 1542 edition,
    with examples of expansions; a discussion of Elyot's in-
    debtedness to Robert Stephanus' Dictionarium Latino-Gallicum

of 1538, the chief source of Elyot's augmentation; a dem-
onstration, on the basis of differences between the 1542
and 1545 editions, that they are different editions. A
final section is devoted to Elyot's importance in the development of a classical Latin-English dictionary; mainly in
his inclusion of "literary features"--i.e., "biographical
sketches, personal reminiscences, pseudo natural history
and mythology, and proverbs and adagia."

9   _____ . "Thomas Cooper's Thesaurus linguae Romanae & Britan-
nicae (1576)." In Renaissance Dictionaries: English-Latin
and Latin-English. Austin: University of Texas Press,
pp. 85-110.
    Slight revision of 1949.3.

1955

1   STARNES, D[EWITT] T[ALMAGE]. "Sir Thomas Elyot and the
Lanquet-Cooper Chronicle." UISE 34: 35-42.
    Shows that at least thirty-nine brief biographies in the
Lanquet-Cooper Chronicle (1549) were written by Elyot.
This pilfering seems to be Cooper's work. Elyot gathers
his biographical material from a wide range of sources and,
as comparison of the English and Latin shows, he is for
the most part translating. Elyot's work continues to appear, unacknowledged, in later chronicles of Cooper and
Grafton, down to 1569.

1956

1   MAXWELL, J[AMES] C[LOUTTS]. "Julius Caesar and Elyot's Governour." N&Q n.s. 3, no. 4 (April): 147
    II.i.203-08 is indebted to Governour II, xiv, on flat-
tery.

1957

1   BLAND, D. S. "Rhetoric and the Law Student in Sixteenth-
Century England." SP 54, no. 4 (October): 498-508.
    Seeks to answer a question posed at the end of Schoeck's
article (1953.3): to what extent were law students who had
not gone to Oxford or Cambridge given rhetorical training
in the Inns of Court? Argues that rhetoric was not taught
there and suggests that the development of drama in the
Inns may have been compensation for this lack. Claims that
Schoeck has been "over enthusiastic."

1957

2 BULLOUGH, GEOFFREY, ed. <u>Narrative and Dramatic Sources of
   Shakespeare</u>. Vol. 1. <u>Early Comedies, Poems, "Romeo and
   Juliet</u>." London: Routledge and Kegan Paul; New York:
   Columbia University Press, pp. 212-17.
      Quotes from Elyot's "Tale of Titus and Gisyppus" (<u>Gov-
   ernour</u>, II, xii) as a "possible source" for <u>Two Gentlemen
   of Verona</u>.

3 LEHMBERG, STANFORD E. "Sir Thomas Elyot and the English
   Reformation." <u>Archiv für Reformationsgeschichte</u> 48, no. 1:
   91-111.
      Examines Elyot's various comments regarding the Reforma-
   tion. Though he did not object to changes in ecclesiastical organization and though he favored a simplification of
   ceremonies, he nevertheless retained the basic theological
   beliefs of his Roman Catholicism regarding good works and
   freedom of the will.

4 STARNES, D[EWITT] T[ALMAGE]. "Sir Thomas Elyot <u>Redivivus</u>."
   <u>UTSE</u> 36: 28-40.
      Demonstrates the influence of Elyot on four sixteenth-
   and seventeenth-century works: John Bossewell's <u>Workes of
   Armorie</u> (London, 1572; 1597); Thomas Forrest's <u>A Perfite
   Looking Glasse for All Estates</u> (London, 1580); James Cleland's <u>The Institution of a Young Nobleman</u> (Oxford, 1607);
   and <u>Principles for Young Princes</u> (1611) attributed to Sir
   George More. Shows manner in which each writer borrowed
   from Elyot.

1958

1 BOUCK, CONSTANCE W. "On the Identity of Papyrius Geminus
   Eleates." <u>Transactions of the Cambridge Bibliographical
   Soeiety</u> 2, part 5: 352-58.
      Surveys six classes of circumstantial evidence which
   lead to the probability that Elyot is author of the 1522
   <u>Hermathena</u>.

2 MAJOR, JOHN M. "The Moralization of the Dance in Elyot's
   <u>Governour</u>." <u>Studies in the Renaissance</u> 5: 27-36.
      Identifies three stages in Elyot's theory of the dance
   as moral exercise and indicates the contributions of
   Aristotle, Lucian, Plato, and the medieval allegorical
   tradition to the theory. Finds in Elyot an "almost total
   absence of any aesthetic appreciation of dancing."

1959

3   RICE, EUGENE F., JR. The Renaissance Idea of Wisdom. Harvard
      Historical Monographs, 37. Cambridge, Mass.: Harvard
      University Press, pp. 85-92.
        Sees Elyot's Knowledge as belonging to the tradition of
      Sadoleto's "break" with Florentine Neoplatonism; both Elyot
      and Sadoleto define wisdom as a human virtue naturally ac-
      quired. For Elyot, "wisdom is a natural knowledge of
      divine and immutable things, from the intelligibles of
      metaphysics to the 'things invisible' of natural theology.
      It is potential in the soul's knowledge of the ideas innate
      in it; partially perfected in the knowledge, symbolized by
      mathematics, of universal forms; . . . and fully perfected,
      in the contemplation of the divine majesty." For reserva-
      tions, see 1964.2. See index for other passages, which
      discuss Elyot's view of the relation between wisdom and
      experience, or use him to define transformations in the
      concept of wisdom.

                              1959

1   HOGREFFE, PEARL. The Sir Thomas More Circle: A Program of
      Ideas and Their Impact on Secular Drama. Urbana: Univer-
      sity of Illinois Press, pp. 59-63, 130-34, 180-83.
        The most substantial discussions occur in chapters en-
      titled "The Bases of True Nobility," "Law and Government,"
      and "Education in General." The first shows how Elyot's
      aristocratic bias distinguishes him from the first genera-
      tion of the "More circle." The second outlines succinctly
      Elyot's ideas on government in Governour and other works
      and points to his concern for law reform in I.xiv. The
      third is a somewhat cursory review of Elyot's educational
      theories. Throughout Hogrefe differentiates Elyot's
      thought from that of More, Erasmus, and Vives.

2   KNOWLES, DOM DAVID. The Religious Orders in England. Vol. 3.
      The Tudor Age. Cambridge: Cambridge University Press,
      pp. 291-302.
        Although alluding only once to Elyot, Chapter 22 ("The
      Act of Suppression and the Case for the Defence") offers
      valuable background for Elyot's involvement in the visita-
      tion of the monasteries in 1535-36, particularly regarding
      climate of opinion among local gentry. Compare 1924.1.

3   ONG, WALTER J., S.J. "Latin Language Study as a Renaissance
      Puberty Rite." SP 56, no. 2 (April): 103-24.
        Argues that the study of Latin was for the schoolboy in
      the Renaissance an initiation; accompanied often by

1960

whippings, it was a process of "toughening" and of separating the boy from the familial past, preparing him for the
rigors of the adult world of men. Education of the child
is for Elyot particularly associated with courage; each
time he mentions the child's age in Governour I, x–xvi, he
comments explicitly on "corage."

1960

1   FERGUSON, ARTHUR B. The Indian Summer of English Chivalry:
    Studies in the Decline and Transformation of Chivalric
    Idealism. Durham, N.C.: Duke University Press, pp. 218–21.
       Elyot reflects "with peculiar clarity" the influences
    shaping a "new social ideal," that of the knight more ef-
    fective with his learning than with his sword.

2   LEHMBERG, STANFORD E. Sir Thomas Elyot: Tudor Humanist.
    Austin: University of Texas Press, xv, 218 pp.
       Ten chapters chronologically arranged, supplemented by
    three appendices, a bibliography which "attempts to list
    all significant writings concerning Elyot," and an index.
    Lehmberg's chief governing assumption is that there is much
    biographical material to be gleaned from the works, which
    must be "studied carefully in light of events contemporary
    with their composition." Argues in Chapter 1 that Elyot
    did attend Oxford. Chapters 3–5 are devoted to Governour:
    to the argument that Elyot wrote it to ingratiate himself
    with Henry, and that I, i–iii, were written later than the
    rest of the book; to an analysis of its contents; to an
    elucidation of Elyot's sources, some commentary on his use
    of language, and a somewhat cursory indication of his in-
    fluence on later writers. The assessment of sources is
    superseded by Major's study (1964.2). Although Lehmberg
    sees the dialogues of 1533 as critical of Henry VIII, he
    stops short of claiming that they were specifically designed
    to defend More. Chapter 8 examines the works of 1532–38,
    arguing that the translation of Plutarch's "How One May
    Take Profit" is by Elyot, that 1534 may be the date of the
    first edition of Bankette, and that the 1539 edition of
    Castel is not the first.
       Chapter 9 examines Elyot's personal religious beliefs
    and his private life after 1532. The final chapter looks
    at the last published works, and sees Defence as a "veiled
    defense of Catherine of Aragon." Appendix II prints
    Elyot's will for the first time. See 1961.4, 1963.3.

1961

1 AMMANN, ROMAN ERNST. Die Verbalsyntax in Sir Thomas Elyots
   "Governour" mit vergleichenden Beispielen aus Roger Aschams
   "Scholemaster." Aarau: Keller, AG, 129 pp.
   In separate chapters describes the verbal inflections
   which appear in Elyot, his use of impersonal verb forms, of
   active and passive voice, of the infinitive and gerund,
   tense, aspect, mode, participials, and the verbs do, may,
   and can. Reaches the following tentative conclusions:
   that the influence of classical Latin is very large and is
   seen both in the syntax and the style of the sentence; that
   both Governour and Scholemaster belong to the transition
   period between middle and modern English; that Elyot is not
   only one of the best representatives of pre-Elizabethan
   English humanism, but also an important developer of modern
   English prose style.

2 BAKER, HERSCHEL. The Image of Man: A Study of the Idea of
   Human Dignity in Classical Antiquity, the Middle Ages, and
   the Renaissance. New York: Harper & Brothers, pp. 231,
   233-34, 277, 286, 288, 295-96, 324.
   Elyot's is "the genuine voice of all conservatives at
   all times," and he is important as an ethical spokesman in
   the sixteenth century. His ethics embody "a class morality
   of noblesse oblige." Originally published as The Dignity
   of Man. See 1947.2.

3 HOLMES, ELISABETH. "The Significance of Elyot's Revision of
   the Governour." RES n.s. 12 (November): 352-63.
   A collation of the first and second editions "indicates
   a modification of Elyot's attitude toward neologisms and
   archaisms, a developing feeling for the structure of the
   English sentence, and a recognition of his own weakness
   for anacoluthon, tautology, prolixity, and naive personal
   reference." Claims that her conclusions will "give point"
   to those of Bult (1951.1) and Gledd (1949.2). See, however, the reservations of Rude (1971.5).

4 SYLVESTER, RICHARD S. Review of Sir Thomas Elyot, Tudor
   Humanist, by Stanford E. Lehmberg. Renaissance News 14,
   no. 3 (Autumn): 178-81.
   Though Lehmberg "has done his job well" in coping with
   the biographical problems, he has not solved everything,
   and in particular the relation with More. Why does More
   never mention Elyot? Finds Lehmberg's attempts to disen-
   tangle the allegory of Elyot's writings from 1533-45 un-
   convincing, particularly the claim that Elyot disapproved

of Anne Boleyn. The claim that Elyot was a better prose
stylist than More is "ludicrous"; "no one of More's pupils
ever surpassed his master." Corrects several errors. <u>See</u>
1960.2.

<u>1962</u>

1   BULLOUGH, GEOFFREY, ed. <u>Narrative and Dramatic Sources of</u>
     <u>Shakespeare</u>. Vol 4. <u>Later English History Plays</u>. London:
     Routledge & Kegan Paul; New York: Columbia University
     Press, pp. 257, 259, 265, 288–89.
         Discusses the relation of <u>Governor</u> to <u>II Henry IV</u> and
     quotes a passage from II, vi as a "possible source" for IV.
     iv.33–41.

2   FREEMAN, ERIC J. "Bibliography of Sir Thomas Elyot (1490?–
     1546)." Bibliography submitted in partial requirement for
     the University of London diploma in Librarianship.
         The front matter contains an introduction, a key to lo-
     cations, a list of authorities, and an index of printers
     and publishers. The text is a primary, descriptive bib-
     liography, divided into two parts: genuine works and works
     attributed to Elyot. The aim is "to record all the extant
     sixteenth- and seventeenth-century editions of Elyot's
     books, and to illustrate their bibliographical relation-
     ships and principal variations," thereby showing "in out-
     line" the publishing history of Elyot's books and providing
     "the raw material for the study of his text."
         The introduction explains in detail Freeman's method.
     The descriptions are "intended to enable the reader to
     identify the particular book described, understand some-
     thing of its printing, recognize its precise contents, and
     identify his own copies." Each description includes the
     following: a quasi-facsimile transcription of the title
     page; the colophon; the collation, representing "as far
     as possible an 'ideal copy' of the edition"; head titles,
     if any; running titles; a description of the contents
     intended to "provide a description of the various parts of
     the book"; a selection of catchwords; notes, including
     such items as STC number, the measure of twenty lines of
     solid text type, a suggestion of the probable copy text,
     the probable date of undated editions, identity of unknown
     printers, and major variations in text.

1963

3   LEHMBERG, STANFORD E.   Introduction to his edition of The
    Book Named Governor.   Everyman's Library.   London: Dent;
    New York: Dutton, pp. v-viii.
        Introduces Elyot and Governor to the general reader,
    claiming that Elyot was educated at Oxford, that his poli-
    tical theory is the most significant part of Governour,
    that the book may have helped shape the ideas of James VI
    about the power of the monarch, that it "set the tone" for
    later writers of courtesy books.   Lehmberg's edition adopts
    modernized spelling, unlike the earlier edition by Foster
    Watson (1907.1).

1963

1   BROOKS, HAROLD F.   "Shakespeare and The Governour, Bk. II,
    ch. xiii: Parallels with Richard II and the More Addition."
    SQ 14, no. 3 (Summer): 195-99.
        Proposes that the passage in Governour is a source for
    Richard's moralisation on the defection of Roan Barbary at
    V.v.77-90.   Also argues that the same chapter, in being a
    source for Hand D's addition to Sir Thomas More, is evi-
    dence that the hand is Shakespeare's.

2   GOTTESMAN, LILLIAN.   "Sir Thomas Elyot, Educator."   Ph.D.
    dissertation, New York University, 182 pp.
        Studies all of Elyot's works as "tracts on education--
    humanistic education, political education, religious edu-
    cation"--and aims to "reintroduce" Elyot's little-known
    works to a modern audience by discussing their contents,
    style, dates of composition, sources, contemporary allu-
    sions, and timeless principles.

3   HOGREFE, PEARL.   "Sir Thomas Elyot's Intention in the Opening
    Chapters of the Governour."   SP 60, no. 2, (April): 133-40.
        Rebuts Lehmberg's speculations (see 1960.2) that Elyot
    wrote Chapters 1-3 in support of unlimited power for Henry
    VIII and perhaps at insistence of Cromwell: verb tenses
    suggest a "looking forward" rather than something inserted,
    and Elyot's demand that a king "rule with justice and
    wisdom, act for the common welfare, avoid tyranny, and
    bring England to excellence as a public weal" is at odds
    with an espousal of absolute power.   Furthermore, these
    ideas grow to a natural climax in the rest of the work.
    (See also 1967.3.)

1963

4   RYAN, LAWRENCE V. Roger Ascham. Stanford: Stanford Univer-
    sity Press; London: Oxford University Press, pp. 61–65,
    260–62, 282–83.
        Finds Ascham indebted to Elyot for Toxophilus--for in-
    spiration to write on archery, for several particular
    ideas, for incentive to write in English. Sees in Schole-
    master a "strong kinship in ideals" between Ascham and
    Elyot.

1964

1   BULLOUGH, GEOFFREY, ed. Narrative and Dramatic Sources of
    Shakespeare. Vol 5. The Roman Plays. London: Routledge
    & Kegan Paul; New York: Columbia University Press, pp. 22–
    23, 166–68.
        Cites references to Caesar in Governour, "a book which
    Shakespeare seems to have known well," and claims that a
    passage on "affability" (II.v), among others, may have in-
    fluenced Shakespeare. Quotes three passages as analogues
    to the play: II.v, III.xvi, and III.vi.

2   MAJOR, JOHN M. Sir Thomas Elyot and Renaissance Humanism.
    Lincoln, Neb.: University of Nebraska Press, xii, 276 pp.
        The only book-length critical study, examines Elyot's
    sources in detail. An initial section on the "plan" of
    Governour is followed by chapters on Elyot's indebtedness
    to Italian humanists, Erasmus, More, classical authors
    other than Plato, and Plato. Major finds the "loose and
    sprawling structure" of Governour to result from Elyot's
    "determination to be encyclopedic," from the absence of a
    prior model in English, and from its unfinished state.
    The chapter on the Italians examines the compatibility in
    the thinking of Elyot and Castiglione and assesses the in-
    fluence of Machiavelli. Of all Elyot's near-contemporaries,
    Erasmus wielded the strongest influence. Major believes
    that Elyot's works between 1532 and 1535 are all "defenses"
    of More and that Governour, heavily influenced by More, is
    an "anti-Utopia." Elyot is "unusual" in the Renaissance
    for his high admiration of Aristotle, and his "governor"
    resembles Cicero's "orator" more than any other literary
    or historical type. The final three chapters discuss
    Plato's influence on Elyot's political ideas (his theories
    of order, kingship, and equity), on his psychology (Elyot's
    epistemology is "wholly Platonic" and suggests first-hand
    knowledge of Timeaus and Phaedo), and on his ethics.

1965

3   PINCKERT, ROBERT CARL. "Sir Thomas Elyot's The Image of Gov-
    ernance (1541): A Critical Edition." Ph.D. dissertation,
    Columbia University, 417 pp.
        Based on the first edition, collates copies of five
    early editions in the Folger Library. Differs from H. E.
    Joyce's rotograph edition of 1926 (see 1926.1) in providing
    a lengthy introduction; footnotes for variant readings,
    emendations, and other textual matters; end notes for
    comments on the substance of the text; glossary of archaic
    words; and an appendix on the canon of Elyot's works. The
    "Introduction" claims that Image is a "complement" to
    Governour and that it is also a "literary fraud" in which
    Elyot "deceives his readers." Traces the tradition of the
    speculum principis from Xenophon to Guevara and compares
    Image with More's Utopia. Calls Image "a document of the
    first importance for the comprehension of English human-
    ism," as well as "an artistic and original work of realis-
    tic prose fiction."

                              1965

1   British Museum General Catalogue of Printed Books. Photo-
    lithographic Edition to 1955. Vol. 61. London: Trustees
    of the British Museum, cols. 338-41.
        Cites fifty-nine imprints, distributed as follows:
    Sermon (1534); Image (1541, 1544, 1549, 1556); Doctrinal
    (1534); Education [1535?]; Bankette (1539, 1542, 1545,
    1557); Governour (1531, 1537, 1544, 1546, 1553, 1565,
    1580, 1834, 1880, 1907); Castel (1539, 1541, 1547, [1560?],
    1561, 1572, 1580, 1594, 1610, 1936); Defence (1545, 1912);
    Dictionary-Bibliotheca (1538, 1542, 1545, 1548, 1552,
    1559); Knowledge (1533, [1552?], 1946); Pasquil (1540);
    Preservative (1545); lists also a few secondary sources
    with selections.

2   CHARLTON, KENNETH. Education in Renaissance England. London:
    Routledge & Kegan Paul; Toronto: University of Toronto
    Press, pp. 82-85, 115-17, 242-43.
        Compares Elyot and Castiglione as models of their re-
    spective kinds, influential on the literature of their
    respective languages throughout the sixteenth century;
    locates the importance of Elyot's dictionary among those
    in common use in grammar schools; discusses his attempts
    to purify the legal language of the day; and assesses his
    translations. See index for other, frequent, citations.

1965

3   FERGUSON, ARTHUR B.   The Articulate Citizen and the English
      Renaissance. Durham, N.C.: Duke University Press,
      pp. 162-99, passim.
         Although Elyot is not the sole subject of Chapter VII,
      "The Intellectual and the Problem of Counsel," in the
      course of describing the emergence of "a new figure . . .
      the intellectual . . . more often than not a layman,
      widely read in the secular culture of the antique world,
      and confident in the broadening beneficence of such
      studies in the actual ordering of the commonwealth," Fer-
      guson draws at length upon Elyot's Governour and Knowledge,
      claiming that in the 1530s it was Elyot who "became the
      truly effective apostle of humanism to the English govern-
      ing class." Governour is a "landmark" in the "history of
      'applied' humanism in England."

4   McCONICA, JAMES KELSEY.   English Humanists and Reformation
      Politics Under Henry VIII and Edward VI. Oxford: Clarendon
      Press, pp. 121-23, 182-83, 196-99.
         Discusses Elyot in context of Cromwell's "semi-official"
      sponsorship of church and state reform along Erasmian doc-
      trinal and political lines. Sees Governour as "a magis-
      terial statement" of the Erasmian program, and Elyot as "an
      almost ideally representative figure of the moderate re-
      forming party." At the same time Elyot's is an "independ-
      ent voice among Cromwell's humanist writers," as attested
      by the disapproval of the royal divorce in Pasquil the
      Playne.

5   ONG, WALTER J., S.J.   "Oral Residue in Tudor Prose Style."
      PMLA 80, no. 3 (June): 145-54.
         Sees in Elyot examples of the use of "parallelisms which
      are formulaic in a highly oral way, often incremental."

6   PHIALAS, PETER G.   "Shakespeare's Henry V and the Second
      Tetralogy." SP 62, no. 2 (April): 155-75.
         Cites Elyot as an example of the main idea of the tetral-
      ogy, that success in public life depends on an ability to
      reconcile its demands with the claims of individual,
      personal life.

1966

1   GORDON, IAN.   The Movement of English Prose. London: Long-
      mans, pp. 76-77.
         Sees Elyot as one of two types of "ink-horn men," one
      who "wrestled with the 'inadequacy' of English," and whose

"linguistic tact" was such that "we could not do without
the many words . . . for which the NED can find no earlier
record than The Governour."

2   NEWKIRK, GLEN ALTON.   "The Public and Private Ideal of the
    Sixteenth Century Gentleman: A Representative Analysis."
    Ph.D. dissertation, University of Denver, 345 pp.
        Traces the classical concept of the virtuous man trained
    to serve his state and analyzes the "gentlemanly ideal,"
    which was undeveloped in England before the arrival of the
    humanists in Oxford but which in the course of the century
    was assimilated into "the more imaginative literature,"
    where it "received a more valid representation."

3   PEPPER, ROBERT D.   Introduction to his edition of Four Tudor
    Books on Education. Gainesville, Fla.: Scholars' Facsim-
    iles & Reprints, pp. ix-xii.
        Calls Peri Paidon Agoges (attributed to Plutarch),
    which Elyot translated as The Education or Bringing Up of
    Children (1533), "one of the most influential treatises
    in the history of European educational theory." Discusses
    probable date, omissions and additions to Greek text, use
    of other sources in translating, and influence on later
    writers, notably Lyly and Will Kempe.

4   RYDÉN, MATS.   Relative Constructions in Early Sixteenth Cen-
    tury English, with Special Reference to Sir Thomas Elyot.
    Acta Universitatis Upsaliensis. Studia Anglistica Upsali-
    ensia 3. Uppsala: Almqvist & Wiksells, lvi, 384 pp.,
    with 24 unpaginated tables of frequency surveys.
        A descriptive-analytic study of Elyot's use of relative
    constructions, to which are added "a number of other rep-
    resentative prose texts from the period." While making
    no claim to exhaustiveness, surveys sufficient data to
    indicate reliably the use of relatives in the literary
    language of the period 1520-60. The introduction contains
    a brief life of Elyot and a list of his writings. The
    bibliography, which aims to present a complete listing of
    previous work on relative constructions in English, lists
    items overlooked by Lehmberg (1960.2). Rydén reaches the
    following conclusions: "In the main, Elyot can be said to
    be a fairly true exponent of the literary language of the
    time. . . .   Remarkable features of Elyot's usage are . . .
    a comparatively high frequency of who and of restrictive
    which, the extreme rarity of the which . . . of preposition
    + which, and of zero. Distributional patterns do not dif-
    fer very greatly in the various books. There are no funda-
    mental differences between his original works and his

translations. . . . Among characteristics of individual
books is the high proportion of which in Castel and Sermon
and of that in Doctrinall and Bankett. . . . The Prefaces
and Prohemes . . . are often more complicated in sentence-
structure than the books themselves." As regards the dis-
puted works, Profit and Dialogue, in both "the combination
that that is strikingly common." And three features are
found in Profit which do not occur in Elyot's authentic
works: objective personal the which, whence without
preposition from, and anticipatory that that.

5 SIMON, JOAN. Education and Society in Tudor England. Cambridge: Cambridge University Press, pp. 150-56.
In a chapter entitled "Education and the State: Some
Proposals for Reform," discusses Elyot's position as a
conservative spokesman "at a time when events and ideas
were unfolding apace." He "proposed refurbishing a familiar form of upbringing by giving a humanist content to
instruction in the household." Briefly summarizes Elyot's
main educational tenets, and observes that his "complicated
programme of classical studies" was the exception rather
than the rule, citing the program followed by Gregory
Cromwell. See Index for frequent passim references.

1967

1 BROOKE, [C. F.] TUCKER. "The Renaissance." In A Literary
History of England. Edited by Albert C. Baugh. 2d ed.
New York and London: Appleton-Century-Crofts, pp. 329-32.
Text unchanged from the first edition (1948.2); bib-
liography revised.

2 GOTTESMAN, LILLIAN. Introduction to her edition of Four
Political Treatises . . . by Sir Thomas Elyot. Gaines-
ville, Fla.: Scholars' Facsimiles & Reprints, pp. vii-xiv.
Brief introduction to Doctrinal, Pasquil, Bankette, and
Image. Claims Doctrinal was written in 1533 shortly after
Elyot's return from the Emperor's court; it precedes
Pasquil. Speculates as to the historical figures repre-
sented in Pasquil. Summarizes dispute over the source of
Image without attempting a resolution. All four works
share a concern with the utilization of learning in prac-
tical service to the state.

3 HOGREFE, PEARL. The Life and Times of Sir Thomas Elyot,
   Englishman. Ames: Iowa State University Press, xii,
   410 pp.
      Using a technique that she terms "account of probable
   mental events," seeks to achieve three aims, speculating
   at times freely on the available evidence, including "mostly
   unpublished wills": to indicate Elyot's relationship to
   the major events of the period; to give "as complete" an
   account of Elyot's life and writings "as remaining materials permit"; and to "emphasize the English elements in his
   life and in his writings." The first seven chapters cover
   the years to the publication of Governour in 1531, with
   more emphasis on the "times" than on the "life"; for
   example, Chapter IV presents a composite picture of the
   ideas and attitudes of "westcountry landed gentry" on the
   assumption that the people described "must have exerted an
   influence on the life and thinking of Elyot." Corrects
   earlier biographers by showing that Richard Fettiplace had
   twelve children not seven, and, on the basis of four statements by Elyot about his education, concludes that he did
   not have a university education, but studied at one of the
   Inns of Chancery in preparation for entering the Middle
   Temple, and that he also studied with both Linacre and
   More. In a chapter on Elyot's clerkship on Wosley's
   Council, speculates as to why he would have served six and
   a half years without pay. Chapters VII and VIII analyze
   the contents, sources, and influence of Governour, with
   stress on its "Individual and English Ideas." Disagrees
   with Lehmberg (1960.2) about Elyot's motives for writing
   I.i-iii and claims that the book's stress on sexual
   morality "seems to be something unique in manuals for the
   education of a gentleman." Claims further that Elyot was
   not dependent on "sources" for his ideas about music,
   dancing, archery, painting, carving, and law, but "had only
   to look at English life." Chapter IX shows that Elyot's
   tenure as ambassador was normal for the period, suggests
   that he was appointed to the post because of his ability
   to argue tactfully and persuasively, and rejects Major's
   suggestion (1964.2) that Elyot was in the pay of Charles V.
   Chapters X-XV are devoted to analysis of or commentary on
   Elyot's works. She sees in Governour, Pasquil, and Knowledge a "cumulative development based on Elyot's effort to
   influence his king." She reads St. Cyprian and Pico's
   Rules as offering consolation for the troubled times
   brought on by Henry's treatment of the religious orders.
   She concludes that Profit and Lucian are probably by Elyot
   and that they, as well as Education and Doctrinal, were

1968

begun as "exercises . . . when Elyot was training himself
in the use of Greek and Latin." Doctrinal is the most
significant piece of translation from Greek before the
1580s. She argues, contra Lehmberg, that Defence contains
no specific reminders of Catherine of Aragon. Image is
perhaps the "second volume" of which Elyot speaks in Governour, and in it Elyot may be consciously following the
ideas of More's Utopia "on a realistic basis." The final
chapter provides a good summary of Elyot's personality and
succinctly answers the question "Why is Elyot important?"

1968

1 BROWN, MARICE COLLINS. "A Descriptive Grammar of the Early
   Sixteenth Century as Ascertained from the Corpus, The
   Castel of Helth by Sir Thomas Elyot." Ph.D. dissertation,
   Louisiana State University, 119 pp.
       Discusses four major word classes defined by paradig-
   matic sets (nouns, pronouns, verbs, adjunctivals) and two
   classes defined by relationships with other words, phrases,
   or clauses (prepositions and conjunctivals). Finds that
   the "most promising" line for further study is a "system
   of signalling that controlled clause structure."

2 O'MALLEY, C[HARLES] D[ONALD]. "Tudor Medicine and Biology."
   HLQ 32, (November): 1-27.
       Although it contains only a paragraph on Castel, it is
   one of the few works available which "places" Elyot in the
   larger context of writings about medicine in the Tudor
   period.

1969

1 CREETH, EDMUND. Introduction to his edition of Tudor Prose,
   1513-1570. Garden City, N.Y.: Doubleday & Co., pp. xviii-
   xxii.
       A general introduction to Knowledge (reprinted complete,
   pp. 177-274), discussing its sources, and claiming that it
   adopts Plato's dialogues "directly and accurately, without
   medievalisms, for the first time in English."

2 MAJOR, JOHN M. Introduction to his edition, abridged, of Sir
   Thomas Elyot's "The Book Named the Governor." Classics in
   Education, no. 40. New York: Teachers College Press,
   Columbia University Press, pp. 1-27.

Surveys the life of Elyot, emphasizing the "complicated" nature of the times in which he produced Governour and the three works of 1533 on "counsel." Analyzes the "plan of education for the nobleman's child" laid forth in Governour, Book I, through which Elyot is "seeking to mold the complete English gentleman . . . and through him, a flourishing English society."

3   The National Union Catalog, Pre-1956 Imprints. A Cumulative Author List Representing Library of Congress Printed Cards and Titles Reported by Other American Libraries. Vol. 159. Chicago and London: Mansell, pp. 160-68.

Cites 135 separate imprints (including at least one imprint of each of Elyot's works), distributed as following: 12 of Bankette, 11 of Bibliotheca, 9 of Governour, 45 of Castel, 6 of Defence, 3 of Dictionary, 1 of Education, 12 of Image, 9 of Knowledge, 5 of Pasquil, 1 of Preservative, 1 of Sermon.

1970

1   CAREY, JOHN. "Sixteenth and Seventeenth Century Prose, Part I, Prose before Elizabeth." In History of Literature in the English Language. Vol. 2. English Poetry and Prose, 1540-1764. Edited by Christopher Ricks. London: Barrie and Jenkins, pp. 353-54.

A brief assessment of Elyot as "dedicated to the imaginative possession, through the words, of what he takes in hand." His prose "achieves an integration of the natural, human, and political which challenges comparison with, say Marvell's 'Little T. C. in a Prospect of Flowers.'"

2   MacDONALD, MICHAEL JOSEPH. "A Study of Sir Thomas Elyot's Pasquil the Playne." Ph.D. dissertation, University of Toronto.

Sees "four facts as essential to an understanding of Pasquil: it is a description; it is written in the vernacular; it owes a debt to 'the sayenges of moste noble autors' . . . ; and it is informed by practical experience." Examines each in turn. The third section stresses the fact that Pasquil "reflects a commonplace structure ordered in the very nature of the young governor"; it thus "resembles a handbook." The most important issue in Pasquil is language; the work aims to instruct how to use words in their "trew" and "proper signification" in counsel. See 1973.1.

1970

3   PARTEE, MORRISS HENRY. "Sir Thomas Elyot on Plato's Aesthet-
      ics." Viator: Medieval and Renaissance Studies 1: 327-35.
         Beginning with the apparent contradiction in which Elyot
      uses Plato to approve of poetry in Governour and condemn it
      in Defense, shows that the problem arises from an apparent
      inconsistency in Plato's own aesthetics. Says in conclu-
      sion that "Elyot glosses over a distinction between the
      divine beauty of poetry and the effects of poetry on fal-
      lible men, a problem never fully even solved by Plato."
      Shows that Elyot "consistently gives poetry more credit
      than does Plato." See 1941.1.

4   RIERDAN, RICHARD COTTER. "Sir Thomas Elyot: A Theory and
      Practice of Written Communication in the Early Sixteenth
      Century." Ph.D. dissertation, University of California at
      Los Angeles, 210 pp.
         Develops the thesis that Elyot has "a clearly articulat-
      ed theory of communication based on Plato's idea of the
      relationship of knowledge to virtue and Cicero's distinc-
      tion between a rhetorician and an orator." Like Plato,
      Elyot believes that wisdom is innate in man but is gradu-
      ally forgotten; his works are written to remind man of this
      loss. Chapters 2-4 treat the sources by which a governor
      can learn the proper use of language; examine Elyot's
      reliance on letter-writing manuals for the form of his
      prefaces; and analyze his techniques as a translator. The
      final chapter discusses style, structure, and characteri-
      zation in Elyot's three dialogues.

5   SKOV, JOHN VILLADS. "The First Edition of Sir Thomas Elyot's
      Castell of Helthe, with Introduction and Critical Notes."
      Ph.D. dissertation, University of California at Los Angeles,
      439 pp.
         A facsimile reproduction of the first edition (which
      survives in a single copy) with textual notes providing a
      critical study of the text and introduction discussing the
      date of the first edition and the sequence of succeeding
      editions. Castel belongs to a loosely defined class of
      medical writings called regimina and reflects the influ-
      ence of medical humanism, that is, a return to original
      Greek and Roman texts. Since the legacy of Castel extends
      to imaginative writers like Shakespeare and Spenser, it
      is "one of the significant minor works of the early Tudor
      period."

6   SLAVIN, ARTHUR J.   "Profitable Studies: Humanists and Govern-
    ment in Early Tudor England."   Viator: Medieval and Ren-
    aissance Studies 1: 307-25.
        Surveys twenty-five representative humanists who flour-
    ished during the period of Henry VIII, among them Elyot, to
    ask in what specific ways they realized the humanist ideal
    of service to government in actual practice, how they came
    into the positions, how they were remunerated.

7   WIERUM, ANN.   "'Actors' and 'Play Acting' in the Morality
    Tradition."   Renaissance Drama, n.s. 3: 189-214.
        As a "shrewd observer of the Tudor court," Elyot "con-
    tinually stresses the flatterer's skill as 'actor'"; in
    this respect he "perfectly describes the false face of the
    flattering Vice" of the morality plays. See especially
    pp. 197-98.

*8 WOOLGER, M. N.   "Sir Thomas Elyot's The Image of Governance:
    Its Sources and Political Significance."   B. Litt. thesis,
    Oxford University.
        Cited in Index, vol. 21 (1973), p. 14.

1971

1   CONNIFF, JAMES JOSEPH, JR.   "Humanism and Reform in Tudor
    England."   Ph.D. dissertation, Columbia University, 332 pp.
        Elyot's Governour represents one of two broad classes
    of humanistic reform writing after More's Utopia, that
    dealing with the education of the ruler and his advisors
    (the other class advocates specific reforms, in the manner
    of Starkey's Dialogue). While such humanist reforms had an
    impact on Tudor policy, they failed to gain entrance to
    England's elite; they became increasingly tied to the mon-
    archy and by early seventeenth century they ceased to be
    an important factor in politics.

2   COOGAN, ROBERT C.F.C.   "Petrarch's Latin Prose and the English
    Renaissance."   SP 68, no. 3 (July): 270-91.
        Contrasts the attitudes of the More circle toward
    Petrarch with those of earlier, medieval period, and finds
    Elyot influenced by Petrarch's major political treatise,
    De republica optime administranda (p. 279).

3   KINGHORN, A[LEXANDER] M[ANSON].   The Chorus of History:
    Literary-Historical Relations in Renaissance Britain, 1485-
    1558.   New York: Barnes & Noble, pp. 91-101, 170-71, 179-
    80, 297-98.

1971

Governour is concerned with "personal morality in service to the 'state,' itself a new concept. The standards of
conduct appropriate to a feudal knight and summed up in
the chivalric code were by Elyot softened and modified into
the practical pursuit of fresh ideals of service in a different cause, a secular and abstract concept sanctioned by
the King's Court." Governour "reveals its author's grasp
of the essential fact of political evolution. . . . Elyot
could perceive that the old order . . . was not going to
be able to maintain its authority unless it acquired new
skills."

4   REDMOND, JAMES PATRICK. "A Critical Edition of Sir Thomas
    Elyot's Pasquil the Playne." Ph.D. dissertation, Purdue
    University, 192 pp.
       Collates the Folger Library copy of the 1540 edition
    with 1533 editions at the Bodleian, Huntington, and Pepys-
    ian libraries and the British Library 1540 edition. An
    assumed 1532 edition is a ghost. Introductory chapters
    conclude that the work is not an attack on Henry VIII or
    Cromwell, nor a defense of More, but rather an attempt to
    enhance Elyot's own status; that Elyot shows little famil-
    iarity with the "pasquinade" tradition; that Pasquil can
    be appreciated for its dramatic quality.

5   RUDE, DONALD WARREN. "General Introduction," in his "Critical
    Edition of Sir Thomas Elyot's The Boke Named the Governour."
    Ph.D. dissertation, University of Illinois at Urbana-
    Champaign, pp. v-cli.
       Contains a life of Elyot, a critical assessment of Gov-
    ernour, a full bibliographical description and analysis of
    the four editions collated, including a detailed discussion
    of Elyot's revisions, and, finally, an account of the text-
    ual principles followed. Of greatest interest is the third
    section, which notes more than 500 changes between the
    first and second editions, ranging in scope from "the al-
    teration of inflectional endings of nouns and verbs to the
    deletion of numerous lengthy passages." Is strongly
    critical of Holmes (1961.3): "While Miss Holmes' misrepre-
    sentations and errors in interpretation are distressing,
    her tendencies to confuse accidental variations with sub-
    stantive variations in the text and to create nonexistent
    variations are more irritating." Finds it "unsound to
    draw sweeping generalizations about Elyot's changes in
    diction," and sees "little evidence" that Elyot "attempted
    a systematic grammatical revision of the text." Through
    his revisions, Elyot sought a "more simplified, direct mode
    of expression." The Biographical section provides evidence

for dating Education and Dictionary and for the contention
that the list of works in Image is not chronological.

*6   SALAMON, LINDA BRADLEY. "The Mirrors for The Scholemaster:
      Erasmus, Castiglione, Elyot, Ascham and the Humanistic
      'Speculum.'" Ph.D. dissertation, Bryn Mawr College.
      Cited in ADD, 1970-71, p. 220. See 1973.2.

                              1972

1   STROZIER, ROBERT M. "Roger Ascham and Cleanth Brooks: Ren-
      aissance and Modern Critical Thought." Essays in Criti-
      cism 22, no. 4 (October): 396-407.
           Argues that for Elyot, as well as Ascham and Sidney, a
      concern with literary art is a means toward some higher
      end. A critic "uses" a work to "resolve a problem." In
      this respect Elyot is like a "new critic."

                              1973

1   MacDONALD, M[ICHAEL] J[OSEPH]. "Elyot's The Boke Named the
      Governour and the Vernacular." In Acta Conventus Neo-
      Latini Lovaniensis: Proceedings of the First International
      Congress of Neo-Latin Studies, Louvain, 23-28 August 1971.
      Edited by Joseph IJsewijn and Eckhard Kessler. Munich:
      Wilhelm Fink; Louvain: Louvain University Press, pp. 365-
      69.
           Contending that Elyot's "first concern" in Governour is
      "the precise and effective use of words," argues that in
      Valla's Elegantiae Elyot found a model for "a method which
      allows him to integrate a way of developing the vernacular
      with his actual description of a humanist education."
      Elyot is "constantly developing his medium as he writes."
      See 1970.2.

2   SALAMON, LINDA BRADLEY. "A Gloss on 'Daunsinge': Sir Thomas
      Elyot and T. S. Eliot's Four Quartets." ELH 40, no. 4
      (Winter): 584-605.
           Argues that the influence of Governour is more pervasive
      in Four Quartets than in just the "daunsinge" section.
      Showing that Elyot sees history as a series of "timeless
      moments," that he speaks for "an old outlook of timeless
      balance and order which once required acquiescence of every
      moral man," and that for him the dance is a "model for . . .
      controlled action," explores the intersection of his think-
      ing and Eliot's "East Coker, I," noting differences. Though

                               61

1973

to Eliot's narrator Elyot's vision is "old fashioned," the
elder writer is not mocked; there is sympathy.

3 WILSON, KENNETH JAY. "The Early Tudor Dialogue." Ph.D. dissertation, Yale University, 308 pp.
    Compares themes and methods in Knowledge, Ascham's
Toxophilus, and More's Dialogue of Comfort to define the
"art" of the Tudor dialogue. A first chapter analyzing the
mimetic art of Plato's and Cicero's dialogues, which are
"hybrid," between drama and dialectic, is followed by suc-
cessive chapters on Elyot, Ascham, and More. Argues that
the main concerns of Knowledge have their origins in the
author's striving for personal recognition. Concludes that
dialogues "enlarge our insight into humanist ways of
thought" and should be "ranked high among the achievements
of humanist art."

1974

1 GALIGANI, GIUSEPPE. "Il Boccaccio nel Cinquecento ingelse."
In Il Boccaccio nella culture inglese e anglo-americana.
Edited by Giuseppe Galigani. Florence: Leo S. Olschki,
pp. 37-40.
    Analyzes Elyot's version of "Titus and Gissypus" in
Governour II, xii; stresses his "amplificazione iperbolica"
and his "intensificazione del pathos."

2 M[cCONICA], J[AMES] K[ELSEY], comp. "Sir Thomas Elyot, 1499?-
1546." In The New Cambridge Bibliography of English Literature. Vol. 1. 600-1660. Edited by George Watson.
Cambridge: Cambridge University Press, cols. 1818-19.
    Cites forty-one items published between 1903 and 1966.
Seems idiosyncratic in listing four Starnes articles but
not the book in which two of them are reprinted, and a
third, of greater importance, appears (1954.7-9). Includes
Schoeck (1953.3) but not Bland's replay (1957.1).

1975

1 ANON. "Elyot, Thomas." In The New Encyclopaedia Britannica
in 30 Volumes. Micropaedia, Vol. 3. 15th ed. Chicago,
London, Toronto, Geneva, Sydney, Tokyo, Manilla, Seoul, and
Johannesburg: Encyclopaedia Britannica, Helen Hemingway
Benton, Publisher, p. 868.
    Very brief and general account: "The end of all Elyot's
works was usefulness: he brought classics and Italian

authors to the general public . . . he provided practical
instruction in his own writings, and he added many new
words to the English language." Mentions Governour, Castel, Dictionary among Elyot's works. Compare 1929.1,
1878.1.

2　FOREMAN, JOEL [EDWARD]. "An Unacknowledged Use of the Cratylus by Thomas Elyot." N&Q, n.s. 22, no. 12 (December):
532-34.
　　Notes that in the preface to the 1538 Dictionary Elyot
includes a passage from Cratylus for a purpose different
from Plato's own and asks whether Elyot understood the
linguistic and epistemological implications; he did.

3　GOTTESMAN, LILLIAN. Introduction to her edition of "Bibliotheca Eliotae" (1548), Augmented by Thomas Cooper. Delmar,
N.Y.; Scholars' Facsimiles & Reprints, no pagination.
　　Briefly traces the development of the dictionary to
1548, provides examples to indicate the nature and extent
of Cooper's augmentations, indicates sources for both Elyot
and Cooper, and discusses the influence on later dictionaries (especially regarding adages and biographical sketches)
and on sixteenth-century English writers. See 1954.7-8.

4　McLEAN, ANDREW M. "Castiglione, Cicero, and English Dialogues, 1533-1536." Romance Notes 16, no. 2 (Winter): 450-
54.
　　In assessing briefly the indebtedness of Thomas Starkey's
Dialogue between Pole and Lupset, presents the "conjectural
evidence" that Starkey knew Knowledge and Pasquil.

5　STREITBERGER, W. R. "Ideal Conduct in Venus and Adonis." SQ
26, no. 3 (Summer): 285-91.
　　"I conclude, then, that the courser and jennet episode
is a double-edged exemplum, that Venus presents a moral
threat to Adonis . . . that the striking similarities between Elyot's and Shakespeare's treatments of the material
point to the fact that the seduction attempt is of real
dramatic interest. . . ."

1976

1　DEES, JEROME S[TEELE]. "Recent Studies in Elyot." ELR 6,
no. 2 (Spring): 336-44.
　　Provides descriptive analyses of critical studies and
editions of Elyot between 1945 and 1973, categorized as
follows: biographical studies; general critical studies;

studies of language, style, poetics, and influence; studies
of individual works and of the Elyot canon. Assesses the
state of criticism, offers a critique of the standard editions, describes other editions. A section entitled "See
also" lists additional studies in an attempt to provide a
"reasonably complete" bibliography for the period.

2   FOREMAN, JOEL EDWARD. "The Contributions of Plato, Cicero,
     and Quintilian to Sir Thomas Elyot's Theory of Language."
     Ph.D. dissertation, George Washington University, 192 pp.
        The common denominator for the four writers is their
     concern with the distinctions between idea and expression.
     In the Cratylus Plato holds language to be a "poor instru-
     ment for the communication of knowledge because the sounds
     which convey thought to the intellect through the senses
     lack fixed difinitions." Though Cicero is concerned
     throughout his career with distinctions between ideas and
     one's manner of expressing them, his emphasis shifts in
     his last works from a primary concern for "matter" to a
     concern more for "words and elocution." Quintilian devel-
     ops Cicero's later ideas. Elyot "selectively incorporates
     the ideas of Plato, Cicero, and Quintilian in a theory of
     language which has its own identity." For him words are
     "containers of ideas." He relates the distinction between
     sounds and thought to that between sense and intellect.
     The ears receive forms of expression while the mind "appre-
     hends the intended meaning." These distinctions between
     outer and inner inform all his discussions of language,
     including such matters as the nature of eloquence, the
     method for arriving at definitions, and the function of
     poetry.

3   PARKS, GEORGE B. "Pico della Mirandola in Tudor Translation."
     In Philosophy and Humanism: Renaissance Essays in Honor of
     Paul Oskar Kristeller. Edited by Edward P. Mahoney. New
     York: Columbia University Press, pp. 352-69.
        Describes, analyzes briefly, and provides biographical,
     dating, and publication information for six translations of
     Pico made in England in the sixteenth century. Elyot's is
     number five, pages 365-66.

4   WILSON, K[ENNETH] J[AY]. Introduction to his edition of "The
     Letters of Sir Thomas Elyot." SP 73, no. 5 (December):
     ix-xxx.
        Introduces a critical edition of Elyot's twelve surviv-
     ing letters, dating from 1528 to 1538, to which Wilson adds
     as an appendix all the English prologues of first editions
     of Elyot's works. Much of the Introduction concentrates on

the prologues, which, according to Wilson, "reveal the same personal preoccupations" as the letters. Together these private and public documents reveal a "shape" to Elyot's life, one which moves from an "incomplete assimilation of personal desires within social aims" to a more "mature" stage" in which conflicts between authority and experience are almost resolved.

1977

1   HALL, ANNE DRURY.   "Tudor Prose Style: English Humanists and the Problem of a Standard." ELR 7, no. 3 (Autumn): 267-96.
    Of the four classes of diction recognized by classical rhetoricians--proper words, coinages, archaisms, and metaphors--a "standard" or "central" language should be drawn predominantly from the first. Since the store of proper words in sixteenth-century English was inadequate, it was necessary to build it by borrowing foreign terms. Borrowings are not the same as "coinages" in classical theory, however, so classical rules could not be used to govern "inkhorn terms." Rhetoricians were thus torn between too strict a reliance on native words, which resulted in a style lacking in urbanity and sophistication, and too liberal a commitment to foreign terms, leading to artificiality and affectedness. Not until Jonson's Discoveries do we encounter a mind able to "liberalize English rhetoric by subtly and consistently applying classical standards to the expressive needs of the time." Within the context of this dilemma, Elyot's task in Governour of making English a more "abundantly expressive" language by giving it a greater store of distinguished proper words was an "immensely complicated" one, because he was "creating a language and a rhetoric for that language at the same time."

2   RUDE, DONALD W[ARREN].   "On the Date of Sir Thomas Elyot's The Education or Bringinge Up of Children." PBSA 71, no. 1: 61-65.
    Quotes a letter from Martin Tyndall to Thomas Cromwell that offers "conclusive" external evidence that Education was in print by midsummer 1533.

1978

1   HALE, DAVID.   "Sir Thomas Elyot and 'Noble Homere.'" In The Early Renaissance. Acta, vol. 5. Edited by Aldo Bernardo.

1978

Binghamton, New York: Center for Medieval and Early Renaissance Studies, State University of New York at Binghamton, pp. 121-31.
   Elyot's varied use of Homer, including an extended
statement of praise and translations of three brief passages (apparently the first translations published in
English), suggests the need for a more precise study of
the arrival of Greek literary culture in England. Elyot's
interest in Homer is in those aspects which can be of use
to a future governor--political ideas, desirable personal
qualities, and suitable recreational activities. Though
Erasmus may be the cause, directly or indirectly, of
Elyot's knowledge of Eustathius's commentary on Homer,
Elyot's "enthusiastic use" of him is not closely linked to
the work of any of his contemporaries.

2   HARNER, JAMES L[OWELL]. English Renaissance Prose Fiction,
    1500-1600: An Annotated Bibliography of Criticism. A Ref-
    erence Publication in Literature. Boston: G. K. Hall &
    Co., pp. 152-53.
       Lists editions and studies of Elyot's Titus & Gissypus.

3   PRINCISS, G. M. "The Old Honor and the New Courtesy: I Henry
    IV." Shakespeare Survey 31:85-91.
       Cites the standards of conduct recommended in Governour
    and Castiglione's Courtier to argue that Hotspur represents
    a code that is obsolete whereas Hal embodies a newer con-
    cept of "courtesy": "talents and skills Elizabethans
    looked for in the best representatives of nobility."

1979

1   SASAKI, KUNIYA. "Notes on Thomas Elyot's View of Virtues."
    Essays and Studies in English Language and Literature
    (Sendai, Japan) 68-69 (November): 1-19.
       In an attempt to "clarify Elyot's view of the governors'
    [sic] morals," provides a summary analysis of the first
    seven chapters of Book II of Governour. The following is
    typical of the writing throughout: "In the first Book . . .
    Elyot criticises the nobleman's laziness, their desire for
    pleasure only, and their indifference to their son's edu-
    cation." Depends heavily upon Caspari (1954.2) and Hogrefe
    (1959.1 and 1967.3).

Roger Ascham
(1515?-1568)

Writings About Roger Ascham

1576

1 [GRANT, EDWARD.] "Ad Adolescentulos Latinae Linguae Studiosos,
   E. G. Oratio de Vita Obitu Rogeri Aschami, ac Eius Scrip-
   tionis Laudibus." In Dissertissimi Viri Rogeri Ascham
   Angli, Regiae Olim Maiestati a Latinus Epistolis, Famil-
   iarum Epistolarum Liber Tres. . . . London: Pro Francisco
   Coldocko, sigs. L12^r-O62^r.
   The first "biography" of Ascham, the basis for all sub-
   sequent lives. Reprinted in Giles' edition; see 1865.1.

1662

*1 FULLER, THOMAS. The History of the Worthies of England.
    Endeavored by Thomas Fuller. London: Printed by
    J. G. W. L. and W. G.
    See 1840.2.

1684

1 [FULLER, THOMAS.] Anglorum Speculum: Or the Worthies of
   England in Church and State. Alphabetically Digested into
   the Several Shires and Counties Therein Contained; Wherein
   Are Illustrated the Lives and Characters of the Most Emi-
   nent Persons since the Conquest to this Present Age.
   London: John Wright, Thomas Passinger, and William Thack-
   ery, p. 901.
   "Preface" signed "G. S." [George Sandys]; so cited in
   Wing and catalogued in some libraries. Characterizes
   Ascham as "an honest man, a good archer, and much delighted
   with Cock-fighting."

1694

*1 STRYPE, JOHN. <u>Memorials of the Most Reverend Father in God</u>
<u>Thomas Cranmer</u>. London: Printed for R. Chiswell.
<u>See</u> 1840.3.

1703

*1 ASCHAM, ROGER. <u>Rogeri Aschami Epistolarum, Libri Quatuor.</u>
<u>Accessit Johannis Sturmii, Aliorumque ad Aschamum,</u>
<u>Anglosque Alios Eruditos Epistolarum Liber Unus.</u> <u>Editio</u>
<u>Novissima, Prioribus Auctior.</u> Edited by William Elstob.
Oxford: Henry Clements, 506 pp.
　　The edition used by all eighteenth- and nineteenth-
century biographers and critics; superseded by Giles's
edition (1864.1).

1705

*1 STRYPE, JOHN. <u>The Life of the Learned Sir John Cheke, Kt.</u>
London: J. Wyat.
<u>See</u> 1821.1.

1721

*1 WOOD, ANTHONY à. <u>Fasti Oxonienses, or Annals of the Univer-</u>
<u>sity of Oxford</u>, in his <u>Athenae Oxonienses</u>. 2d ed. London:
Printed for F. C. and J. Rivington, et al.
<u>See</u> 1815.2.

1735

1 BAYLE, PIERRE. <u>A General Dictionary, Historical and Critical:</u>
<u>In Which a New and Accurate Translation of That of the</u>
<u>Celebrated Mr. Bayle, with the Corrections and Observations</u>
<u>Printed in the Late Edition at Paris, Is Included</u>. By the
Reverend Mr. John Peter Bernard; the Reverend Mr. Thomas
Birch; Mr. John Lockman; and Other Hands. Vol. 2. London:
James Bettenham, for G. Strahan, et al. pp. 371-78.
　　A substantial encyclopedia biography based mainly on
Grant (1576.1), with some use of Elstob's letters (1703.1),
but with essay-length footnotes on such matters as Ascham's
election to fellowship, his tutorship of Queen Elizabeth,

1761

his marriage, his "character" ("easy and polite behav-
ior . . . undisguised frankness of temper . . . fidelity to
his friends"), and his writings. English version of
1750.1. See also 1747.1.

1747

1   Biographia Britannica: Or, the Lives of the Most Eminent
    Persons Who Have Flourished in Great Britain and Ireland,
    from the Earliest Ages, down to the Present Times . . .
    Digested in the Manner of Mr. Bayle's Historical and Criti-
    cal Dictionary. Vol. 1. London: W. Innys, et al.
    pp. 213-18.
       Very similar to Chauffepié (1750.1) and Bayle (1735.1),
    although details vary slightly and emphases differ some-
    what, especially in the footnotes. The biography most
    often cited by nineteenth-century critics, historians, and
    bibliophiles.

1750

1   CHAUFFEPIÉ, JACQUES GEORGE DE. "Roger Ascham." In Nouveau
    Dictionnaire historique et critique pour servir de supplé-
    ment ou de continuation au dictionnaire historique et
    critique de Mr. Pierre Bayle. Vol. 1. Amsterdam: Z.
    Chatelain, pp. 507-513.
       French version of 1735.1.

1751

*1   A New and General Biographical Dictionary. London: Printed
    for T. Osborne, J. Whiston, et al.
    See 1784.1.

1761

1   JOHNSON, SAMUEL. "Life of Ascham." In English Works of Roger
    Ascham, With Notes and Observations, and the Author's Life.
    Edited by James Bennet. London: R. and J. Dodsley,
    pp. i-xvi.
       Greatly influenced nineteenth-century biographical and
    critical studies. Focuses mainly on Ascham's university
    career, the state of learning in the sixteenth century,

1782

Ascham's financial situation, Toxophilus and Report; written in Johnson's magisterial style; for example, regarding
Ascham's ability to hold office under Mary although a
Protestant: "it is vain to examine the motives of dis-
crimination and partiality . . . if some were punished,
many were forborne . . . and why not, among them, Ascham?"
Praises Ascham's learning, manners, courtesy, benevolence,
liberality, and piety. Source of much later speculation
as to just how poor Ascham was.
    Each work has separate title page: Report, pp. 1-49
(with letter from Asteley to Ascham on pp. 3-4); Toxophilus, pp. 51-178; "Divae Elizabethae," pp. 179-86;
Scholemaster, pp. 187-347; miscellaneous pieces and English
letters, pp. 349-95. Johnson's "Life" reprinted in 1815.1
and 1890.1. See 1956.1.

1782

1   AYSCOUGH, SAMUEL, ed. A Catalogue of Manuscripts Preserved in
    the British Museum Hitherto Undescribed. Vol. 1. London:
    John Rivington, pp. 179, 215.
        Item 26, p. 179, lists "Letters of Mr. Roger Ascham,
    transcribed by the Rev. Mr. Tho. Baker from the origi-
    nals . . .," located in Vol. 5 of a "Collection of copies
    of Letters chiefly relating to State Affairs." Item 10,
    p. 215, lists a letter from Ascham to Cecil.

1784

1   A New and General Biographical Dictionary; Containing an His-
    torical and Critical Account of the Lives and Writings of
    the Most Eminent Persons in Every Nation; Particularly the
    British and Irish. Vol. 1. A New Edition . . . Greatly
    Enlarged and Improved. London: Printed for W. Strahan
    et al., pp. 341-46.
        Roughly same as 1735.1, 1747.1, and 1750.1. First edi-
    tion, 1751.1.

1801

1   ROBERTS, T[HOMAS]. "The Art and Practice of Archery, Includ-
    ing a Comment upon the Toxophilus of Ascham." In The Eng-
    lish Bowman, or Tracts on Archery: To Which Is Added the
    Second Part of the Bowman's Glory. London: C. Roworth,
    pp. 115-229. Reprint, with a new introduction by E. G.
    Heath. London: EP Publishing, 1973.

An attempt to "methodise" Toxophilus, consisting mainly
of a commentary on lengthy extracts, designed to modernize
Ascham's archaic prose, so that contemporary archers could
study Ascham's still-valuable precepts. Chapter titles are
indicative of Roberts' method: "Of the String," "Of the
Bow," "Of Arrows," "Of Nocking," etc.

1807

1   BURNETT, GEORGE. "Roger Ascham." In Specimens of English
    Prose-Writers, from the Earliest Times to the Close of the
    Seventeenth Century, with Sketches Biographical and Liter-
    ary, Including an Account of Books as Well as of Their
    Authors. Vol. 2. London: Longman, Hurst, Rees & Orme,
    pp. 84-111.
        A general biography, which discusses Toxophilus and
    Report in the context of Ascham's life, but refers to
    Scholemaster as an "other work," and speaks of it as though
    he knew Book I only. Ascham is "among the most distin-
    guished scholars of his time" and the first man other than
    More to publish "any piece of consequence" in the sixteenth
    century.

1809

*1   DIBDIN, THOMAS FROGNALL. Bibliomania; or Book-Madness: Con-
     taining Some Account of the History, Symptoms, and Cure of
     This Fatal Disease. London: Printed for Longman, Hurst,
     Rees, Orme & Brown.
         See 1876.1.

2   HODGSON, FRANCIS. Lady Jane Grey, A Tale, in Two Books; with
    Miscellaneous Poems in English and Latin. London:
    T. Bensley for T. Mackinlay, pp. 1-18 passim, 47-49.
        Ascham appears as Jane's "good preceptor" in this verse
    tale, with speeches on pp. 7, 8, 10-11.

1811

*1   Biographie universelle ancienne et moderne, ou histoire, par
     ordre alphabétique. Paris: Michaud.
         See 1854.1.

1812

1 CHALMERS, ALEXANDER. The General Biographical Dictionary:
   Containing an Historical and Critical Account of the Lives
   and Writings of the Most Eminent Persons in Every Nation.
   Vol. 3. A New Edition, Revised and Enlarged. London:
   Printed for J. Nichols & Son, et al., pp. 28-35. Reprint.
   New York: AMS Press; Kraus Reprint Co., 1969.
      A routine dictionary biography, derivative of 1735.1,
   1747.1, 1740.1, although without their customary footnotes.

1815

1 [COCHRANE, J. G.], ed. The English Works of Roger Ascham.
   New Edition. London: White, Cochrane, & Co., xxviii,
   391 pp.
      Contains Johnson's "Life of Ascham," pp. iii-xxviii, and
   texts, with separate title pages of Report, Toxophilus,
   Scholemaster, and English letters. The letter to Elizabeth
   is printed as though it were separate from Scholemaster.
   The text of Scholemaster is identified as "Corrected and
   Revised, with Explanatory Notes, by James Upton," but none
   of the other texts are identified as to editor.

2 WOOD, ANTHONY á. Fasti Oxonienses, or Annals of the University of Oxford. A New Edition, with Additions and a Con-
   tinuation by Philip Bliss. The First Part. London:
   F. C. and J. Rivington, et al., cols. 114-16.
      Notes a supplicate made for "one Roger Haskham" to be
   incorporated M. A. in July 1541, but finds no record of
   actual incorporation. Follows this with a brief biography
   and list of publications. First edition, 1721.1.

1816

1 WRANGHAM, FRANCIS. "Roger Ascham." In The British Plutarch.
   London: J. Mawman, pp. 410-35.
      An appreciation, based largely on Grant's Oratio and
   Johnson's "Life," which stresses Ascham's character and his
   importance as an historian: both Report and the letters
   reveal him "an accurate observer of men and manners," and
   contain "a very great choice of historical matter . . .
   hardly preserved anywhere else." Ascham "rendered essential service to posterity by promoting correct taste and
   sound learning."

1819

*1 [ELLIS, SIR HENRY, and DOUCE, FRANCIS], eds. A Catalogue of
    the Lansdowne Manuscripts in the British Museum. With
    Indexes of Persons, Places, and Matters. London: Printed
    by R. and A. Taylor.
        Cited in Tannenbaum (1946.1) and in NUC, vol. 76, p. 470.

1821

1 STRYPE, JOHN. The Life of the Learned Sir John Cheke, Kt.
   First Instructor, Afterwards Secretary of State, to King
   Edward VI. New Edition, Corrected by the Author. Oxford:
   Clarendon Press, pp. 5-21 passim and 47-53.
        General account of Ascham's connection with Cheke until
   the latter's leaving Cambridge in 1544; summary of Ascham's
   perceptions of the state of learning and religion on the
   continent. This is Vol. 11 of Strype's Collected Works
   (1820-40); first edition, 1705.1.

1822

1 ANON. "Toxophilus, the Schole or Partitions of Shooting . . .
   Anno 1571. Imprinted at London . . . by Thomas Marshe."
   The Retrospective Review 4: 76-87.
        An appreciative introduction to Toxophilus and to the
   character and spirit of its author. The writer is so taken
   by the "many highly touched traces of nature" and the
   "spirited handling of [Ascham's] pen in the detached pictures" of Toxophilus that he can only with difficulty focus
   on his main purpose, to extoll Ascham's "splendid delinea-
   tion of the delights and advantages" of archery.

2 H., E. "Bradgate Park, the Residence of Jane Grey." London
   Magazine 5 (February): 166-74.
        Account of the author's visit to Bradgate Park; quotes
   passage from Scholemaster, characterizes Ascham as Jane's
   "pleasant tutor," and remarks that he "sojourned in the
   neighborhood."

3 HOWARD, GEORGE [Laird, Francis Charles]. Lady Jane Grey and
   Her Times. London: Sherwood, Neely, and Jones, pp. 165-71.
        Rehearses Ascham's account of his visit to Lady Jane Grey
   in the autumn of 1550 and quotes in translation the letter
   to her from Augsburg, January 1552 (new calendar).

<u>1824</u>

*1   LANDOR, WALTER SAVAGE. "Roger Ascham and the Lady Jane Grey."
     In <u>Imaginary Conversations of Literary Men and Statesmen</u>.
     Vol. 2. London: Printed for Taylor and Hessey.
        See 1826.2.

 2   WATT, ROBERT. <u>Bibliotheca Britannica; or a General Index to</u>
     <u>British and Foreign Literature</u>. Vol. 1. Edinburgh:
     Archibald Constable & Co.; London: Longman, Hurst, Rees,
     Brown & Green, pp. 49a–49b.
        Printing history of <u>Toxophilus</u>, <u>Scholemaster</u>, <u>Apologia</u>,
     <u>Dissertissimi</u>, <u>Report</u>, <u>Works</u>. Contains errors.

<u>1826</u>

*1   [GORTON, JOHN.] <u>A General Biographical Dictionary, Containing</u>
     <u>a Summary Account of the Lives of Eminent Persons of All</u>
     <u>Nations</u>. Vol. 1. London: Hunt & Clark.
        <u>See</u> 1851.1.

 2   LANDOR, WALTER SAVAGE. "Roger Ascham and the Lady Jane Grey."
     In <u>Imaginary Conversations of Literary Men and Statesmen</u>.
     Vol. 2. 2d rev. ed. London: Henry Colburn, pp. 77–84.
        Imagines Ascham and Lady Jane Grey conversing on the
     eve of her marriage: Ascham speaks on state of matri-
     mony and love; recalls some verses that Lady Jane Grey
     reputedly wrote some years earlier; cautions her to watch
     out for the dangers of court; urges her to "lay aside
     books" and to devote her energies to "minding" her husband:
     "Lead him from ambition," for "men of high estate grow
     tired of contentedness." First edition, 1824.1.

<u>1828</u>

*1   The <u>London University Press; or Remarks upon a Late Publica-</u>
     <u>tion, Entitled, "A Popular System of Classical Instruction,</u>
     <u>Combining the Method of Locke, Ascham, Milton</u>. Bath: n.p.
        Cited in <u>BM</u> (1965.1) vol. 140, col. 597; erroneously
     attributed by Tannenbaum (1946.1) to Locke.

1832

1   VARRO [Disraeli, Isaac]. "Of the Three Earliest Authors in
    our Vernacular Literature." The New Monthly Magazine and
    Literary Journal 35 (September), 243-54.
        The other two authors are More and Elyot; the portion
    on Ascham occupies pp. 249-54. An appreciation, stressing
    Ascham's works in the context of his life as student and
    public servant. Similar in content to 1841.1, 1842.1, and
    1881.4.

1833

*1   COLERIDGE, HARTLEY. Biographia Borealis, or Lives of Distin-
     guished Northerns. London: Whitaker, Tracher & Co.;
     Leeds: F. E. Bingley.
         See 1852.1.

1834

*1   LOWNDES, WILLIAM THOMAS. The Bibliographer's Manual of Eng-
     lish Literature, Containing an Account of Rare, Curious,
     and Useful Books. London: W. Pickering.
         See 1871.1.

1835

1   ANON. Review of The Worthies of Yorkshire and Lancashire by
    Hartley Coleridge. The Quarterly Review 54 (September)·
    345-50.
        Though mainly an appreciative summary of Ascham's life,
    with lengthy quotations from Coleridge to illustrate the
    biographer's charm, scholarship, and taste, contains a
    technical discussion of Ascham's notions about the pronun
    ciation of Greek. See 1833.1, 1852.1.

1836

1   "The Schoolmaster: An Analytical Account of Ascham's School-
    master." In The Schoolmaster: Essays on Practical Educa-
    tion. Vol. 1. London: Charles Knight, pp. 1-105.
        Prefixed by a brief biography and by Cardinal Wolsey's
    letter of instructions to the masters of Ipswich School
    (1 September 1528) as an "appropriate introduction," offers

1837

a summary analysis of Scholemaster, with lengthy quotations and with occasional discursive commentary which draws on analogues or glosses from Toxophilus.

1837

1　CUNNINGHAM, GEORGE GODFREY, ed. Lives of Eminent and Illustrious Englishmen, from Alfred the Great to the Latest Times. Vol. 2. Glasgow: A. Fullerton & Co., pp. 251–55.
　　Events of Ascham's life focused to illustrate the "tone and character" of his time.

*2　HALLAM, HENRY. Introduction to the Literature of Europe in the Fifteenth, Sixteenth, and Seventeenth Centuries. London: J. Murray.
　　See 1855.1.

1839

1　TYTLER, PATRICK FRASER. England Under the Reigns of Edward VI. and Mary, with the Contemporary History of Europe, Illustrated in a Series of Original Letters Never before Printed. Vol. 2. London: Richard Bentley, pp. 120–32, 144–45, 294–95.
　　Quotes, with occasional comment: Ascham's letter to John Astely enumerating the criteria for good history writing; portions of the January 1551 letter-diary to Edward Raven; the portrait in Report of Albert, Margrave of Brandenburg; and the account of Lady Jane Grey in Scholemaster.

1840

1　AINSWORTH, WILLIAM HARRISON. The Tower of London: A Historical Romance. London: Richard Bentley, pp. 478–87.
　　A fictional account of a conversation between Ascham and Jane Grey in the tower before her death. Ascham consoles Jane by telling her that her name "will be a beacon and a guiding star to the whole Protestant Church" in years to come.

2　FULLER, THOMAS. The History of the Worthies of England. Vol. 3. New ed., edited by P. Austin Nuttall. London: Printed for Thomas Tegg, pp. 430–31. Reprint. New York: AMS Press, 1965.

Principal source (following Camden) of the oft-repeated legend that Ascham died impoverished from cock-fighting. Originates the claim that Ascham's "Toxophilus is accounted a good book for young men, his Scholemaster for old men, his Epistles for all men." First edition, 1662.1.

3 STRYPE, JOHN. Memorials of the Most Reverend Father in God Thomas Cranmer, Sometime Lord Archbishop of Canterbury. Vol. 1. New ed. Oxford: Oxford University Press, pp. 230-43 passim.

Details, in a chapter entitled "The Archbishop's Care of the University," Ascham's involvement in the religious and political issues at Cambridge in 1547. This is Vol. 9 of Strype's Collected Works (1820-40). First edition, 1694.1.

1841

*1 DISRAELI, ISAAC. "Roger Ascham." In Amenities of Literature, Consisting of Sketches and Characters of English Literature. London: E. Moxon.

See 1842.1 and 1881.4; also 1832.1.

1842

1 [DISRAELI, ISAAC.] "Roger Ascham." The Mirror n.s. 1 (7 May): 301-3.

Apparently a verbatim reproduction of Disraeli's remarks on Ascham in Amenities of Literature. See 1841.1 and 1881.4; also 1832.1.

1843

*1 "Roger Ascham." In Cyclopaedia of English Literature: Consisting of a Series of Specimens of British Writers in Prose and Verse. Edinburgh: W. and R. Chambers.

See 1901.1.

1844

1 SOUMET, ALEXANDRE, and DALTENHEYM, GABRIELLE. "Jane Grey, Tragédie en cinq actes et en vers." Magasin Théatral 37: 1-27.

Text of a play presented 30 March 1844 at the Odéon theatre, in which Ascham appears in Acts I, IV, and V in

1848

major speaking roles. At first he is spokesman for the
values of knowledge, by means of which "tout renaît, tout
vit, tout se féconde." Later, as defender of Jane against
Mary's death, he is used to heighten the pathos of Jane's
situation: "O reine! à votre tour montrez-vous magnime;/
Dieu pour vous éprouver vous livre la victime! . . ."

1848

1   ROSE, HUGH JAMES. A New General Biographical Dictionary.
    Vol. 2. London: B. Fellows, et al., pp. 230-31.
        A routine dictionary biography, extolling Ascham's
    "learning and ingenuity . . . accompanied . . . with a
    certain easiness and joyousness of spirit, and a fondness
    for the recreations of life." Compare 1784.1 and 1735.1.

1851

1   GORTON, JOHN. "Ascham." In A General Biographical Diction-
    ary. Vol. 1. New ed. London: Henry G. Bohn, no pagina-
    tion.
        A general "life," pointing to the conclusion that Ascham
    was "a very amiable and benevolent man; somewhat careless
    and indiscreet in worldly manners, but highly to be hon-
    oured as a scholar and a promoter of correct taste and
    sound learning." First edition, 1826.1. Compare 1784.1,
    1735.1.

1852

1   COLERIDGE, HARTLEY. "Roger Ascham." In Lives of Northern
    Worthies. Vol. 2. New ed. with marginal observations of
    S. T. Coleridge. London: Edward Moxon, pp. 85-160.
        Perhaps the most influential biography between Johnson
    and Giles. Little interested in factual accuracy, more in
    generalizing about Ascham's personality, about the times,
    or about "human nature," particularly with respect to
    class distinctions and religion. Typical generalizations
    include: "He had that disposition which, above all things,
    qualifies the conscientious and successful teacher, for he
    delighted rather to discover and call forth the talents of
    others, than to make a display of his own"; and "The real
    grounds of the Marian persecution were political, not re-
    ligious." A reissue of 1833.1.

[1853?]

1   BARTLETT, DAVID W.   The Life of Lady Jane Grey.   Philadelphia:
    Porter and Coates, pp. 143-48.
        An "imaginary conversation" between Ascham and Lady Jane
    Grey, based on Landor's Imaginary Conversations.   See
    1824.1 and 1826.2.

1854

1   Biographie universelle (Michaud) ancienne et moderne, ou his-
    toire, par ordre alphabétique, de la vie publique et privée
    de tous les hommes qui se sont fait remarquer par leurs
    écrits, leurs actions, leurs vertus ou leurs crimes.   Vol.
    2.   New ed.   Paris: Chez Madame C. Desplaces et Chez M.
    Michaud, p. 315.
        Routine brief biography, interesting in that it is
    shorter than that for Elyot (See Elyot, 1854.1), seemingly
    indicative of a difference in English and French taste.
    First edition, 1811.1.

2   MAYOR, J[OHN] E. B.   "Roger Ascham and His Letters."   N&Q 9
    (24 June): 588-89.
        Enumerates letters discovered and printed since Elstob's
    edition (1703.1); announces three Cambridge University MSS
    containing additional Ascham letters; asks for information
    regarding other unpublished Ascham MSS in anticipation of
    a forthcoming edition.

3   _____.   "Roger Ascham's Letters."   N&Q 10 (22 July): 75.
        Announces the discovery of an Ascham letter, dated
    Landau, 1 October, 1552, in the Hardwicke Papers, vol. 1,
    p. 48.
        Notes that editor of Zurich Letters (2d ser., nos. 30
    and 40) prints as "new" two letters which had previously
    appeared in the 1703 edition.

1855

1   HALLAM, HENRY.   Introduction to the Literature of Europe in
    the Fifteenth, Sixteenth, and Seventeenth Centuries.
    Vol. 2.   5th ed.   London: John Murray, pp. 293-94.
        The primary treatment of Ascham is in a chapter on
    "Polite Literature in Prose."   Ascham's style is "without
    grace or warmth," though it is "plain and strong."   First
    edition, 1837.2.

1857

1   ANON. "Biography of Roger Ascham." <u>American Journal of Edu-</u>
    <u>cation</u> 3 (March): 23-40.
        A "sketch of the author's life," drawn mainly from
    Coleridge's <u>Northern Worthies</u> (<u>see</u> 1852.1), intended as an
    "introduction" to <u>Scholemaster</u>, which is to begin in the
    next number (<u>see</u> 1857.2). Interesting for chatty asides
    and for the values implied in its generalizations; for
    example, when discussing Ascham's tutorship to the Queen:
    "the learning of languages is emphatically a female talent."
    Appends Landor's essay from <u>Imaginary Conversations</u> (<u>see</u>
    1824.1 and 1826.2).

2   ANON. "<u>The Schoolmaster, or a Plain and Perfect Way of Teach-</u>
    <u>ing Children to Understand, Write and Speak the Latin</u>
    <u>Tongue.</u>" <u>American Journal of Education</u> 4 (September):
    155-66.
        Prints and annotates Ascham's "Preface" to 1571 edition,
    identifying the speakers present at Burleigh's dinner as
    well as persons and titles named later in the preface.
    Includes in the three densely packed pages on Burleigh the
    text of his "Advices to his son, Robert Cecil."

3   ANON. "<u>Toxophilus; The Schole of Shootinge.</u>" <u>American Jour-</u>
    <u>nal of Education</u> 3 (March): 41-46.
        "A brief notice and a few specimens of <u>Toxophilus</u>" de-
    signed as "introduction" to <u>Scholemaster</u>, to follow in the
    next number. Presents Ascham's "views of the fitness and
    utility of manly sports, and recreating amusements for
    those who lead a sedentary life." Relates Ascham's ideas
    to Sidney's <u>Apology</u> and Fuller's <u>Holy State</u>.

4   KIRSTEN. <u>Ueber Ascham's Leben und Schriften.</u> Programm bei
    herzoglischen Realgymnasiums zu Gotha. Gotha: Englehard-
    Renher, 23 pp.
        A general survey of the subject designed as a lecture to
    an academic audience. See 1901.3.

5   "LETHREDIENSIS." "Portrait of Ascham." <u>N&Q</u>, 2d ser., 3
    (23 May): 415.
        Says there is no original portrait of Ascham and that
    the print by Burghers representing Ascham reading a manu-
    script to Queen Elizabeth is "doubtful." See 1861.2.

1858

*1   ALLIBONE, S[AMUEL] AUSTIN. A Critical Dictionary of English
     Literature and British and American Authors, Living and
     Deceased. Vol. 1. Philadelphia: J. B. Lippincott,
     pp. 72-73.
        See 1878.1.

 2   COOPER, CHARLES HENRY, and COOPER, THOMPSON. "Roger Ascham."
     In Athenae Cantabrigienses. Vol. 1. 1500-1585. Cam-
     bridge: Deighton, Bell & Co.; London: Bell & Daldy,
     pp. 263-68, 555.
        A succinct chronology emphasizing events and persons
     connected to Cambridge, followed by brief testimonies of
     Johnson and Hallam, and by Camden's assertion that gambling
     caused Ascham's pecuniary straits. The list of Ascham's
     works contains some spurious items, although it is general-
     ly accurate on publishing facts.

                            1859

*1   GRAESSE, JEAN GEORGE THÉODORE [Graesse, Johann Georg Theodor].
     Trésor des livres rares et précieux, ou nouveau diction-
     naire bibliographique. Dresden: R. Kuntze, et al.
        See 1950.1.

 2   MAYOR, JOHN E. B. "Letters of Roger Ascham, Communicated by
     John E. B. Mayor, M.A. Fellow of St. John's College."
     Antiquarian Communications: Being Papers Presented at the
     Meetings of the Cambridge Antiquarian Society. Vol. 1.
     Cambridge: Cambridge University Press; London: Deighton,
     Bell, & Co. and Macmillan & Co., pp. 99-124.
        Prints the text of and copiously annotates six letters,
     dating from 1553-67, which to that time had not appeared
     in print, identifying MS sources. See 1854.2 and 1854.3
     for announcement of discovery. The letters subsequently
     appear in Giles's edition (see 1864.1), without annotations.

                            1861

 1   [MORLEY, JOHN.] Review of The Dramatic Works of John Lilly
     (the Euphuist): With Notes, and Some Account of His Life
     and Writings, by F. W. Fairhold. Quarterly Review 109,
     no. 218, 350-83.
        Discussion of Ascham (pp. 358-60) promotes thesis that
     "there is reason for suggesting, if not for believing, that

1861

John Lyly drew from [Scholemaster] both the motive and the
title of his fashionable novel," quoting in support Ascham's
passage on Euphues.

2   RIMBAULT, EDWARD F.   "Roger Ascham."   N&Q, 2d ser. 11 (11 May):
    378.
        Notes the "engraved portrait" by Burghers of Ascham
    reading to Queen Elizabeth prefixed to Elstob's 1703 edi-
    tion of Epistles.   Also claims "an indistinct recollection"
    of having once seen an oil portrait of Ascham.   See 1857.5.

1862

1   [BARNHARD, HENRY], ed.   "Roger Ascham."   In Education, the
    School, and the Teacher, in English Literature.   Repub-
    lished from Barnard's "American Journal of Education."
    2d ed.   Philadelphia: J. B. Lippincott & Co., pp. 21-76.
        Consists of a "Biography of Roger Ascham," pp. 23-38; a
    "brief notice and a few specimens of his Toxophilus,"
    pp. 39-44; Ascham's "Preface to the Reader," from The
    Schoolmaster, with annotations identifying speakers, and
    an abstract of Book I, pp. 45-76.   Same as 1857.1-3.

2   DAGLEISH, W. SCOTT.   "Ascham and His Scholemaster."   Museum:
    A Quarterly Magazine of Education, Literature, and Science
    1 (January): 421-30.
        Reviews Ascham's career, with emphasis on his "shrewd-
    ness and sense, great warmth of heart, liberality of spir-
    it, and naiveté of manner," then summarizes contents of
    Scholemaster, emphasizing the digressions which disclose
    the same personality.

3   MAYOR, JOHN E. B.   "Quotations in Roger Ascham's Scholemaster."
    N&Q, 3rd ser.   1 (1 February): 89.
        Asks for correct identification of a quotation which
    Ascham misattributes to Aristotle's Rhetoric, for explana-
    tion of a proverb, and for identification of a "Mr. Brokke."

1863

1   ANON.   "Ascham's Schoolmaster."   Saturday Review (London) 15
    (18 April): 503-4.
        Ostensibly a review of J. E. B. Mayor's edition of
    Scholemaster (see 1863.4), though more accurately a general
    introduction to Ascham's work, with primary emphasis on
    "the more general points of interest" in Book I.   Claims

84

that Ascham's discussion of classical meters is "pleading hard for blank verse." Calls attention to the "relevance" of Scholemaster to educational and social theories of the day. Faults Mayor for retaining archaic spelling, and finds in his notes little that is "animated or entertaining."

2   CUNNINGHAM, GEORGE GODFREY. "Roger Ascham." In The English Nation; or a History of England in the Lives of Englishmen. Vol. 1. Edinburgh and London: A. Fullarton & Co., pp. 739-43.
    Offers judgments largely unencumbered by supporting evidence on the major issues of Ascham's life: whether he was adequately or poorly remunerated by the sovereigns he served, whether he compromised himself in serving Mary, whether he was addicted to gambling; recounts the circumstances surrounding the origins of Toxophilus and Scholemaster.

3   DARGAUD, J[EAN] M[ARIE]. Histoire de Jane Grey. Paris: Librairie de L. Hachette, pp. 332-40.
    Rehearses the account of Ascham's visit to Jane in 1551.

4   MAYOR, JOHN E. B., ed. "The Scholemaster," by Roger Ascham. London: Bell & Daldy, xxiv, 296 pp. Reprint. New York: AMS Press, 1967.
    Mayor's notes, pp. 201-67, identifying allusions to writers, historical figures, and events, and quoting analogues and explanatory anecdotes from contemporary sources, make this still the standard edition of Scholemaster. In addition to the notes, Mayor has collected, pp. 268-80, "testimonies" to Ascham and his works and provides a list of editions of Ascham's works to be found in the St. John's College library.

1864

1   GILES, J[OHN] A[LLEN]. "The Life of Ascham," in his edition of The Whole Works of Roger Ascham, Now First Collected and Revised, with a Life of the Author. London: John Russell Smith, pp. ix-c. Reprint. New York: AMS Press, 1965.
    The first biography of Ascham to make extensive use of his Latin correspondence, though with errors in dating because, like other biographers and editors, Giles did not understand that Ascham used two systems of dating depending on whether the letter were personal or public. Divided

1865

into three parts: to 1550; his sojourn in Germany and the period of Mary's reign; the period of Elizabeth's reign to his death. Giles' method is to summarize in his own words what is generally known of Ascham's actions and movements or to speculate about his motives (e.g., how he, a Protestant, could serve as Mary's secretary), and then to quote lengthy passages, translated from the Latin letters, as offering insight into his interests, attitudes, and character. Concludes, "It is much to be feared that the real truth of Ascham's character is still to be discovered."

1865

1   GRANT, EDWARD. "Grant's Oration on the Life and Death of Roger Ascham." In The Whole Works of Roger Ascham, Now First Collected and Revised. Vol. 3. Edited by J[ohn] A[llen] Giles. London: John Russell Smith, pp. 294-355. Reprint. New York: AMS Press, 1965.
      Reprinted from 1576.1.

1867

1   ANON. "Selected Pictures. From the Picture in the Collection of John Hick, Esq., Bolton. Lady Jane Grey and Roger Ascham." The Art Journal 29 [n.s. 6]: 154.
      Analytic description of the painting by J. C. Horsley, based on the account of Ascham's visit to Lady Jane recorded in Scholemaster. Plate, opposite, unpaginated, contains painting.

1868

1   ARBER, EDWARD. Introduction to his edition of Toxophilus, 1545. English Reprints. Westminster: A. Constable & Co., pp. 3-10.
      Provides a "chronicle of some of the principal events in the life, works, and times" of Ascham, and stresses his achievement as a prose stylist, based on the assumption that "the absence of any antecedent literature left him without any model of style."

*2   QUICK, ROBERT HERBERT. "Ascham (1515-1568)." In Essays on Educational Reformers. London: Longmans, Green & Co.
      See 1902.4.

1870

*1   ARBER, EDWARD. Introduction to his edition of The Schole-
    master. Birmingham: n.p., 1870.
       See 1888.1.

1871

1   LOWNDES, WILLIAM THOMAS, and BOHN, HENRY G. The Bibliogra-
    pher's Manual of English Literature, Containing an Account
    of Rare, Curious, and Useful Books, Published in or Relat-
    ing to Great Britain and Ireland. Vol. 1. New ed. Lon-
    don: Bell & Daldy, pp. 78-79.
       Lists Works of 1761 and 1815; Epistolarum, Grant's 1578
    and Elstob's 1703 editions; Scholemaster, 1570 and Upton's
    1711 edition; Report, 1552; Toxophilus, 1545 and 1788 edi-
    tions; each with brief description, including later pub-
    lishing history where applicable. First edition, 1834.1.

2   RUSSELL, W[ILLIAM] CLARK, ed. "Roger Ascham. 1505 [sic] -
    1568." In The Book of Authors: A Collection of Criticism,
    Ana, Mots, Personal Descriptions, Etc., Etc., Etc., Wholly
    Referring to English Men of Letters in Every Age of English
    Literature. London and New York: Frederick Warne & Co.,
    pp. 12-13.
       Six appreciative quotations of from one to six sentences
    by Hallam (1855.1), Hartley Coleridge (1852.1), Alexander
    Nowell, Queen Elizabeth, Johnson (1761.1), and Richard
    Hurd.

1872

1   SCHOLZ, A. Ueber Roger Ascham's "Schoolmaster." Jahres-
    Bericht über die Realschule erster Ordnung zu Osterode.
    Osterode: J. Ginschagel, 12 pp.
       Summary analysis of the contents of Book 1, aimed at a
    general academic audience. See 1901.3.

1873

*1   DAMON, KARL. Einige Gedanken aus Roger Ascham's "The Schole-
    master" über Erziehung, besonders über Behandlung der
    Schüler. Karlsruhe, 56 pp.
       Cited in Tannenbaum (1967.3). See also 1901.3, p. 223;
    copy apparently no longer at Columbia.

1873

2   H., R. "Roger Ascham and Sir John Denham." N&Q, 4th ser. 12
        (20 December): 493-94.
            Claims that the lines "Oh could I flow like thee . . ."
        from Cooper's Hill are plagiarized from an Ascham letter
        to Sir William Petre.

                            1875

1   ADAMS, W[ILLIAM] DAVENPORT. "Ascham's Schoolmaster." In
        Famous Books: Sketches in the Highways and Byeways of
        English Literature. London: Virtue, Spalding & Co.,
        pp. 86-113.
            A brief account of "some of the most important points in
        the life of Ascham," followed by a summary analysis of Book
        I of Scholemaster, stressing its moral aspects. Calls
        Ascham's criticism of Italianate Englishmen "a little harsh
        and uncalled for."

                            1876

1   DIBDIN, THOMAS FROGNALL. Bibliomania; or Book-Madness: A
        Bibliographical Romance. London: Chatto & Windus,
        pp. 254-56.
            Characterizing Ascham as "among the most renowned bib-
        liomaniacs of the age," cites passages from Ascham's let-
        ters which refer to his love of books. First edition,
        1809.1.

                            1878

1   ALLIBONE, S[AMUEL] AUSTIN. A Critical Dictionary of English
        Literature and British and American Authors, Living and
        Deceased, from the Earliest Accounts to the Latter Half of
        the Nineteenth Century. Vol. 1. Philadelphia: J. B.
        Lippincott & Co., pp. 72-73.
            An anecdotal "Life," with brief uneven accounts of Toxo-
        philus, Scholemaster, Apologia, Epistolarum and Report.
        In each case, though at greater length for Toxophilus and
        Scholemaster, Allibone quotes appreciations from Wood,
        Fuller, Johnson, Campbell, Dibdin, and others. First edi-
        tion, 1858.1.

1879

2   ANON. "Ascham, Roger." In The Encyclopaedia Britannica: A
     Dictionary of Arts, Sciences, and General Literature.   Vol.
     2.   9th ed.   New York: Samuel L. Hall, pp. 677-79.
         Survey of Ascham's life with emphasis on the Cambridge
     period.   Discussion of Toxophilus, Report, and Scholemaster
     records circumstances of composition, of publication, or of
     reception, with no literary judgments.   Compare 1929.1 and
     1975.1.

3   MORLEY, HENRY.   "Ascham's Scholemaster." In Sketches of
     Longer Works in English Verse and Prose, Selected, Edited
     and Arranged.   Cassell's Library of English Literature.
     London, Paris, and New York: Cassell, Petter, Galpin & Co.,
     pp. 282-86.
         An abstract, with several lengthy quotations, of Schole-
     master.

4   ____.   Shorter Works in English Prose, Selected, Edited and
     Arranged.   London, Paris, New York and Melbourne;   Cassell
     & Co., pp. 40-44.
         Although primarily an edition of Ascham's Preface to
     Scholemaster, the preface is introduced and followed by
     some commentary, particularly on the relation between
     Scholemaster and Lyly's Euphues.

                              1879

1   KATTERFELD, ALFRED.   Roger Ascham: Sein Leben und seine Werke:
     Mit besonderer Berücksichtigung seiner Berichte über
     Deutschland aus den Jahren 1550-1553.   Strasburg: Karl J.
     Trübner; London: Trübner & Co., xi, 369 pp.
         Until the appearance of Ryan's Roger Ascham (1963.3),
     the authoritative biography.   The two central chapters,
     comprising the bulk of the work, analyze Report and give a
     detailed account of Ascham's travels on the continent,
     tracing his itinerary and providing accounts of important
     people with whom he came into contact.   Gives less atten-
     tion to Toxophilus and Scholemaster.   In two appendices,
     examines the evidence regarding Ascham's birth date and the
     fate of his family after his death and surveys the reprint-
     ing history of his works.   Argues that Ascham was born be-
     tween 3 July and 30 December 1516; establishes that Report
     was almost certainly not published in 1553, as earlier
     biographers claimed; and argues for 1575 as the date for
     the first edition of Ascham's Latin letters.   See 1900.3.

1879

2 MORLEY, HENRY, and TYLER, MOSES COIT. "Roger Ascham." In A
   Manual of English Literature . . . Thoroughly Revised.
   New York: Sheldon & Co., pp. 208-13.
       General survey of life and writings, hardly distinguish-
   able in places from Davenport Adams's account in 1883.1 and
   1884.1.

3 PHELPS, WILLIAM FRANKLIN. Roger Ascham and John Sturm.
   Chautauqua Textbooks, no. 17. New York: Phillips & Hunt;
   Cincinnati: Hitchcock & Walden, pp. 5-23.
       A brief biographical sketch, followed by a general ac-
   count of Ascham's "leading idea," that "to learn thoroughly
   one should also teach."

1880

*1 WALLENFELS, A. Roger Ascham. Jahres-Bericht der Höheren
    Bürgerschule zu Weisbaden. 16 pp.
        Cited in NUC, vol. 646, p. 475.

1881

1 ARNSTADT, FR[IEDRICH] AUG[UST]. Roger Ascham: Ein englischer
   Pädagog des XVI Jahrhunderts, und seine Geistverwandtschaft
   mit Johannes Sturm. Plauen: F. E. Neupert, 33 pp.
       Contains a brief "life" and survey of Ascham's works,
   an account of the state of Latin instruction during
   Ascham's lifetime, analysis of both books of Scholemaster,
   and evaluation of Ascham's relation to Sturm.

2 BALDWIN, JAMES. "An Old School-Master." The Western, n.s. 7
   (September): 428-44.
       An appreciation, bordering at times on fulsomeness, of
   those qualities and accomplishments which make Ascham an
   ideal "schoolmaster." Confidently attributes motives and
   describes events for which evidence is inconclusive or
   lacking; e.g., Ascham's reputation was so great at Cambridge that "his chamber was constantly thronged," or his
   "strong and spacious manhood . . . scorned whatever seemed
   in the smallest degree to smack of effeminacy."

*3 BROWNING, OSCAR. An Introduction to the History of Education-
    al Theories. London: K. Paul, Trench & Co.
        See 1905.4.

4   DISRAELI, ISAAC. "Roger Ascham." In <u>Amenities of Literature,</u>
     <u>Consisting of Sketches and Characters of English Litera-</u>
     <u>ture</u>. Vol. 1. New ed., edited by the Earl of Beacons-
     field. London and New York: Frederick Warne & Co.,
     pp. 359-67.
          An appreciation, liberally sprinkled with the word
     <u>genius</u> and given to excessive claims (e.g., <u>Scholemaster</u>
     "may be placed by the side of its great Latin rivals, the
     <u>Orations</u> of Cicero, and the <u>Institutes</u> of Quintillian"),
     but not without an occasional incisive critical judgment.
     Sees Ascham the writer of <u>Report</u> as a "profound observer
     at an interesting crisis in modern history," capable of
     offering "new views and many strokes of character" to his-
     torians of Disraeli's own time. First edition, 1841.1.
     <u>See</u> 1842.1.

5   HOLZAMER, JOSEF. "Roger Ascham, sein Leben und Wirken." In
     <u>Roger Ascham's Schulmeister, Einleitung, Übersetzung, und</u>
     <u>Commentar von Josef Holzamer</u>. Pädagogische Klassiker,
     vol. 9. Vienna: A. Bichler's Witwe & Sohn, pp. 111-xx11.
          A general introduction, with lengthy quotation and
     paraphrase. Speculates that Ascham could not have served
     Mary without some "restraint" of his Protestant opinions.
     <u>See also</u> pp. 130-70 for Holzamer's extensive annotations
     to the text.

                              1882

1   WODHAMS, J. R. "Ascham and Lady Jane Grey." <u>N&Q</u>, 6th ser. 6
     (23 December): 515-16.
          Inquires whether Ainsworth (1840.1) had any authority
     for Ascham's interview with Jane shortly before her execu-
     tion.
          <u>See</u> 1883.4.

                              1883

1   ADAMS, W[ILLIAM] H[ENRY] DAVENPORT. "Roger Ascham." In <u>Good</u>
     <u>Samaritans; or, Biographical Illustrations of the Law of</u>
     <u>Human Kindness</u>. London: W. Swan Sonnenschein & Co.,
     pp. 26-33.
          Brief and relatively accurate general introduction to
     life and works, with emphasis on the first; less attentive
     to the idea of "humaneness" than the book's title implies.
     <u>See</u> 1884.1.

1883

2   KATTERFELD, ALFRED. "Roger Aschams pädagogische Ansichten."
    <u>Paedagogium: Monatsschrift für Erziehung und Unterricht</u>,
    5: 476-504.
       By comparing Ascham to later pedagogical theorists such
    as Locke and Rousseau, aims to make him better known to the
    German public. In three parts: the first discussing such
    aspects as the importance of education, the effect of
    original sin on the learner, the relation of study to ex-
    perience, and quick and slow learners; the second comparing
    Ascham's thoughts on ten educational subjects (history,
    drama, mathematics, etc.) with those of German pedagogues;
    the third briefly surveying the contents of <u>Scholemaster</u>.

3   MORLEY, HENRY. <u>A First Sketch of English Literature</u>. London,
    Paris, and New York: Cassel & Co., pp. 305-7, 351-55.
       Brief summary analyses of <u>Toxophilus</u> and <u>Scholemaster</u>;
    quotes the passage on <u>Euphues</u>, and dwells at some length
    on the Italianate Englishmen. Substantially the same as
    1892.4.

4   TERRY, F. C. BIRKBECK. "Ascham and Lady Jane Grey." <u>N&Q</u>,
    6th ser. 7 (10 March): 194.
       Responds to the query in 1882.1; Ascham's account of
    Lady Jane Grey in <u>Scholemaster</u> makes it certain that he
    could <u>not</u> have conversed with her immediately before her
    execution.

<u>1884</u>

1   ADAMS, W[ILLIAM] H[ENRY] DAVENPORT. <u>A Book of Earnest Lives</u>.
    London: Swan Sonneschein & Co., pp. 26-33.
       Identical to 1883.1.

2   [BULLEN, GOERGE], ed. <u>Catalogue of Books in the Library of</u>
    <u>the British Museum Printed in England, Scotland, and Ire-</u>
    <u>land, and of Books in English Printed Abroad, to the Year</u>
    <u>1640</u>. Vol. 1. London: Trustees of the British Museum,
    pp. 57-58.
       Cites eighteen copies of five separate works, including
    early editions of <u>Epistolarum</u>, <u>Report</u>, <u>Scholemaster</u>,
    <u>Toxophilus</u>, and Giles's <u>Whole Works</u>.

3   MEAD, EDWIN D. "Queen Elizabeth's Schoolmaster." In <u>The</u>
    <u>Washingtons' English Home and Other Stories of Biography</u>.
    Edited by Rose G. Kingsley. Boston: D. Lathrop & Co.,
    pp. 73-100.

An introduction to Ascham and his times ("the age of the Renaissance . . . when the old world was waking up from its middle-age torpor") spoken by an avuncular "I" to some boys and girls. Typical of its tone and style is the following: "[he] was the forerunner, you see, of Otto and Ollendorf and the men who are relieving us of the drudgery of the grammars."

4 MULLINGER, JAMES BASS. The University of Cambridge from the Royal Injunction of 1535 to the Accession of Charles the First. Cambridge: Cambridge University Press, pp. 1-100 passim. Reprint. New York and London: Johnson Reprint Co., 1969.
    Invaluable educational, political, religious, and personal background information for Ascham's longstanding connections with the university. Compare 1958.1. Although the title page carries no volume number, this is usually Vol. 2 of a three-volume set, and is so reprinted above.

1885

*1 L[EE] [SIR] S[IDNEY]. "Ascham, Roger." In Dictionary of National Biography. Vol. 2. Edited by Leslie Stephen. London: Smith, Elder & Co.
    See 1908.2.

2 SINKER, ROBERT. A Catalogue of the English Books Printed before MDCI Now in the Library of Trinity College Cambridge. Cambridge: Deighton, Bell & Co.; London: George Bell & Sons, pp. 43, 56, 248, 252.
    Provides bibliographical description of copies owned of Toxophilus (items 90, 671), Report (item 118), Scholemaster (item 672), Epistolarum (item 662).

1886

1 ATKINSON, ERNEST G. "Roger Ascham." The Athenaeum, no. 3071 (4 September): 304-5.
    Summarizes contents of two documents, dated 1590 and 1599, relating to the leasing of Salisbury Hall, which "correct" Sidney Lee's DNB article (1885.1). See 1886.2-4.

2 _____. "Roger Ascham." The Athenaeum, no. 3075 (2 October): 432-33.
    Rejoinder to Lee's charge (1886.3) that he had confused Ascham with one Roger Ascham, yeoman of the queen's chamber. See 1886.1, 3-4.

1886

3   LEE, SIDNEY L.   "Roger Ascham."   The Athenaeum, no. 3073
        (25 September): 309.
            Replies to Atkinson's charge (1886.1) that he erred in
        calling Dudley Ascham's youngest son; charges Atkinson
        with confusing two Roger Aschams.   See 1886.1-2, 4.

4   _____.   "Roger Ascham."   The Athenaeum, no. 3077 (16 October):
        499-500.
            Lee's final response to the controversy begun in 1886.1,
        citing a document to demonstrate Elizabeth's favor toward
        Roger Ascham, yeoman.   See 1886.1-3.

*5 QUICK, ROBERT HERBERT.   Schools of the Jesuits: Ascham, Mon-
        taigne, Ratich, Milton.   Pedagogical Biography, no. 1.
        Syracuse, N.Y.:   C. W. Bardeen, pp. 19-26.
            Of two locations cited in NUC, vol. 447, p. 330, the
        only copy is apparently in New York Public Library.
        Probably the same as 1902.4.

1887

1   SAINTSBURY, GEORGE.   "Roger Ascham."   In A History of Eliza-
        bethan Literature.   London and New York: Macmillan & Co.,
        pp. 30-33.
            Ascham's style is "clear, not inelegant, invaluable as a
        kind of go-cart to habituate the infant limbs of prose
        English to orderly movement; but it is not original or
        striking or characteristic or calculated to show the native
        powers and capacities of the language."

1888

1   ARBER, EDWARD.   Introduction to his edition of The Schole-
        master.   English Reprints.   Boston: Willard Small, pp. 5-
        40.   Reprint.   Norwood, Pa.:   Norwood Editions, 1977.
            Depicts, largely by quotations from original sources of
        the day, the influences on Ascham's early life, notably
        conditions at St. John's Cambridge and the impact of John
        Cheke on its intellectual life.   Argues that materials for
        Scholemaster were merely collected before Sackville's death
        and that the actual planning and writing of the book was
        carried out in the last six or eight months before Ascham's
        death.   Contains also an analysis of Ascham's method of
        teaching Latin and a bibliography.   First printed, 1870.1.

2   HAZLITT, W[ILLIAM] CAREW. Schools, School-books and School-
    masters: A Contribution to the History of Educational
    Development in Great Britain. London: J. W. Jarvis &
    Son, pp. 220-23.
        Calls Scholemaster "so celebrated" that to judge its
    "character and merits" would be "supererogatory." Though
    it is "a literary treatise" rather than a "technical one,"
    it is still "a manual of valuable . . . counsels" for the
    teacher.

3   TURNER, J[OSEPH] HORSFALL, ed. Yorkshire Bibliographer.
    1: 87-89. [Bingley, Eng.: T. Harrison & Sons.]
        Brief descriptions of or comments on original editions
    and reprints of Ascham's works (including a Report, London:
    John Daye, 1552, quarto, described as "the scarcest of
    Ascham's publications; 36 leaves"); see 1879.1. Some lo-
    cation information.

1889

1   Catalogue of Additions to the Manuscripts in the British
    Museum in the Years 1882-1887. London: Trustees of the
    British Museum, p. 405. Reprint. 1967.
        Cites a prospectus for an edition of Ascham's English
    works, 1758; copies of letters 1545-68; a petition from
    London citizens in Ascham's hand; a letter from Elizabeth
    in favor of Ascham.

2   GILL, JOHN. "Roger Ascham." In Systems of Education: A
    History and Criticism of the Principles, Methods, Organiza-
    tion, and Moral Discipline Advocated by Eminent Education-
    ists. Boston: D. C. Heath & Co., pp. 4-13.
        Calling Ascham "the father of school method," explores
    briefly the principles of instruction found in Scholemaster
    Book I, which are "few but pregnant." For example, teacher
    should teach to pupil's "understanding," and not to the
    completion of tasks; instruction should be thorough as well
    as intelligent; it should progress a small amount at a
    time; examples should precede rules; etc. See 1899.2.

3   WILLE, JUSTUS. Die Orthographie in Roger Ascham's "Toxo-
    philus" und "Scholemaster," mit besonderer Berücksichtigung
    der für den Volksismus sich ergebenden Resultate. Marburg:
    Georg Schirling, 64 pp.

Examines vowel sounds in the two works in order to supplement the conclusions of Ellis and Sweet concerning
pronunciation in sixteenth-century English.

1890

1   CARLISLE, JAMES H., ed. Two Great Teachers: Johnson's Memoir
of Roger Ascham and Selections from Stanley's Life and
Correspondence of Thomas Arnold of Rugby. Syracuse, N.Y.:
C. W. Bardeen, pp. 1-54.
Following a ten-page introduction by Carlisle, Johnson's
Memoir occupies pp. 11-34. This is followed by a "Chapter
II," containing "a few extracts from [Scholemaster],
rather to show the author's style than to furnish an abstract of his views on the best methods of teaching the
languages." These include Ascham's "Preface" and such
anecdotal passages as those on Lady Jane Grey, on Italianate Englishmen, on Sallust, etc.

*2   JUSSERAND, [ADRIEN ANTOINE] J[EAN] J[ULES]. The English Novel
in the Time of Shakespeare. Translated by Elizabeth Lee.
London: T. Fisher Unwin.
See 1966.2.

1891

1   SCHELLING, FELIX E. Poetic and Verse Criticism of the Reign
of Elizabeth. Philadelphia: University of Pennsylvania
Press, pp. 9-11. Reprint. New York: Haskell House, 1965.
Quoting at some length Ascham's statements on classical
meters, concludes that he would have needed "a prophetic
vision" to have thought differently.

1892

1   FISCHER, THOMAS A. "Roger Ascham: Eine Studie aus dem
Zeitalter der Königen Elisabeth." In Drei Studien zur
englischen Litteraturgeschichte. Gotha: Friedrich Andreas
Berthes, pp. 3-46.
A survey of Ascham's life and summary analysis of his
major works. Comments on the digressive aspects of Toxophilus, claiming that Ascham often forgets the Greek form
of the dialogue. Sees Report as having historical value to
Germans; it is also written in the style of a journal and

indicates "exceptional" aspects of Ascham's character. Scholemaster marks a "long step forward" in both pedagogical theory and prose style.

2   HUNT, THEODORE W. "Roger Ascham--English Old and New." In Ethical Teachings in Old English Literature. New York, London, and Toronto: Funk & Wagnalls Co., pp. 328-39.
An appreciation which finds two outstanding characteristics in Ascham: a lifelong aim to defend and extend the vernacular and a "controlling ethical purpose" which aligns him with "Tyndale and Latimer among the Old English Reformers." Suggests a similarity between Scholemaster, Chaucer's Astrolabe, and Milton's Of Education. Calls Ascham "a self-appointed mediator between Rome and Geneva."

3   LAURIE, S[IMON] S[OMERVILLE]. "Roger Ascham, the Humanist." In Teachers' Guild Addresses and the Registration of Teachers. London: Percival & Co., pp. 130-68.
Quotes at length from Thomas Fuller's "Life" (1840.2) and provides a summary analysis of Ascham's thinking in Scholemaster and Toxophilus on the method of teaching and learning Latin; on contemporary teaching methods; on the importance of knowing more than one language; on school discipline; on the relation between virtue and learning; and on the importance of physical exercise and music. See 1905.5.

4   MORLEY, HENRY. English Writers: An Attempt towards a History of English Literature, vol. 8. From Surrey to Spenser. London, Paris, and Melbourne: Cassell & Co., pp. 167-70, 298-305.
Recounts the main facts of Ascham's life and sees in Toxophilus "the manly simplicity of Ascham's own English," which is in "good accord with his right doctrine." Discusses the circumstances leading to the composition of Scholemaster and provides a summary analysis, with emphasis on the passages in Book I which influenced Lyly's Euphues, on poor manners among contemporary youth, and on Italianate Englishmen. See 1883.3.

5   PAYNE, JOSEPH. "Ascham." In Lectures on the History of Education, with a Visit to German Schools. Edited by Joseph Frank Payne. London and New York: Longmans, Green & Co., pp. 57-63.
Brief biography, with discussion of the state of women's education in sixteenty-century England, of Ascham's method of teaching Latin ("far superior . . . to the ordinary grammar-school method of our own days"), and of "imitation."

6   SCHMID, K[ARL] A[DOLF], and SCHMID, GEORG. "Roger Ascham."
     In Geschichte der Erziehung vom Anfang an bis auf unsere
     Zeit. Stuttgart: J. G. Cotta, pp. 349-72.
          Brief life and summary analysis of Scholemaster, aimed
     at showing Ascham's "detailed observation of human nature
     and healthy opinion of it." Compares Ascham and Sturm on
     imitation: Sturm is more detailed about how imitation
     should be practiced.

7   SKINNER, HERBERT MARSHALL, ed. "Roger Ascham." In The School-
     master in Literature. New York, Cincinnati, and Chicago:
     American Book Co., pp. 13-15.
          An introduction to selections from Toxophilus and
     Scholemaster quotes appreciations by Isaac Disraeli and
     Charles D. Cleveland; claims for Ascham the rank of an
     English classic, a degree higher than that of Elyot or
     More.

                              1893

1   Catalogue of Original and Early Editions of Some of the Poet-
     ical and Prose Works of English Writers from Langland to
     Wither, with Collations & Notes, & Eighty-Seven Facsimiles
     of Titlepages and Frontispieces. New York: Grolier Club,
     pp. 4-8. Reprint. New York: Cooper Square Publishers,
     1963.
          Bibliographical descriptions of the first four editions
     of Scholemaster, with collation (1570, 1571, 1579, 1789);
     of the 1571 and 1589 editions of Toxophilus; and of the
     1552 [sic] Report.

2   CRAIK, HENRY, ed. "Roger Ascham." In English Prose: Selec-
     tions with Critical Introductions by Various Writers.
     Vol. 1. Fourteenth to Sixteenth Century. New York and
     London: Macmillan Co., pp. 267-70.
          Briefly introduces and evaluates Ascham as humanist and
     stylist. He illustrates, "perhaps more completely than
     any other in his generation . . . that eager curiosity and
     vigorous outlook which he kept upon all the current topics
     of the day," and he is "almost" our "first purely literary
     man." His love of the classics and distrust of modern
     Romance languages accounts for "the almost pedantic sim-
     plicity of his style."

1894

1 LEWIS, EDWIN HERBERT. The History of the English Paragraph. Chicago: University of Chicago Press, pp. 34-42 passim, 77-80.

Cites Ascham's Toxophilus in several tables indicating comparative paragraph and sentence length among seventy-five different writers. Analysis of Ascham's paragraphing methods in Toxophilus and Scholemaster shows that there was no essential change in the twenty years separating them; that Ascham has a weak sense of the paragraph as a rhetorical unit; that his paragraph rhythm is "monotonous."

2 SKINNER, HERBERT M[ARSHALL]. The Schoolmaster in Comedy and Satire. New York, Cincinnati, and Chicago: American Book Co., pp. 34-42.

General introduction preceding selections from Schole-master; recounts Ascham's relations to Lady Jane Grey, John Whitney, and Queen Elizabeth. Selections designed for "teachers' reading circles and round tables."

1896

1 PARMENTIER, JACQUES. Histoire de l'éducation en Angleterre: Les doctrines et les écoles depuis les origines jusqu'au commencement du XIXe siècle. Paris: Perrin et Cie, Libraires-Éditeurs, pp. 39-57.

Chapter 3, "Roger Ascham," decries the fact that Ascham is virtually unknown in France, and provides a ten-page summary of the main events of his life before proceeding to an analysis of Ascham's methods of teaching Latin in Scholemaster. Observes that Ascham's principles were not merely theoretical but had been tested on his own pupils and proposes that his method of double translation "nous paraît aussi digne d'attention aujourd'hui qu'au temps passé."

1897

1 RUSHTON, WILLIAM LOWES. Shakespeare an Archer. Liverpool: Lee & Nightingale, 118 pp. passim.

Argues that Toxophilus was the origin of many passages in Shakespeare's works having to do with archery. Isolates words or phrases within lengthy passages by Shakespeare, parallels them with the same words or phrases from a

lengthy passage by Ascham, and claims direct influence;
also interprets some Shakespearean language by means of
technical terminology in Toxophilus and in several places
suggests emendations; occasionally extends his claims to
non-technical vocabulary.

1898

*1 ACKERMAN, W. A. "Roger Ascham and His Relation to Education."
    Master's thesis, Columbia University, 59 pp.
        Contains chapters on Ascham's life, on sixteenth-century
    education in England, and on Scholemaster.

2   DOUGLAS, ROBERT LANGTON. Introduction to his edition of
    Matteo Bandello, Certain Tragical Discourses of Bandello,
    trans. Geoffrey Fenton. Vol. I. Tudor Translations, 19.
    London: David Nutt, pp. xlvi-1.
        Argues that Geoffrey Fenton's translation is the chief
    object of Ascham's attack on Italian novelle in Schole-
    master. "In advocating the licensing of books . . .
    Ascham . . . was endeavoring to promote 'Papish' practices
    in England," whereas Fenton "was the more consistent
    Protestant of the two."

3   SAINTSBURY, GEORGE. A Short History of English Literature.
    London: Macmillan & Co., pp. 237-41. Reprint. London:
    Macmillan & Co.; New York: St. Martin's Press, 1966.
        Ascham is a "very agreeable specimen of a good type of
    Englishman," and his three major works (Toxophilus, Schole-
    master, and Epistolarum) entitle him to a "very important
    place" in the history of English prose. Though the letters
    "rank lowest" of the three, they nevertheless show that
    Ascham's mother tongue was "a vehicle of literature . . .
    capable of being immensely improved." Ascham's style is
    "struck out on classical models," and is thereby "the first
    accomplished plain style in English." His greatest im-
    portance is the personal contribution which his writing
    made to the larger wave of "classicizing" that led to
    Hooker.

1899

1   Catalogue of the Printed Books and Manuscripts in the John
    Rylands Library. Manchester: John Rylands Library,
    pp. 90-91.

Lists eleven imprints, including first editions of Toxophilus, Scholemaster, and Report, and Elstob's Epistolarum.

2   GILL, JOHN. "Roger Ascham: Father of School Method." In
     Mulcaster and Ascham: Two English Schoolmasters. The
     Pedagogic Quarterly, vol. 1, no. 2. New York and Chicago:
     E. L. Kellogg & Co., pp. 18-26.
     Analysis of selected principles from Book I of Schole-
     master; essentially the same as 1889.2. Difficult to
     locate; usually cited under Foster Watson, author of the
     chapter on Mulcaster.

3   SEELEY, LEVI. "Ascham (1515-1568)." In History of Education.
     New York, Cincinnati, and Chicago: American Book Co.,
     pp. 190-92.
     Ascham is "the most celebrated English educator of the
     sixteenth century," and Scholemaster is the "first educa-
     tional classic in English." Though Sturm "made some
     use" of the method of double translation, "Ascham is en-
     titled to full credit" for it.

1900

1   Catalogue général des livres imprimés de la Bibliothèque
     Nationale. Vol. 4. Paris: Imprimerie Nationale, cols.
     781 83.
     Cites ten imprints, including five original editions of
     the letters, one of Scholemaster, and two of Toxophilus.

2   FITCH, SIR JOSHUA [GIRLING]. "Ascham and the Schools of the
     Renaissance." In Educational Aims and Methods: Lectures
     and Addresses. New York and London: Macmillan Co.,
     pp. 215-48.
     Only pp. 223-29 deal directly with Ascham, touching on
     the following: the condition of learning in the sixteenth
     century; Scholemaster; Ascham's relationship to Lady Jane
     Grey and Queen Elizabeth; his attitude to Italy; his "other
     writings" (with no reference to Toxophilus!); and his
     "place" in history of education. See 1905.2.

3   WEIDEMANN, GERHARD. Roger Ascham als Pädagoge. Berlin:
     Gustav Schade, 77 pp.
     Provides a systematic outline of Ascham's theories of
     education using all of his available works. Claims that
     in his desire to have his works accepted, Ascham presented
     his ideas as though they were unoriginal, citing classical

1901

authorities. In crediting Pliny the Second for his notion
of double translation, Ascham misread what Pliny says, and
as a result his technique is "indeed original." Gives
considerable attention to Ascham's "undoubtable" influence
on Locke. Notes several instances in which Katterfeld
(1879.1) misrepresents Ascham's ideas.

<u>1901</u>

1 ANON. "Roger Ascham." In <u>Chambers's Cyclopaedia of English
   Literature</u>. Vol. 1. New ed. by David Patrick. London
   and Edinburgh: W. & R. Chambers, pp. 144-48.
      Quotations from <u>Toxophilus</u>, <u>Scholemaster</u>, and the let-
   ters, illustrating different aspects of Ascham's personality and style. Some of his letters make Ascham "one of
   the very earliest of 'picturesque tourists' on the Rhine."
   First edition, 1843.1.

2 <u>Catalogue of Additions to the Manuscripts in the British
   Museum in the Years 1894-1899</u>. London: Trustees of the
   Britsh Museum, p. 600. Reprint. 1967.
      Cites a letter book, 1554-58, and letters written in
   1551 to fellows of St. John's.

3 <u>Columbia University Library Bulletins, No. 2: Books on Education in the Libraries of Columbia University</u>. New York:
   Printed for the University, pp. 102-3, 222-23.
      The first section, listing thirteen imprints, mostly
   German, is biographical; the second cites editions and
   critical studies of <u>Scholemaster</u>. Lists some items which
   apparently may be found only at Columbia; see 1857.4,
   1872.1, 1873.1.

4 MOULTON, CHARLES WELLS, ed. "Roger Ascham." In <u>The Library
   of Literary Criticism of English and American Authors</u>.
   Vol. 1. Buffalo, New York: Moulton Publishing Company,
   pp. 288-91.
      A collection of quotations from over twenty biographers,
   critics, and historians from 1582-1899 concerning Ascham
   the man, <u>Toxophilus</u>, and <u>Scholemaster</u>, for example,
   "Ascham is a thorough bred philologist, and of the purest
   water," by T. F. Dibdin, <u>The Library Companion</u> (1824).

5 SAINTSBURY, GEORGE. <u>The Earlier Renaissance</u>. New York:
   Charles Scribner's Sons, pp. 259-63.
      Treats Ascham as one of the leaders of a "remarkable
   Cambridge group" who made mid-sixteenth century "one of

the greatest turning points in English prose." Excuses
Ascham's literary "pecadillos"--his advocacy of classical
meters, his prudery and Puritanism--as "patriotism a little
gone wrong." As for Ascham's prose, "for sureness, vivid-
ness, correctness, command of method, no forerunner had
equalled him."

1902

*1 CUBBERLEY, ELLWOOD P[ATTERSON]. Syllabus of Lectures on the
    History of Education, with Selected Bibliographies. New
    York and London: Macmillan Co.
       See 1904.2.

2   KEMP, ELLWOOD L. "Extension of Educational Activity." In
    History of Education. Lippincott Educational Series.
    Philadelphia: J. B. Lippincott Co., pp. 180-83.
       Scholemaster is the "most charming" educational treatise
    of the period 1550-75, a period characterized by "growth of
    interest in the use of the native language." It embodies
    the "rare good sense" with which Ascham "worked out a com-
    prehensive theory of Latin teaching."

^3 MOODY, WILLIAM VAUGHAN, and LOVETT, ROBERT MORSS. A History
    of English Literature. New York: Charles Scribner's Sons.
       See 1918.2.

4   QUICK, ROBERT HERBERT. "Ascham (1515-1568)." In Essays on
    Educational Reformers. New York. D. Appleton & Co.,
    pp. 80-89, 486.
       Analyzes Ascham's method of double translation. Although
    the method is sound and, for the advanced pupil, "excel-
    lent," it imposed on the beginning student, "it leads to
    unintelligent memorizing." Ascham is one of the three
    English educational theorists to have influenced other
    nations, not by brilliance of thought, but by the "charm"
    of his style. First edition,1868.2. See also 1886.5.

5   SAINTSBURY, GEORGE. "Ascham." In A History of Criticism and
    Literary Taste in Europe from the Earliest Texts to the
    Present Day. Vol. 2. From the Renaissance to the Decline
    of Eighteenth Century Orthodoxy. New York: Dodd, Mead &
    Co.; Edinburgh and London: William Blackwood & Sons,
    pp. 153-62.
       Distinguishing between what he "thought as a critic,"
    and what he "did as a writer," chastises Ascham for the

1903

"moral craze" which prompted him to condemn romances, for his addiction to that "Delilah of alliteration," and for his part in preferring classical meters to rhyme--"a necessary, if morbid, stage in the development of English prosody."

1903

1   GARNETT, RICHARD. English Literature: An Illustrated Record. Vol. 1. From the Beginnings to the Age of Henry VIII. London: William Heinemann; New York: Macmillan Co., pp. 329-32.
      See 1906.1.

2   LAURIE, S[IMON] S[OMERVILLE]. "Roger Ascham, the Humanist; b. 1515, d. 1568." In Studies in the History of Educational Opinion from the Renaissance. Cambridge: Cambridge University Press, pp. 58-85.
      See 1905.5.

3   SYMMES, HAROLD S. Les débuts de la critique dramatique en Angleterre jusqu'à la mort de Shakespeare. Paris: Ernest Leroux, pp. 26-28.
      Ascham's statements about drama in Scholemaster, although largely parenthetical, have "a considerable import for the development of dramatic criticism in England." Most important are his opinions concerning tragedy. Ascham's taste is for classical drama, never for the native "interludes barbares."

4   WATSON, FOSTER. "Notices of Some Early English Writers on Education--Part II." In Annual Reports of the Department of the Interior for the Fiscal Year Ended June 30, 1902. Report of the Commissioner of Education. Vol. 1. Washington: Government Printing Office, pp. 492-501.
      A brief chronology, followed by: a selective annotated bibliography of lives and commentary; a list of Ascham's works; and descriptions, with lengthy quotations, of Toxophilus and Scholemaster.

1904

1   ASCHAM, ROGER. English Works: "Toxophilus," "Report of the Affaires and State of Germany," "The Scholemaster." Edited by William Aldis Wright. Cambridge: Cambridge University Press, 324 pp.

The most reliable modern edition with original spelling
and punctuation. Contains no notes or other apparatus,
save a preface and list of errata in the originals. <u>See</u>
1908.5 and 1967.2.

2   CUBBERLEY, ELLWOOD P. <u>Syllabus of Lectures on the History of</u>
<u>Education, with Selected Bibliographies and Suggested</u>
<u>Readings</u>. 2d ed., rev. New York and London: Macmillan
Co., pp. 195-97.
Merely an outline of a lecture to be given on Ascham's
life and times and on <u>Scholemaster</u>. Most valuable for the
list of secondary references, some of which do not appear
in Tannenbaum (1946.1). First edition, 1902.1.

3   CURRY, JOHN T. "'Three Guns.'" <u>N&Q</u> 10th ser. 2, no. 8
(27 August): 169.
Explains a passage in Strype's <u>Life of Smith</u> by reference to <u>Toxophilus</u>.

4   EMKES, MAX ADOLF. <u>Das Erziehungsideal bei Sir Thomas More,</u>
<u>Sir Thomas Elyot, Roger Ascham und John Lyly</u>. Marburg:
R. Friedrich's Universitätsbuchdruckerei, 88 pp.
Compares the thinking of each man under the headings of
"physical," "intellectual," and "moral" education, with
the second subdivided into sections entitled "Who is
qualified to be a tutor, and what is the proper relation
between pupil and tutor and parents and tutor?" and "Particular Disciplines"; under the latter, Emkes summarizes the
substance of Ascham's advice on teaching Latin in Book II.

<u>1905</u>

1   ANON. "Roger Ascham." <u>The Spectator</u> 94 (18 March): 406-7.
Ostensibly a review of Wright's edition (1904.1), it is
instead a paean to <u>Toxophilus</u> and archery ("not since
Xenophon . . . so admirable a treatise on sport"), to which
is added a brief generalization about <u>Scholemaster</u> and
Ascham ("of less interest than his works").

2   [ARCHER, WILLIAM.] "Ascham and Colet." In <u>Let Youth But</u>
<u>Know: A Plea for Reason in Education</u>. London: Methuen &
Co., pp. 240-42.
Quotes from Sir Joshua Fitch (1900.2): Ascham "looked
with fresh eyes upon the traditional methods of teaching."

1905

3 BENNDORF, CORNELIE. Die englische Pädagogik im 16. Jahrhundert, wie sie dargestellt wird im Wirken und in den Werken
von Elyot, Ascham, und Mulcaster. Vienna and Leipzig:
Wilhelm Braumüller, xi, 84 pp.
  Chapter 3 contains a brief account of Ascham's life and
the history of his works, followed by a summary analysis of
Toxophilus and Scholemaster. Chapter 4 compares the impact
of humanism on the thought of the three men and their posi-
tions regarding such matters as physical exercise, the
teaching of languages, and the education of women. Chapter
5 compares their literary qualities and "philosophies."
See 1908.5.

4 BROWNING, OSCAR. An Introduction to the History of Educational Theories. New York and London: Harper & Brothers Publishers, pp. 85-90.
  Dividing educational theory into three "schools," the
Humanists, the Realists, and the Naturalists, treats
Ascham as representative of the first school and considers
him "probably overrated." Concludes from Ascham's advice
on the teaching of Latin that he is "little else than a
mere schoolmaster . . . with no extended views or aims."
First edition, 1881.3.

5 LAURIE, S[IMON] S[OMERVILLE]. "Roger Ascham, the Humanist;
b. 1515, d. 1568." In Studies in the History of Educational Opinion from the Renaissance. Cambridge: Cambridge
University Press, pp. 58-85.
  Same as 1892.3. First edition, 1903.2.

6 PLATT, JAMES, JR. and SALMON, DAVID. "Roger Ascham: 'Schedule.'" N&Q, 10th ser. 4 (9 September): 216.
  Two separate contributions asserting that the pronunciation of Ascham's name is Askham.

7 SNELL, F[REDERICK] J[OHN]. The Age of Transition, 1400-1580.
Vol. 2. London: George Bell & Sons, pp. 119-25.
  Brief evaluation of Ascham as "a maker of English
prose," stressing his "charm," and "naiveté."

8 WILSON, JOHN DOVER. John Lyly. Cambridge: Cambridge University Press, pp. 537-39. Reprint. New York: Haskell House
Publishers, 1970.
  On Ascham's style as a precursor of euphuism, transverse
alliteration, classical allusions, and balanced sentence
structure.

1906

1 GARNETT, RICHARD. English Literature: An Illustrated Record.
   Vol. 1. From the Beginnings to the Age of Henry VIII.
   London: William Heinemann; New York: Macmillan Co.,
   pp. 329-32.
       Evaluation of Ascham's life, personality, and works.
   Suggests comparison between Toxophilus and Walton's Com-
   pleat Angler. In Scholemaster, Ascham "displays an enlightened spirit in advance of his time." Ascham's
   "pedantry" concerning rhyme is deplorable. First edition,
   1903.1.

1907

1 MONROE, PAUL. A Brief Course in the History of Education.
   New York and London: Macmillan, pp. 179-80, 221-23.
       As a typical humanist, follower of Sturm, Ascham's
   stress on "method" leaves the impression of "narrowness."
   Ascham's conservative English distrust of travel contrasts
   with Montaigne's more "socially realistic" advocacy of it.

1908

*1 BURCHERS, MICHAEL. "Roger Ascham and Princess Elizabeth"
   [Plate]. In Catalogue of Engraved British Portraits Pre-
   served in the Department of Prints and Drawings in the
   British Museum. Vol. 1. London: Trustees of the British
   Museum, p. 79.
       Cited in 1946.1 and in NUC, vol. 76, p. 487.

2 L[EE], [SIR] S[IDNEY]. "Ascham, Roger." In Dictionary of
   National Biography. Vol. 1. Edited by Leslie Stephen and
   Sidney Lee. New York: Macmillan Co.; London: Smith,
   Elder & Co., pp. 622-31.
       A reissue of 1885.1, in which the Ascham article was in
   vol. 2, with errors corrected and bibliographies revised.
       Apparently independent of the "Life" in Giles' edition
   (1864.1), to which Lee does not refer, although he cites
   the letters in that edition frequently. Organized by
   identifiable "periods" in Ascham's life, with emphasis more
   on externals than on his intellect and personality. Begins
   with details of known or suspected members of the Ascham
   family from 1313 to Roger Ascham's time; enumerates
   Ascham's chief teachers, pupils, and acquaintances at
   Cambridge; and throughout places considerable emphasis on

his financial situation, on the misfortunes in his life,
and on his constant solicitations for patronage. Relatively brief accounts of Toxophilus, Scholemaster, and
Report. The claim that Ascham's translation of Oecumenius'
commentaries on Titus and Philemon was "published" in 1542
is misleading, as they only exist in a MS exhibiting
Ascham's handsome penmanship. Suggests that the Roger
Ascham returned to Parliament for Preston in 1563 may have
been Ascham. See 1963.3.

3   SAINTSBURY, GEORGE. A History of English Prosody from the
Twelfth Century to the Present Day. Vol. 2. London:
Macmillan & Co., pp. 170-72. Reprint: New York: Russell
& Russell, 1961.
    Scholemaster is the "earliest manifesto" on subject of
classical meters.

4   SANDYS, JOHN EDWIN. A History of Classical Scholarship.
Vol. 2. From the Revival of Learning to the End of the
Eighteenth Century. Cambridge: Cambridge University
Press, pp. 231-36 passim.
    Although the discussion of Ascham does not stick en-
tirely to the subject of his classical scholarship, it
places him in context of the reformation of both Greek
and Latin pronunciation in England; also demonstrates
Ascham's continued preference for Cicero over Quintilian
regarding the method of language instruction.

5   SCHOTT, WILHELM. Review of English Works of Roger Ascham,
edited by William Aldis Wright; of Cornelie Benndorf,
Die englische Pädagogik im 16. Jahrhundert; and of Wiener
Beiträge zur englischen Philologie, vol. 22, edited by
J. Schipper. Anglia, Zeitschrift für englische Philologie.
Beiblatt. Mitteilungen über englische Sprache 19 (January): 22-32.
    Wright's edition (1904.1), although an important contri-
bution to the study of Ascham's major works, would have
been better had it contained a chronology of Ascham's life
and a selection of the important letters. Although
Benndorf's book (1905.3) is readable and of some help to
the specialist, it falls short of scholarly excellence and
is contradictory in its appraisal of Ascham and Mulcaster.

6   TAYLOR, I[DA] A[SHWORTH]. Lady Jane Grey and Her Times.
New York: D. Appleton & Co., pp. 141-44.
    Recounts Ascham's visit to Lady Jane Grey in summer of
1550, with the claim that it provides "one of the most
distinct glimpses of the girl that we possess." Takes

Ascham's account of her speech as indicative of her "command of the vernacular . . . equal to her proficiency in the dead languages," rather than as Ascham's own style.

7   WATSON, FOSTER. "Ascham and Brinsley." In The English Grammar Schools to 1660: Their Curriculum and Practice. Cambridge: Cambridge University Press, pp. 362-67. Reprint. London: Frank Cass & Co., 1968.
    Compares the two in some depth; whereas Brinsley speaks "from the experience of the classroom," Ascham writes "from the aspiration of the scholar," and shows "greater intellectual breeding."

8   WOELK, GEORG KONRAD. Geschichte und Kritik des englishen Hexameters. Königsberg: Hartungsche Buchdruckerei, pp. 7-8.
    A brief summary of Ascham's statements in Scholemaster concerning classical meters.

1909

1   DAVEY, RICHARD. The Nine Days' Queen: Lady Jane Grey and Her Times. London: Methuen & Co,, pp. 172-77.
    Quotes letter of 18 January 1551, asking whether Ascham could have been "in love with" Lady Jane Grey; there must have been "some politic motive" for a letter "so fulsome and so extravagant."

2   MOORE, J[OHN] L[OWRY]. Die theoretische Stellungnahme der englischen Schriftsteller zur Fremdwörterfrage während der Tudor-Stuartzeit. Göttingen: Dietrich Univ.-Buchdruckerei, 38 pp.
    A condensation of 1910.2.

3   WARD, A[DOLPHUS] W[ILLIAM], and WALLER, A[LFRED] R[AYNEY], eds. The Cambridge History of English Literature. Vol. 3. Renascence and Reformation. Cambridge: Cambridge University Press, pp. 290-94, 432-36.
    The first selection, by Saintsbury, briefly evaluates Ascham as a critic: he shows "best" both the "strengthening power of the critical sense" in the middle of the century and its "lack of education and direction," the latter in his doctrine of imitation and in his advocacy of classical versification.
    In the second selection, W. H. Woodward provides a more general introduction, finding in Ascham a "nationalism which is characteristic of English humanism of the finer

type." He judges Ascham's method of double translation "of slight importance in the history of instruction," but says that Ascham's view of historical writing "far transcends the superficial aspect of it which confronts us in Italian humanists prior to the later Patrizi." He presents a more charitable view of Ascham's theory of imitation than does Saintsbury.

1910

1   JUSSERAND, [ADRIEN ANTOINE] J[EAN] J[ULES]. A Literary History of the English People. Vol. 2. From the Renaissance to the Civil War. 2d ed. New York and London: G. P. Putnam's Sons, pp. 106-9.
    Treats Ascham as "the first English essayist," whose "catholicity of interests" makes him "seem very modern." Ascham's "readiness of wit and good humour . . . already suggest the kindly remonstrances of wise Addison." For passim references to Ascham's ideas concerning the English language, history, travel, Italy, versification, see Index Vol. 3, p. 572.

2   MOORE, J[OHN] L[OWRY]. Tudor-Stuart Views on the Growth, Status, and Destiny of the English Language. Studien zur englischen Philologie, no. 41. Halle a.S.: Max Niemeyer, pp. 10-12, 14-24, 33-34, 38-41, 44-50 passim.
    Cites Ascham frequently in chronicling the views among users of early modern English as to "the powers, capacity and relative worth of the mother-tongue, what was surmised of its past, what hoped and feared for its future." See 1909.2.

1911

1   CURRY, JOHN T. "Roger Ascham and Ioannes Ravisius Textor." N&Q, 11th ser. 3 (10 June): 441-43.
    Provides biographical information for the "Textor" whom Ascham attacks in Toxophilus: Jean Tixier, seigneur de Ravisi, ca. 1480-1524. Claims that Ascham had carefully read his best work, Officina, vel Naturae Historia per Locos (1522). One cannot be certain why Ascham reviles Textor, but perhaps Textor was impugning English bowmanship.

1912

1 SAINTSBURY, GEORGE. A History of English Prose Rhythm.
   London: Macmillan & Co., pp. 119-23. Reprint. Blooming-
   ton: Indiana University Press, 1965.
      "If you take Fisher before, Hooker after, and Latimer as
   a trace-horse running with a very loose rein at the side
   . . . the origin and the object of Ascham's writing will
   soon become clear." "I should certainly assign [the
   term] 'Father of English Prose' rather to Ascham than to
   Wyclif."

1913

1 BAYNE, THOMAS. "Proposed Emendation in Ascham." N&Q,
   11th ser. 7 (28 June): 517.
      Supplements 1913.6; describes juncus articulatus or
   Scottish "spratt" as having "some bearing" on the subject
   of "loamey/ioney." See also 1913.5-6.

2 LONG, PERCY WALDRON. "From Troilus to Euphues." In Anni-
   versary Papers by Colleagues and Pupils of George Lyman
   Kittredge. Edited by F. N. Robinson. Boston and London:
   Ginn & Co., pp. 367-76.
      Argues that "Lyly's indebtedness to Ascham has been
   understated"; euphuism is most immediately and clearly
   anticipated by the style of John Grange's Golden Aphro-
   ditis, and "this style . . . is . . . the 'anatomie' of
   Ascham's abstract Euphues."

*3 MILLER, ERMA ESTHER. "Roger Ascham as a Literary Figure in
   the Sixteenth Century." Master's thesis, Columbia University, iii, 58 pp.
      Cited in 1946.1.

4 MILLER, G[EORGE] M[OREY]. The Historical Point of View in
   English Literary Criticism from 1570-1770. Anglistische
   Forschungen, no. 35. Heidelberg: Carl Winter, pp. 44-46.
   Reprint. Amsterdam: Swets & Zeitlinger, 1967.
      Calls Ascham "the father of dogmatic criticism," claim-
   ing that "his standard is wholly aristocratic," and that
   his "classicist's contempt" for the "lawlessness" of Italian romance was "taught him, directly or indirectly, by the
   orthodox Italian humanists." Ascham has no historical
   point of view apart from his patriotism and his quotation
   of Cheke.

1913

5 MOORE SMITH, G[EORGE] C[HARLES]. "'Joncy.'" MLR 8, no. 1
   (January): 97.
      Proposes "ioncy" = "rushy" in place of "ioney" in
   Ascham's 20 January 1551 letter to Raven. See also
   1913.1, 6.

6 STRACHAN, L[IONEL] R[ICHARD] M[ORTIMER]. "Proposed Emendation in Ascham." N&Q, 11th ser. 7 (7 June): 445.
      Proposes "lomey" = "loamy" for "ioney" in the 20 Jan-
   uary 1551 letter to Raven. See also 1913.1, 5.

                              1914

1 BOAS, FREDERICK S. University Drama in the Tudor Age.
   Oxford: Clarendon Press, pp. 62-64.
      Enumerates what Ascham ("really our only source of in-
   formation") has to say about Thomas Watson's Absalom.
   Says Ascham's comments in Scholemaster may have been
   written to induce Watson to put his play before the public. See 1964.3.

2 LANG, ANDREW. "Ascham." In History of English Literature
   from "Beowulf" to Swinburne. London and New York: Longmans, Green & Co., pp. 175-76.
      Brief evaluative introduction, slightly more space
   devoted to such biographical matters as Ascham's reputation for gambling and his dislike of romances and Italy
   than to his works. Toxophilus "to our age, appears pedantic," and Ascham's advocacy of Greek meters is "absurd."

3 LEGOUIS, ÉMILE. "Les éducateurs: Roger Ascham." Revue des
   cours et conférences (5 May): pp. 384-89.
      A general introduction and evaluation which finds in
   Ascham's style a "rather cramped simplicity. But beneath
   this weighty garb we can get at the man himself, with his
   sincerity, his good sense, his good humor. Even his
   [stylistic] stiffness can't disguise the advantage that
   English prose gained in being put to school by him to the
   classics. If at times it lost in facility, it gained in
   maturity." Analyzes Ascham's attitude toward Italianate
   Englishmen to show how it exhibits simultaneously "l'hor-
   reur du puritanisme naissant pour l'Italie et la passion
   des contemporaines pour les choses italiennes."

4   THOMPSON, GUY ANDREW. Elizabethan Criticism of Poetry.
     Menasha, Wis.: George Banta Publishing Co., pp. 1, 11,
     19-20, 36, 37, 41, 49, 54, 61, 94, 95, 114, 124, 142, 143,
     147n, 153n, 191, 192, 119n, 203, 208.
          Cites Ascham to illustrate the following: the unsatis-
     factory state of poetry in English at mid-sixteenth cen-
     tury, its causes, and ways to remedy that state;
     Elizabethan concepts of the function of poetry; ideas
     regarding its form, style, and diction. The author's
     Ph.D. dissertation, University of Chicago, 1914.

                              1915

1   ANON. "A Great Tutor." The Saturday Review (London) 119
     (6 March): 249-50.
          An appreciative survey of Scholemaster, introduced by
     the claim that "today one must seek it in the old book
     store."

2   HETTLER, ALBERT. Roger Ascham: Sein Stil und seine Beziehung
     zur Antike. Ein Beiträge zur Entwicklung der englischen
     Sprache unter dem Einfluss des Humanismus. Elberfeld:
     Wuppertaler, 100 pp.
          Aims to point out the "most obvious peculiarities" in
     Ascham's style. Claims that Report is often written in a
     "journalistic" style and that Toxophilus may be character-
     ized as "stylistic propaganda." Ascham wants to "pour
     English into the mold of the antique," and his goal is to
     rid the language of as many foreign words as possible.
     Both sentence structure and rhetoric follow classical
     lines. Considers Ascham one of the most important "artis-
     tic" writers of the age.

3   KRAPP, GEORGE PHILIP. The Rise of English Literary Prose.
     New York: Oxford University Press, pp. 292-99. Reprint.
     New York: Frederick Ungar, 1963.
          Surveying "several respects" in which Ascham is "signi-
     ficant" for the development of English style, concentrates
     on Ascham's wish to "write easily and humanely in the Eng-
     lish tongue," and on the Isocratean element in Ascham's
     sentence development; also touches on possible connections
     between Ascham and euphuism. See index for frequent
     passim references.

1915

4 PATTERSON, HERBERT. "The Humanism of Roger Ascham: A Quan-
titative Study of Classical References in Ascham's Scholemaster." The Pedagogical Seminary 22, no. 4 (December):
546-51. [Date on the title page is erroneously given as
1914 and so recorded by Tannenbaum (1946.1).]
Tabulates occurrences of all personal names in Scholemaster. A typical conclusion: "If repetitions be included, there are 782 classical references out of a total of
1035 references, which is more than seventy-five percent.
The Greek and Latin classics were much studied by the
scholars of the Renaissance humanistic period."

1916

1 CROLL, MORRIS WILLIAM and CLEMONS, HARRY, eds. "Euphues:
The Anatomy of Wit," "Euphues & His England" by John Lyly.
London: George Routledge & Sons; New York: E. P. Dutton
& Co., pp. xviii-xxiii passim, xlvi-xlvii, lx-lxi.
Explores the "intimate relation" between Euphues and
Scholemaster: both aim to "rally the scholarship of the
national party against the Italianizing influences which
were so busy in the letters and life of the court," and
both are strongly characterized by a bourgeois aspect.
As for Ascham's significance in the development of euphuism
as a prose style, especially its characteristic use of
parison and paramoion, he is ultimately unimportant; the
main line of influence comes not from classical imitation
but from the medieval rhetorical tradition. Compare
1961.2 and 1962.2. Re-edited as 1966.1.

2 LUCKY, GEORGE WASHINGTON ANDREW. "Roger Ascham (1515-1566)
and Classical Learning." In Outlines of the History of
Education. 3rd ed., rev. Lincoln: University of Nebraska
Press, pp. 95-98.
A thirty-seven item bibliography, followed by a set of
discussion questions and some extracts from Scholemaster.
Works listed are not always in full bibliographical form,
some having been listed in earlier sections, and there is
no cross reference. I can find no listing for a first or
second edition.

3 WHIPPLE, T. K. "Isocrates and Euphusim." MLR 11, no. 1
(January): 15-27; no. 2 (April): 129-35.
Questions the "complete harmony of opinion" that euphu-
ism was the outgrowth of humanistic study of Greek and
Latin oratorical style. Considers the "whole bulk of
early sixteenth-century prose," asking whether the

knowledge and use of the euphuistic figures coincide at
all with the humanist movement; they do not. While the
most blatant use of the Gorgianic figures occurs in the
popular prose of the time, sermons and pamphlets, humanists like Ascham were learning from Isocrates that "the
chief virtues of style are smoothness, clarity, restraint,
and that the schemes of structure--isocolon and parison--
are to be preferred to those which depend on the chime of
like sounds." Isocrates "explains the differences between
Ascham and Lyly--but not the similarities."

1918

1   Catalogue of the Printed Books in the Library of the Univer-
       sity of Edinburgh. Vol. 1. Edinburgh: Edinburgh Univer-
       sity Press, T. and A. Constable, p. 173.
          Lists thirteen items, including first editions of
    Scholemaster, Toxophilus, and Epistolarum.

2   MOODY, WILLIAM VAUGHN, and LOVETT, ROBERT MORSS. "Roger
       Ascham." In A History of English Literature. Rev. ed.
       New York, Chicago, and Boston: Charles Scribner's Sons,
       pp. 83-84.
          Sees Toxophilus as "ostensibly written in praise of
    archery . . . but . . . really a defense of a sound, well-
    balanced life." Scholemaster exemplifies Ascham's view
    of life, which is "thoroughly English," praising learning
    "not for its own sake, but because it furnishes discipline
    for character and examples for conduct." First edition,
    1902.3.

3   SHAFER, ROBERT. The English Ode to 1660; An Essay in Lit-
       erary History. Princeton: Princeton University Press,
       pp. 73-74. Reprint. New York: Gordian Press, 1966.
          Though Ascham knew Pindar, his frequent references to
    the Greek poet in Scholemaster (quoted by Shafer) yield
    no information that would aid an English poet in writing
    odes.

1920

1   ANON. "Roger Ascham." The Times Educational Supplement
       (London), 14 October: 545.
          Offers a brief appreciation by way of decrying the fact
    that in "the latest history of education" Ascham is dis-
    missed in fewer than eleven lines. Concerned to show

1920

Ascham's relevance to educational issues of the present
day, sees him as a "precursor of the public school spirit," and as the "most noteworthy and effective enthusiast
in changing the old oral method of teaching to the new
method of making use of paper books." He "ought to re-
ceive credit as initiating the modern practice of written
exercises" and would "certainly confirm the attitude of
reformers who wish to improve the general handwriting of
the schools."

2 BERDAN, JOHN M. Early Tudor Poetry, 1485-1547. New York:
   Macmillan Co., pp. 305-42 passim. Reprint. [Hamden,
   Conn.]: Shoe String Press, 1961.
       Views Ascham as representing a third stage in the devel-
   opment of humanism, in which its varied elements, not yet
   perfectly assimilated in Elyot's generation, have become
   "fused," with the consequence that the "personality of the
   writer has free play." Also assesses Ascham's place,
   along with Elyot's and Vives', in the transmission of
   humanistic "doctrine." Although much of the Ascham material consists of quotations to illustrate general points,
   there is consistent comparison of the three men, both
   explicit and implicit.

3 SCHROEDER, KURT. Platonismus in der englischen Renaissance
   vor und bei Thomas Eliot, nebst Neudruck von Eliot's
   "Disputacion Platonike," 1533. Palaestra, 83. Berlin:
   Mayer & Müller, pp. 116-28.
       Chapter 7, "Roger Ascham," provides a brief biography,
   cites all quotations from and references to Plato in
   Toxophilus and Scholemaster, and identifies sources. This
   is followed by an analysis of the nature and extent of
   Plato's influence on Ascham. Though Ascham makes little
   use of Plato's metaphysics, his pedagogy shows a strong
   influence, chiefly from the Republic. In his aesthetics,
   Ascham is more dependent on Plato than any previous
   sixteenth-century writer, including Elyot.

*4 TAYLOR, HENRY OSBORN. Thought and Expression in the Sixteenth
    Century. Vol. 2. New York: MacMillan Co.
        See 1930.2.

1921

1 OMOND, T[HOMAS] S[TEWART]. English Metrists: Being a Sketch
   of English Prosodical Criticism from Elizabethan Times to
   the Present Day. Oxford: Clarendon Press, pp. 1-4, 8-12
   passim.

"What does seem extraordinary, and from any point of
view unfortunate, is that in these initial experiments by
a respected teacher the basis of English quantity was not
clearly laid down and illustrated for future use."

1922

1 CLARK, DONALD LEMEN. Rhetoric and Poetry in the Renaissance:
   A Study of Rhetorical Terms in English Renaissance Literary
   Criticism. New York: Columbia University Press, pp. 65,
   67, 70, 77, 87, 92, 98, 141-42. Reprint: New York:
   Russell & Russell, 1963.
      Brief discussions of Ascham's importance in the trans-
   mission of knowledge about Cicero's Orator and Aristotle's
   Poetics; of Ascham's poetic theories; of Ascham as "fore-
   most of the scholarly type" of critical writer; and of
   Ascham as representing "the advance guard in England
   against allegory."

2 SAINTSBURY, GEORGE, ed. "Roger Ascham (1515-1568)." In A
   Letter Book: Selected with an Introduction on the History
   and Art of Letter-Writing. London: G. Bell & Sons;
   New York: Harcourt Brace & Co., pp. 116-22.
      Two extracts, from letters of 20 January 1551 to Edward
   Raven and 24 March 1553 to Lord Cecil, preceded by a brief
   introduction, which comments on how Ascham's gradual change
   from Latin to English over the long course of his letter-
   writing "acknowledges the peculiar character of the genuine
   letter--that, though it may be a work of art, it should
   not be one of artifice--that it is a matter of 'business or
   bosome,' not of study or display."

1924

*1 HIGGINS, RACHAEL JENNINGS. "The First English Essay: Toxo-
    philus by Roger Ascham." Master's thesis, Columbia Uni-
    versity, i, 51 pp. Cited in Tannenbaum (1946.1).

2 THOMPSON, ELBERT N[EVIUS] S[EBRING]. Literary Bypaths of the
   Renaissance. New Haven: Yale University Press; London:
   Humphrey Milford, Oxford University Press, pp. 148-51.
      On the place of Scholemaster in the "courtesy book"
   tradition. Ascham "turned from the court to the world to
   find true manhood," and in so doing "altered noticeably
   the old ideals."

1926

*1 LEGOUIS, ÉMILE [HYACINTHE], and CAZAMIAN, LOUIS [FRANCIS].
A History of English Literature. London and Toronto:
J. M. Dent & Sons.
See 1935.3.

2 MARIQUE, PIERRE J[OSEPH]. History of Christian Education.
Vol. 2. New York: Fordham University Press, pp. 68-69.
Scholemaster "though purporting to be a general discussion of humanistic education . . . is chiefly devoted
to a discussion of the method to be used in the teaching
of the classics," and Ascham's method of double translation is "specially worthy of note."

*3 MITCHELL, MARY. Lady Jane Grey [A tragedy in ten scenes].
Newton: Welsh Outlook Press, 50 pp.
Cited in Tannenbaum (1967.3) and in NUC, vol. 388,
p. 63; copies in New York Public Library and at Harvard.

4 POLLARD, A[LFRED] W[ILLIAM], and REDGRAVE, G[ILBERT] R[ICHARD].
A Short-title Catalogue of Books Printed in England, Scotland, & Ireland and of English Books Printed Abroad, 1475-
1640. London: Bibliographical Society, p. 20. Reprint.
1946.
Cites fifteen imprints, distributed as follows:
Apologia 1 (1577); Epistolarum 4 (1576, 1578, 1581, 1590);
Report 2 (1570?, 1570); Scholemaster 5 (1570, 1571, 1571,
1573, 1589); Toxophilus 3 (1545, 1571, 1589). Supplemented by 1933.1.

1927

1 CONLEY, C[AREY] H[ERBERT]. The First English Translators of
the Classics. New Haven: Yale University Press; London:
Humphrey Milford, Oxford University Press, pp. 5, 9, 11n,
12, 15, 16, 30, 57, 78n, 79n, 80n, 118n, 119, 135, 140,
150, 151, 152, 153.
Ascham cited by name or quoted as evidence for attitudes, conditions, and trends in the sixteenth century.

2 SHEPPARD, J[OHN] T[RESSIDER]. Aeschylus & Sophocles: Their
Work and Influence. New York: Longmans, Green & Co.,
pp. 120-25.
Discusses Ascham's preference for Sophocles over
Seneca. His preference for Greek is "genuine and based on
knowledge."

1928

1   AINSWORTH, OLIVER MORLEY, ed. Milton on Education: The
    Tractate "Of Education," with Supplementary Extracts from
    Other Writings of Milton. Cornell Studies in English,
    vol. 12. New Haven: Yale University Press; London:
    Humphrey Milford, Oxford University Press, pp. 34-36.
       Brief account of the contents of Scholemaster, stress-
    ing points of emphasis shared by Ascham and Milton. See
    also p. 327.

2   McKNIGHT, GEORGE H., with the assistance of EMSLEY, BERT.
    Modern English in the Making. New York and London: D.
    Appleton-Century Co., pp. 117-23 passim.
       Assesses Cheke's influence on Ascham's decision to write
    in English. Ascham's "guiding principle in writing is in
    accord with the ideas of Cheke."

3   NATHAN, WALTER LUDWIG. Sir John Cheke und der englische
    Humanismus. Bonn: Rheania-Verlag, pp. 68-97 passim.
       Although the primary emphasis is on Cheke's impact on
    the development of humanism in England, provides valuable
    background material for the student of Ascham concerning
    the study of Greek at Cambridge. Provides analysis of why
    certain texts were preferred. Discusses Cheke's theories
    of language and his significance as a translator. Con-
    tends that Ascham's prose helped disseminate Cheke's ideas.

1929

1   ANON. "Ascham, Roger (c. 1515-1568)." In The Encyclopaedia
    Britannica. Vol. 2. 14th ed. London and New York:
    Encyclopaedia Britannica Co., pp. 500-501.
       Biographical survey, with some errors of fact and date
    (e.g., the claim that Ascham was Cambridge's first Regius
    Professor of Greek), and brief discussions of Toxophilus
    and Scholemaster only. Suggests that Toxophilus may have
    been a model for Walton's Compleat Angler and says of
    Ascham's method of double translation, that "as a method
    of education in school nothing more deadening could be
    conceived." Claims that Ascham may have imitated Boccaccio
    in the "Preface" to Scholemaster. Compare 1878.2, 1975.1.

2   Encyclopedia italiana di scienze, lettere ed arti. Vol. 4.
    Milan and Rome: Bestetti & Tumminelli, p. 797.
       A routine encyclopedia biography claiming that Ascham
    is "fortemente dominato dall'influenza italiana,"

1929

> particularly by Castiglione, who provides "un modello
> d'ideale educativo." Goes on to explain that such influ-
> ence is not inconsistent with Ascham's famous diatribe
> against "Italianate Englishmen."

3 KELSO, RUTH. The Doctrine of the English Gentleman in the
   Sixteenth Century, with a Bibliographical List of Treatises
   on the Gentleman and Related Subjects Published in Europe
   to 1625. Urbana: University of Illinois Press, pp. 24,
   46, 70, 114, 118, 119, 121, 126, 128, 131, 137, 142, 150,
   151, 154, 159, 160, 161. Reprint. Gloucester, Mass.:
   Peter Smith, 1964.
   Cites or quotes Ascham regarding many aspects of the
   "doctrine of the gentleman," particularly his moral code,
   education, and recreation.

1930

1 MILLER, FLORENCE GRAVES. "The Humanistic Theory of Education." Master's Thesis, University of Oklahoma, pp. 147-
   68.
   Summarizes the educational theories contained in Toxophilus and Scholemaster and discusses the popularization
   of Ascham's theories in Lyly's Euphues.

2 TAYLOR, HENRY OSBORN. Thought and Expression in the Sixteenth
   Century. Vol. 2. 2d ed., rev. New York: Macmillan Co.,
   pp. 17-19, 186, 198.
   Introduces Ascham as a "diligent man with a retentive
   memory," whose books betray "the thoroughly English satis-
   faction . . . at the privilege of associating with those
   of better birth than himself." Treats him as one of several examples leading to the conclusion that "when [Eng-
   lishmen] confine themselves to pure scholarship, and the
   production of polite pseudo-classic literature, the result
   is empty." First edition, 1920.4.

3 VINES, SHERARD. "Roger Ascham." In The Course of English
   Classicism from the Tudor to the Victorian Age. London:
   Hogarth Press, pp. 12-15.
   Considers Ascham important in the development of a
   spirit of classicism which was to mature in the late
   seventeenth century; he "made the first serious effort at
   English criticism," even if he "did not succeed in dis-
   entangling the issues of art from those of morals."

1931

1   ATKINSON, B[ASIL] F[ERRIS] C[AMPBELL]. "Whittlesford Rectory
    and the Ascham Family." Proceedings of the Cambridge
    Antiquarian Society, n.s. 39: 47-50.
        Citing documents which concern the leasing history of
    Whittlesford Rectory down to 6 March 1621, at which time
    it passed from the hands of the Ascham family, provides
    biographical information relating to the heirs of Ascham,
    thereby correcting several statements in DNB (1908.2).

2   RADFORD, LEWIS B. "Roger Ascham." The Quarterly Review 256
    (January): 96-110.
        An introduction to and appreciation of the life, works,
    and achievement of Ascham for the general reader, couched
    in such generalizations as "there is a note of reality in
    writings on education which were written . . . in England
    . . . [which] is not merely the practical simplicity of
    common sense . . . [but] the unformulated and unforgettable
    sense of . . . service of God and Queen and country."

1932

1   GREG, W[ALTER] W[ILSON], ed. English Literary Autographs,
    1550-1650. Oxford: Oxford University Press, 1932, plate
    63. Reprint. Nandeln, Liechtenstein: Kraus Reprint,
    1968.
        Reproduces and transcribes four samples of Ascham's
    "fine humanistic hand": letters to Cecil from 1552-53,
    three in English, one in Latin. See 1960.1 and 1962.1.

2   NUGENT, JOHN RICHARD. "The Utopian Ideals in English Prose
    of the Renaissance." Master's thesis, University of Okla-
    homa, pp. 42-44, 62-67, 78-80, 91-93, 104-5, 111-12.
        Governed by the assumption that Scholemaster "shows . . .
    the Utopian ideal," surveys Ascham's contributions
    toward Utopian thought under the categories, respectively,
    of "Domestic Life," "Education," "Religion," "Morals,
    Private and Public," "Politics," and "Science."

1933

1   EDMONDS, C[ECIL] K[AY]. "Supplement to the Short Title Cata-
    logue." Huntington Library Bulletin, no. 4 (October),
    p. 11.
        Supplements 1926.4; adds four items (825, 827, 835,
    844).

1933

2   HOYLER, AUGUST. Gentleman-Ideal und Gentleman-Erziehung; Mit
     besonderer Berücksichtigung der Renaissance. Erziehungs-
     geschichtliche Untersuchungen: Studien zur Problemge-
     schichte der Pädagogik. Leipzig: Felix Meiner, pp. 144-
     48 and 178-92 passim.
         Argues that the humanists' belief in the value of
     knowledge led to a split between religion and scholarship,
     between theology and intellectual theory, and sees Ascham's
     orientation consistently toward scholarship or "theory."
     Considers Ascham "the most important representative of
     those who wanted to alter the direction of the ideal of
     nobility by introducing an intellectual component into it."

3   SCHIRMER, WALTER F. Antike, Renaissance und Puritanismus:
     Eine Studie zur englischen Literaturgeschichte des 16. und
     17. Jahrhunderts. Munich: Max Hueber, pp. 93-101, 112-
     14, and 123-26.
         Views Ascham against the background of Cambridge human-
     ism, which, Schirmer feels, "prefigured" English Puritan-
     ism. Claims that Ascham felt Henry's opposition to Rome
     "did not go far enough" and that Ascham was not opposed to
     the destruction of the monasteries.

4   YOUEL, DONALD BRUCE. "The Style of Roger Ascham's Prose in
     The Scholemaster." Master's thesis, Northwestern Univer-
     sity, 54 pp.
         Examines Ascham's style from two points of view: his
     attitude toward and efforts to achieve "clearness"; and
     his use of ornamentation. In the first case, considers
     Ascham's overall grasp of organization, his diction, and
     the characteristic features of his sentences and para-
     graphs; in the second, discusses "structural ornament,"
     "sound ornament," and "ornament of idea."

                              1934

*1   ANDERSON, J. J. "Classical Metres in England from Roger
     Ascham to Samuel Daniel." Master's thesis, New York
     University.
         Cited in Tannenbaum (1946.1).

*2   HAYES, ALBERT McCHARG. "The English Letters of Roger Ascham."
     Ph.D. dissertation, Princeton University.
         Cited in DDAAU, vol. 1, p. 83. According to Ryan
     (1963.3), "carefully edited," with helpful annotations.

1935

3   WHIMSTER, D[ONALD] C[AMERON]. Introduction to his edition
     of The Scholemaster. Methuen's English Classics. London:
     Methuen & Co., pp. 1-7.
        General survey of Ascham's life and personality (an
     "attractively normal" man whose "essential simplicity"
     inspired love and admiration) and brief introduction to
     Scholemaster, stressing "double translation" and Ascham's
     prose style.

1935

1   ANDERSON, ELIZABETH K[YRSTEN]. "A Study of the Vocabulary of
     Roger Ascham." Master's thesis, Southern Methodist Uni-
     versity, 114 pp.
        Four chapters. The first discusses Ascham's "position"
     as a scholar and writer in his own day. The second lists
     all the words used by Ascham in a fifty-page sampling from
     Toxophilus and Scholemaster, classified by origin (e.g.
     "Teutonic: Anglo-Saxon," or "Romanic: Latin, Late Latin,
     and Romance Languages through French"). Chapter Three
     comments on the characteristics of mid-sixteenth-century
     English as found in Ascham and discusses those words
     peculiar to Ascham or introduced by him into English.
     Chapter Four advances general conclusions about vocabulary,
     syntax, and orthography.

2   KANE, W[ILLIAM TERRENCE], S.J. "Roger Ascham (1515-1568)."
     In An Essay Toward a History of Education, Considered
     Chiefly in Its Development in the Western World. Chicago:
     Loyola University Press, pp. 357-59.
        A brief, critical account of Ascham's educational
     theory: Scholemaster is "narrow in scope," and Ascham's
     chief point of method, double translation, is "borrowed
     from Vives." "In reality, he had comparatively little to
     offer."

3   LEGOUIS, ÉMILE [HYACINTHE], and CAZAMIAN, LOUIS [FRANCIS].
     A History of English Literature. Translated by Helen
     Douglas Irvine and W. D. MacInnes, rev. ed. (2 vols. in 1).
     New York: Macmillan Co., pp. 215-16, with passim refer-
     ences on 202, 217, 259, 270, 322, 355, 368, 371.
        A brief assessment of Ascham's style and his contribu-
     tion to the development of English prose: "his faults are
     trifling as compared with the benefit prose derived from
     submitting to the discipline of the ancients . . . one of
     the earliest writers of classical English prose." First
     edition, 1926.1. Compare 1914.3.

1935

4 McCUE, GEORGE SUTHERLAND. "Humanistic and Modern Educational
   Theory in The Scholemaster." Master's thesis, University
   of Colorado, iii, 82 pp.
       Chapters on "Continental and English Humanism," Schole-
   master (its aims and the circumstances of composition),
   "Physical Education," "Mental Education," "Moral Education." Sees Ascham as "educating a waning group in ways
   that were destined to be outmoded" and as lacking "the wit
   of Montaigne, the learning of Erasmus, the affability of
   Vittorino de Feltre, the good sense of Mulcaster." Nevertheless, his book is important and his love of learning
   can be contagious to the reader today.

5 WHITE, HAROLD OGDEN. Plagiarism and Imitation During the
   English Renaissance: A Study in Critical Distinctions.
   Cambridge, Mass.: Harvard University Press, pp. 45-48.
       Argues that discussion of imitation in Scholemaster
   seems a direct answer to The Courtier, Ascham being "much
   closer to the narrow Ciceronianism of Bembo and Scaliger
   than to the classic principles as correctly interpreted by
   Castiglione and Hoby." However, Ascham's practical in-
   structions about "the necessarie tooles and instruments,
   wherewith trewe Imitation is rightlie wrought withall" show
   "how clearly he understands the classical principles of
   reinterpretation and improvement, even though he does not
   discuss these points by name."

1936

1 BLACK, J[OHN] B[ENNET]. The Reign of Elizabeth, 1558-1603.
   The Oxford History of England, vol. 8. Oxford: Clarendon
   Press, pp. 276-79.
       Considers Ascham "the greatest educationist of his
   time" and stresses "three great principles" of Ascham's
   theory: the necessity of gentleness in instruction; the
   superiority of hard to quick wits; and the superiority of
   learning to experience as the proper avenue to wisdom.
   Second edition unchanged; see 1959.1.

1937

*1 NOYES, GERTRUDE ELIZABETH. "A Study of Roger Ascham's Lit-
    erary Citations with Particular Reference to his Knowledge
    of the Classics." Ph.D. dissertation, Yale University.
    See Ryan (1963.3), pp. 303, 306, and 334.

1938

1   PARKS, GEORGE B.   "The First Draft of Ascham's Scholemaster."
    HLQ 1, no. 3 (April): 313-28.
        Evidence indicates that MS. Royal B. xxiv, Art. 2, fols.
    47-78 was written in 1563-64 and that it represents a
    stage between rough draft and fair copy. A comparison of
    the MS and printed versions shows the MS over one-third
    shorter than printed version; the printed version having
    added the quick and hard wits section; the middle third
    of the printed version slightly better organized than the
    MS; the printed section on Italy increased by about one
    half. The major "specific omissions" from MS to printed
    version include chiefly "irrelevant passages on matters
    more or less political." The MS indicates that Book I was
    originally intended to be complete; when Ascham added
    Book II cannot be determined--probably 1567-68.

1939

1   BUSH, DOUGLAS.   The Renaissance and English Humanism.   Toronto:
    University of Toronto Press, pp. 75-79, 87, 89, 92.
        Ascham is representative of the humanists' "fervently
    didactic faith in the classical authors as the supreme
    guides," of their insistence on education as training for
    a public life, and of their belief that "good Latin" stood
    for "a whole orthodoxy, cultural, ethical, political, and
    religious."

2   SCHRINNER, WALTER.   Castiglione und die englische Renaissance.
    Neue deutsche Forschungen, Abteilung englische Philologie,
    vol. 14. Berlin: Junker und Dunnhaupt, pp. 51-55 passim,
    70-71, 97-99.
        Argues that Castiglione's Courtier offered a "bridge" by
    which the scholar might become a gentleman and that Ascham
    saw in him a "type of new man, which he yearned for," a
    man whose "ethical greatness, inner self-sufficiency, and
    thoroughly healthy disposition" attracted him despite his
    enmity to Italy.

1940

1   HALL, ROGER SCHULTZ.   "The Influence of Xenophon and Plato
    upon the Educational Principles of Roger Ascham, as shown
    in Toxophilus and The Scholemaster." Master's thesis,
    Columbia University, ii, 38 pp.

1940

Introduction, life, analysis of Scholemaster and Toxophilus, conclusion, short bibliography.

2   ROSENZWEIG, SIDNEY. "Ascham's Scholemaster and Spenser's
     February Eclogue." The Shakespeare Association Bulletin
     15, no. 2 (April): 103-9.
         Argues that a passage in Scholemaster provided Spenser
     "with more than the ungerminated seed" for his fable of
     the Oak and Briar in the February Eclogue: Ascham's sen-
     tences "embody the almost fully developed form of the
     fable" (in particular the reversal of roles for oak and
     briar, which is the noteworthy feature of Spenser's poem).

3   SWEETING, ELIZABETH J. Early Tudor Criticism: Linguistic
     and Literary. Oxford: Basil Blackwell, pp. 66-70 passim,
     88-89, 92-97 passim, 103-4, 120. Reprint. New York:
     Russell & Russell, 1964.
         Cites or quotes Ascham in connection with the imitation
     of Cicero; the importance of Cheke and the Greek pronuncia-
     tion controversy; rhetorical style; and genre theory.

1941

1   R[EED], A. W., comp. "Roger Ascham (1515-1568)." In The
     Cambridge Bibliography of English Literature. Vol. 1.
     600-1660. Edited by F[rederick] W[ilse] Bateson. New
     York: Macmillan Co.; Cambridge: Cambridge University
     Press, p. 671.
         Three brief sections listing collected works; the chief
     separate editions of Toxophilus, Report, Scholemaster,
     Epistolarum, Apologia; and five critical studies, three in
     German. See 1974.6.

2   RUBEL, VERÉ L[AURA]. Poetic Diction in the English Renais-
     sance from Skelton through Spenser. New York: Modern
     Language Association of America; London: Oxford University
     Press, pp. 102-18 passim.
         Chapter 8, "Critical Theories, 1557-1590," contends
     that the "great vogue" of Scholemaster was a "decided
     stimulus" to the movement favoring quantitative verse.

1944

1   BALDWIN, T[HOMAS] W[HITFIELD]. William Shakspere's Small
     Latine & Lesse Greeke. Vol. 1. Urbana: University of
     Illinois Press, pp. 257-80 passim.

1946

Chapter XII, "Educating the 'Prince'; Princess Elizabeth," predominantly an analysis and evaluation of Ascham's
educational theory, sees Ascham as "flogging the dead
horses of his youth in the North." He is "neither a
competent nor a fair witness as to the grammar schools of
his own day." Ascham "could not live in reasonable happi-
ness without someone to lecture to"; he was "to the end
willingly patronized" by Elizabeth; and he was "one of
the greatest of pedants." Less substantial discussions
appear on pp. 437-41, 696-99, 702-4, and 749-51 and on
pp. 253-56 and 261-65 of vol. 2.

1945

1   WILSON, HAROLD S., and FORBES, CLARENCE A.   Introduction to
    their edition and translation of Gabriel Harvey's "Cicero-
    nianus." University of Nebraska Studies, Studies in the
    Humanities, no. 4. Lincoln: University of Nebraska
    Press, pp. 22-29 passim, 90, 92, 132-34.
        Discusses Harvey's criticism of Ascham in the context of
    the two men's different brands of Ciceronianism.

1946

1   TANNENBAUM, SAMUEL A. and TANNENBAUM, DOROTHY R.   Roger
    Ascham: A Concise Bibliography. New York: Samuel A.
    Tannenbaum.
        Organized by Editions (1-51), Selections (52-85), Com-
    mentary (86-323a), Bibliography (324-44), and Addenda
    (345-56), with Index of names and subjects. Remarkably
    complete to 1945, though at the expense of including many
    items containing only a paragraph or less about Ascham.
    Ten to fifteen percent duplication. For frequently re-
    printed works (such as histories) usually cites the most
    convenient edition. Substantial number of errors, and the
    practice of citing authors by one initial often makes
    locating difficult. I have examined and excluded the fol-
    lowing items: 98, 102, 108, 114, 115, 117, 123, 135, 139,
    140, 143, 144, 154, 158, 160, 164, 165, 169, 172, 175, 177,
    183, 188, 193, 204, 205, 208, 212, 216, 218, 220, 222, 226,
    232, 239, 241, 245, 249, 250, 256, 269, 273, 276, 288, 294,
    296, 297, 298, 302, 307, 311, 314, 317, 322, 323, 323a,
    347, 349, 355. Reprinted as 1967.3.

1947

1 ATKINS, J[OHN] W[ILLIAM] H[EY]. English Literary Criticism: The Renascence. London: Methuen & Co., pp. 84-96.
  Surveys Ascham's writings to conclude that his contribution to "rhetorical studies" in the sixteenth century is "of first-rate importance." Most significant is Ascham's contribution to the discussion of imitation, a "raging" European controversy. Ascham's knowledge of Aristotle's poetics is "slight." His theories on versifying formed part of a wider European movement. His literary judgments, particularly on drama and on Chaucer, mark an "advance." His discussion of Sallust's style "represents something new in literary judgment."

*2 CAMPBELL, LILY B[ESS]. Shakespeare's "Histories": Mirrors of Elizabethan Policy. San Marino, Calif.: Huntington Library Press, pp. 65-66, 93-94.
  Reprinted as 1964.1.

1948

1 BARKER, SIR ERNEST. Traditions of Civility: Eight Essays. Cambridge: Cambridge University Press, pp. 149-52.
  Although most of Barker's discussion of Ascham is concentrated into these pages, his entire chapter, "The Education of the English Gentleman in the Sixteenth Century," pp. 124-58, is worth reading for the relations between Elyot, Starkey, Hoby, and Ascham. Ascham is "a curious contrast to the polished Castiglione," with "something of a nipping north-country edge" in his ideas. He is "not in tune with the Italianate fashion which he saw beginning in England." The gentleman that Ascham sought to fashion "had something of [Ascham's] own idiosyncracy."

2 BROOKE, [C. F.] TUCKER. "The Renaissance." In A Literary History of England. Edited by Albert C. Baugh. New York and London: Appleton-Century-Crofts, pp. 333-34.
  Brief and general assessment, erroneously calling Ascham "Regius Professor of Greek." Ascham is the "last humanist," his English style is "markedly simple," and he is a "master" of "graphic detail." See 1967.1.

3 CLARK, DONALD LEMEN. John Milton at St. Paul's School: A Study of Ancient Rhetoric in English Renaissance Education. New York: Columbia University Press, pp. 168-80 passim.

Ascham is quoted frequently, and though there is no extended discussion of his ideas, these pages show the impact
of his thinking on methods by which the school boy is to
imitate--by memorization, by translation, and by paraphrase.

4   HATCH, MAURICE ADDISON. Introduction to his edition of The
    Ascham Letters: An Annotated Translation of the Latin
    Correspondence in the Giles Edition of Ascham's Works.
    Ph.D. dissertation, Cornell University. Published by
    Kentucky Microcards. Series A. Modern Language Series,
    no. 19, pp. xxv-xxxiii. See also Preface, pp. ii-viii.
        In his letters Ascham is revealed "more nearly in the
    round" than in his books. The letters indicate the width
    of Ascham's association with important thinkers on the
    Continent, and they help correct the view of Ascham as
    narrowly puritanical. Analysis of Ascham's Latin shows
    "a steady progression in its ability to express thought."
    Though Ascham could be "blunt, tense, and tart," most
    often he is "easy, colloquial, familiar and direct." His
    Latin style "has a definite affinity with his English,"
    both being "in some respects a step in the development of
    the language of Euphues." In his "Preface," Hatch notes
    that his edition corrects "an endless array" of typo-
    graphical errors in Giles's text and redates letters where
    necessary. Previous editors failed to recognize that
    Ascham dates personal letters using the 1 January New Year,
    public letters using the 25 March New Year.

                              1949

*1 CONNOLLY, P. P. "Roger Ascham." Master's thesis, National
    University of Ireland.
        Cited in Retrospective Index to Theses of Great Britain
    and Ireland, 1716-1950. Vol. 1: Social Sciences and
    Humanities. Edited by Roger R. Bilboul and Frances L.
    Kent. Santa Barbara, Calif.: American Bibliographical
    Center--Clio Press; Oxford: European Bibliographical
    Center--Clio Press, 1975, p. 14.

2   PHILLIPS, ELIAS H. "Humanitas in Tudor Literature." Ph.D.
    dissertation, University of Pennsylvania, 184 pp.
        Argues that Scholemaster, one of eight works or groups
    of works considered, among them Utopia, Governour, and
    Courtier, was "written and read" under the influence of
    Ciceronian humanitas, embodying the ideas that the politi-
    cal order in the commonwealth coincides with the physical
    and moral order in the universe and through paideia man is
    capable of perfection.

1950

1   GRAESSE, JEAN GEORGE THÉODORE [Graesse, Johann Georg Theodor].
    Trésor des livres rares et précieux, ou nouveau dictionaire
    bibliographique. Vol. 1. Milan: G. G. Gorlich, p. 237.
       Cites Bennet's and Cochrane's editions; Epistolarum of
    1578 and 1703; 1570 Scholemaster and 1545 Toxophilus.
    Brief annotations for Elstob, Scholemaster and Toxophilus.
    First edition, 1859.1.

2   HEXTER, J. H. "The Education of the Aristocracy in the Ren-
    aissance." The Journal of Modern History 22, no. 1
    (March): 1-20.
       A seminal article which asks "What . . . was the educa-
    tion of the aristocrats during the Renaissance, how many
    of them received it, when historically did they begin to
    receive it, and what did they want with it?" and provides
    answers which apply to England, France, and the Nether-
    lands. The evidence of attendance at schools, of theoreti-
    cal treatises on education, and of public documents by and
    relating to governmental servants indicates that far from
    acquiescing in ignorance, as is so often the charge, mem-
    bers of the Renaissance aristocracy pursued vigorously the
    learning that would enable them to "perform well their
    duty of service to their prince in council, in embassies,
    and in the governance of the commonwealth." This ideal of
    the end of learning as service remains generally constant
    from the mid-fifteenth century to the late sixteenth; the
    means and methods to achieve it become better understood.
    Although though there is no extended discussion of Ascham,
    provides a concise background for placing his educational
    theories in the larger European socio-political context.

3   McSHANE, [MOTHER] EDITH [ELIZABETH]. Tudor Opinions of the
    Chivalric Romance: An Essay in the History of Criticism.
    [Published on microcards.] Washington: Catholic Univer-
    sity of America Press, 145 pp.
       Analyzes the importance of Ascham's views in the con-
    text of a large number of writings about "function, matter,
    form, and authorship" of the chivalric romances.

1952

1   HEBEL, J[OHN] WILLIAM, HUDSON, HOYT H., JOHNSON, FRANCIS R.
    and GREEN, A. WIGFALL, eds. Prose of the English Renais-
    sance: Selected from Early Editions and Manuscripts.
    New York: Appleton-Century-Crofts, pp. 803-7.

Introduction and notes to selections from Scholemaster
and Toxophilus in standard and influential anthology.

2   MEISSNER, PAUL. England im Zeitalter von Humanismus, Renais-
    sance, und Reformation. Heidelberg: F. H. Kerle, pp. 50,
    51, 54, 93, 103, 104, 107, 146, 149, 151, 173, 217, 317,
    322, 395, 418, 453, 512, 524, 525, 544.
    Although there is no extended discussion of Ascham in
    this standard German history, he is cited frequently for
    comparative purposes regarding educational, social, and
    political theory, literary criticism, and nationalism.

1953

1   HAFNER, MAMIE. "Morals and Ethics in the Works of Roger
    Ascham." Master's thesis, University of North Carolina,
    ii, 78 pp.
    In separate chapters, discusses "personal motives in
    Ascham's public life," his "purposes in writing," his
    views concerning "religion," "patriotism and government,"
    and "right conduct." Contains bibliography.

2   HOFFMAN, C. FENNO, JR. "Roger Ascham and Humanist Education
    in Sixteenth Century England." Ph.D. dissertation, Uni-
    versity of Pennsylvania, 199 pp.
    Assesses Ascham's place in sixteenth-century education,
    with chapters on "The Education of Women, " "Sport,"
    "Science in Education," "Protestantism and Philosophy,"
    and "The Goal of Literary Style" (which treats imitation
    as "a refinement of translation").

1954

1   LEWIS, C[LIVE] S[TAPLES]. English Literature in the Sixteenth
    Century, Excluding Drama. The Oxford History of English
    Literature, vol. 3. Oxford: Clarendon Press, pp. 279-83.
    Ascham possesses "a humanity which his humanism could
    not defeat." Toxophilus is "one of the most genial and
    winning books that had yet appeared in English." In
    Scholemaster, however, Ascham's humanism is too rigid; in
    his doctrine of imitation, "style (and that narrowly con-
    ceived) is coming to be the whole of learning." Ascham is
    not a critic. He is a conscious stylist and, like Elyot,
    is a member of the "refining party," but is "on the other
    wing of that party, a purist like his friend Cheke."
    Ascham's "purist" style, if pressed to an extreme, would
    become euphuism.

1954

2   MAXWELL, J[AMES] C[LOUTTS]. "English Anti-Machiavellianism
    before Gentillet." N&Q n.s. 1, no. 4 (April): 141.
        Calls attention to three references to Machiavelli in
    Report "which make it clear that the Machiavelli legend
    had made considerable progress nearly a quarter of a cen-
    tury before Gentillet's book." See 1964.2.

3   ROPE, H[ENRY] E[DWARD] G[EORGE]. "The 'Italianate' English-
    man." The Month, n.s. 11, no. 1 (January): 93-103.
        Contends from a Roman Catholic point of view that
    Ascham's diatribe against Italianate Englishmen masked an
    "uneasy anxiety about the permanence" of his Protestant
    faith, which Rope characterizes as "the 'true religion'
    set up by politic Machiavellians in 1559."

                            1955

1   HALLAM, GEORGE W. "An Ascham Borrowing from Erasmus." N&Q,
    n.s. 2, no. 3 (March): 97.
        A passage in Report on "the world as a stage" is pos-
    sibly indebted to Chaloner's translation of Praise of
    Folly.

2   ROSENBERG, ELEANOR. Leicester, Patron of Letters. New York:
    Columbia University Press, pp. 46-47, 140-44.
        The earlier passage suggests that Thomas Blundeveille
    may have come under the patronage of Leicester through
    Ascham. The later assesses Leicester's position in the
    troubles Ascham experienced over the prebend of Wetwang,
    chiefly in the final two years before its resolution in
    1566. Ascham apparently held Leicester in part responsi-
    ble for the wrongs he had suffered. Whether Elizabeth's
    direct intervention in Ascham's suit to secure the lease
    may be attributable to Leicester's aid is not clear, but
    the evidence of Ascham's posthumous publication, with
    works dedicated to Cecil, the Queen, and Leicester, sug-
    gests that the extent of his neglect by Queen and patrons
    in his last years has been exaggerated. See 1965.4.

                            1956

1   BRAHAM, LIONEL. "Johnson's Edition of Roger Ascham." N&Q,
    n.s. 3, no. 8 (August): 346-47.
        Quotes letter showing that Dr. Johnson was editor of
    the 1761 edition of Ascham's works, not James Bennet, whose

name appears on the title page. Bennet's contribution
was probably proof-reading. See 1761.1.

2   _____. "Roger Ascham and the Regius Professorships." N&Q,
n.s. 3, no. 9 (September): 373-74.
Corrects the common misconception, still current in
anthologies and general histories, that Ascham was Regius
Professor of Greek; he never held that position.

1957

1   HAFNER, CHARLES YATES. "Foundations of English Poetics,
1570-1575." Ph.D. dissertation, Stanford University,
319 pp.
Argues that the "main principles of English poetics
from Sidney to Dryden stem from the movement of Ciceronian
civic humanism and are transmitted by a group of treatises
composed within the first two decades of the Elizabethan
period," among them Ascham's Scholemaster. The third
chapter discusses Ascham, "whose poetics must be understood
in the context of his humanistic educational program."
His transmission of classical ideas of imitatio, decorum,
and usus "affected the temper and direction of English
poetry and literary criticism in the last years of Elizabeth's reign." The concluding chapter argues that Ascham,
along with Gascoigne and Richard Wills, "laid the founda-
tion for a reformation of English poetry in the sixteenth
century."

2   REANEY, P[ERCY] H[IDE]. "Roger Ascham, Margaret Rampston,
and Salisbury Hall." N&Q, n.s. 4, no. 8 (August): 332-33.
Provides details concerning the leasing of Salisbury
Hall and the man, Thomas Rampston, whom Ascham's widow
married in 1569. Although Mary leased Salisbury to Ascham
on 22 June 1557, Ascham could not take possession until
1564, when the previous lease terminated; therefore Ascham
could not have mortgaged the hall in 1559, as DNB (1908.2)
claims.

1958

1   PORTER, H[ARRY] C[ULVERWELL]. Reformation and Reaction in
Tudor Cambridge. Cambridge: Cambridge University Press,
pp. 41-73 passim.
Although the references to Ascham are few, the chapter
provides essential background material for understanding

1958

the atmosphere and the chief issues during Ascham's association with the university. A revaluation of material
in 1884.4.

2   STATON, WALTER F., JR. "The Characters of Style in Eliza-
    bethan Prose." JEGP 57, no. 2 (April): 197-207.
       Argues that the "plain writing of the 1590s is to be
    explained by the doctrine of the [three] characters of
    style [low, middle, lofty] rather than by a major change
    in literary taste." Uses Ascham to demonstrate the Eliza-
    bethan preference for a middle style, which could be
    varied up or down, then shows how Sidney, Lyly, Green,
    and Nashe were capable of modulating their middle "florid"
    styles into the low when occasion demanded. See 1974.4.

1959

1   BLACK, J[OHN] B[ENNETT]. The Reign of Elizabeth, 1558-1603.
    2d ed. The Oxford History of England, vol. 8. Oxford:
    Clarendon Press, pp. 324-27.
       See 1936.1; the discussion of Ascham remains unchanged.

2   HOGREFE, PEARL. The Sir Thomas More Circle: A Program of
    Ideas and Their Impact on Secular Drama. Urbana: Uni-
    versity of Illinois Press, pp. 134-35 and 184-87.
       Although Ascham is referred to frequently (some fifty
    times in all) these two passages are the only substantive
    discussions, the first on Ascham's typical humanist im-
    pulse to relate his ideas to the good of the commonweal,
    the second a comparison of Ascham's views of education
    with those of More, Erasmus, and Vives.

3   MILLER, EDWIN HAVILAND. The Professional Writer in Eliza-
    bethan England: A Study of Nondramatic Literature.
    Cambridge, Mass.: Harvard University Press, pp. 7, 20, 35,
    38, 79, 82-83, 112, 176-77, 206.
       Cites Ascham regarding the taste of the Elizabethan
    audience, censorship, and the way professional writers
    "abuse" the dedication. Ascham's attack on Italian books
    "borders on hysteria."

4   ONG, WALTER J., S.J. "Latin Language Study as a Renaissance
    Puberty Rite." SP 56, no. 2 (April): 103-24.
       Argues that in the Renaissance the study of Latin was a
    "process preparing [a boy] for adult life by communicating
    to him the heritage of a past in a setting which toughened

him and thus guaranteed his guarding the heritage for the
future." Finds an unrecognized ambivalence toward the
ultimate aims of the educational process in Ascham's plea
for a "soft" schoolmaster and in his use of Lady Jane Grey,
a girl, as his chief example. Analyzes the underlying
assumptions of speakers in the conversation recorded in
preface to Scholemaster to suggest that "beating" was
closely allied to learning as part of a total initiative
process.

5   RYAN, LAWRENCE V. "Roger Ascham's Toxophilus in Heroic Verse."
      HLQ 22, no. 2 (February): 119-24.
        The poem in heroic couplets Archerie Reviv'd, by Robert
      Shottrel and Thomas D'Urfey (1676), is an unacknowledged
      verse paraphrase of the first half of Ascham's book, while
      the prose "Postscript" to the poem is an epitome of the
      second half. Suggests possible reasons for the two men's
      collaboration; shows how they depend exclusively on Toxo-
      philus, following their model point for point; and demon-
      strates how Shottrel and D'Urfey "bring Ascham up to date."
      That the two men could use it unacknowledged suggests that
      Toxophilus was a much less well-known work than Schole-
      master at the time.

6   STATON, WALTER F., JR. "Roger Ascham's Theory of History
      Writing." SP 56, no. 2 (April): 125-37.
        Analyzes point by point the "rules for writing history"
      presented in the "Preface" to Report and assesses the
      degree to which Ascham in that work realized his ideals.
      Concludes that Ascham "believed in and was capable of the
      historical truthfulness that made Italian humanists like
      Polydore Vergil and Paulus Aemilius superior to most
      northerners"; that Ascham was "abreast of his time in dis-
      cerning historical causes"; that he displayed "unusual
      freedom for the sixteenth century in his method of organ-
      izing"; and that he was aware of the trend away from
      certain stylistic devices." Had Ascham written "a full-
      scale account de suo tempore, he would have roughly mea-
      sured up to the highest level of humanist history writing
      in the mid-sixteenth century."

                            1960

1   FAIRBANK, ALFRED, and WOLPE, BERTHOLD. Renaissance Hand-
      Writing: An Anthology of Italic Scripts. London: Faber
      & Faber, pp. 30-33 and Plates 34, 35.

1961

A brief account of Ascham's place in the development of
italic in sixteenth-century England. The plates contain
pages from his Expositiones . . . ad Philemonem (1542) and
an official letter (1555). See 1962.1 and 1932.1.

1961

1   AMMANN, ROMAN ERNST. Die Verbalsyntax in Sir Thomas Elyots
     "Governour" mit vergleichenden Beispielen aus Roger Aschams
     "Scholemaster." Aarau: Keller, 129 pp.
        Provides comparative examples from Ascham in describing
     the verbal inflections which appear in Elyot's Governour,
     his use of impersonal verb forms, of active and passive
     voice, of the infinitive and gerund, tense, aspect, mode,
     participials, and the verbs do, may, and can. Reaches the
     tentative conclusion that Ascham's and Elyot's styles
     represent a transitional stage between late middle English
     and modern English.

2   HORNÁT, JAROSLAV. "Lyly's Anatomy of Wit and Ascham's Schole-
     master." Acta Universitatis Carolinae, Philologica 1.
     Prague Studies in English, 9. Prague: Caroline Univer-
     sity, pp. 3-21.
        Analyzes Ascham's influence on Lyly, adding to English
     writers on the subject a Marxist perspective which views
     both Lyly and Ascham within the context of social theory;
     for example, though Ascham's arguments are "attempts at an
     idealogical breakthrough," they do not "speak for the
     bourgeoisie as a class." Sees Lyly's plan and organization
     a rebuttal of Ascham's views on "experience" in Schole-
     master. See 1916.1, 1962.2, and 1970.4.

3   PARKS, GEORGE B. "The First Italianate Englishmen." Studies
     in the Renaissance 8: 197-216.
        Traces and assesses the gradually emerging connotations
     of the word Italianate from 1545-72. For Ascham, who was
     the first to use the phrase "Italianate Englishman" in
     literature, the word meant only "irreligious, undisciplined,
     immoral," as distinct from its later meaning of "deceitful,
     treacherous," current around 1572. The meaning of "Ital-
     ianate" becomes less determinate after the mid-1570s.

1962

1   FAIRBANK, ALFRED, and DICKENS, BRUCE. The Italic Hand in
    Tudor Cambridge. Cambridge Bibliographical Society Mono-
    graph no. 5. London: Bowes & Bowes, pp. 9-12 passim,
    and Plates 4, 5a, 5b and 7.
        The pages from the introduction detail Ascham's tenure
    as Public Orator of the University and describe his place
    among notable penmen of the day. The plates illustrate
    three different italic styles among the many Ascham com-
    manded. See 1960.1 and 1932.1.

2   HUNTER, G. K. John Lyly: The Humanist as Courtier. Cam-
    bridge, Mass.: Harvard University Press, pp. 49-50, 58.
        A succinct account of the relation between Euphues and
    Scholemaster; Ascham provides "the system of attitudes
    involved in an anatomy of wit." See 1916.1 and 1961.2.

3   SMITH, CONSTANCE I. "Some Ideas on Education before Locke."
    JHI 23, no. 3 (July-September): 403-6.
        Cites Ascham as an example of an educational theorist
    prior to Locke who considers education "in relation to the
    body, to social behavior, and to a thorough knowledge of
    men." Finds an "extremely interesting similarity" between
    Ascham's ideas on Euphues and Locke's general position.

1963

1   COBB, CARL W. "Milton and Blank Verse in Spain." PQ 42,
    no. 2 (April): 264-67.
        Milton's assertion in the preface to Paradise Lost that
    "Spanish poets of prime note have rejected rime" is not
    based on a direct knowledge of the poets themselves since
    none of any significance eschewed rhyme; rather Milton's
    idea is probably from Ascham, who claims in Scholemaster
    that Gonzalvo Periz "avoided the fault of rhyming." See
    1963.3, p. 274.

2   MILLER, WILLIAM E. "Double Translation in English Humanistic
    Education." Studies in the Renaissance 10: 163-74.
        Seeks to explain how double translation probably worked
    as a pedagogical method in the Renaissance, using Ascham's
    account in Scholemaster as a basic text. Outlines the
    history of the concept prior to Ascham, indicates tributes
    paid by other writers to the method, discusses books writ-
    ten to aid second-rate teachers whose Latin was inadequate
    for doing the job on their own.

1963

3 RYAN, LAWRENCE V. Roger Ascham. Stanford: Stanford Univer-
      sity Press; London: Oxford University Press, viii, 352 pp.
         The standard biography. Seeks to "present the story of
      Ascham's life accurately and sympathetically," to "trace
      the generation of his three principal English works," and
      to "assess his contribution to the intellectual heritage
      and prose literature of England." The biographical chap-
      ters treat Ascham's position in the intellectual life of
      St. John's, Cambridge, during the 1530s; the frustration of
      his hopes in the early forties; his attempts to avoid uni-
      versity politics and religious schism later in the decade;
      his tenure as Elizabeth's tutor; his tour of duty as sec-
      retary to Richard Morison in Germany; his services as
      Latin Secretary under Mary and Elizabeth. In each chapter
      Ryan focuses on ambiguity of motive and cause, bringing to
      bear evidence from the letters, from the published works,
      and from a vast store of other primary and secondary
      sources. He finds that Ascham is a "moderate protestant"
      whose thought is "in the spirit of the not yet formulated
      Thirty-Nine Articles," rather than the extreme Puritan
      that many have taken him to be. He also concludes that
      Ascham did not compromise his Protestant religious beliefs
      in order to serve as Mary's Latin Secretary. Finding no
      evidence that Ascham was either addicted to gambling or
      overly importunate to his patrons, Ryan argues that his
      failure to advance under Elizabeth resulted from the rapid
      growth of his family, legal impediments and suits, and his
      "impulsive generosity toward others in need." Chapters 4,
      8, and 11 contain comprehensive analyses of Ascham's three
      major English works. For Scholemaster he analyzes Book I
      in light of events prompting its composition; discusses
      the major sources, with emphasis on Quintilian and Sturm;
      evaluates his importance as a critic and prose stylist;
      and claims that his influence on Sidney is great. For
      Toxophilus, he discusses conditions that would conduce to
      the book's popularity, its sources, influences, style, and
      structure. For the last, he demonstrates the subtlety with
      which Ascham constructed the work upon "three interrelating
      and mutually reinforcing structural patterns." Though for
      Ryan Report is not a "neglected masterpiece," it contains
      the first "clear formulation of an historical method by a
      Renaissance Englishman," and it may have been written to
      influence Edward VI's advisors to "reshape England's for-
      eign alliances." Ryan provides for each work a succinct
      account of its publishing history.

1964

1 CAMPBELL, LILY B[ESS]. Shakespeare's "Histories": Mirrors of
   Elizabethan Policy. London: Methuen & Co., pp. 65-66,
   93-94.
      Claims that Ascham "most truly" saw the place of More in
   the history of English historical writing, and that he
   "formulated as clearly as any one in England basic standards of judgment," by which he judged More. Reprint of
   1947.2.

2 RAAB, FELIX. The English Face of Machiavelli: A Changing
   Interpretation, 1500-1700. London: Routledge & Kegan
   Paul; Toronto: University of Toronto Press, pp. 32-34,
   48-51 passim.
      Ascham's references to Machiavelli, like Pole's, repre-
   sent a viewpoint which, for religious reasons, finds him
   unacceptable; in contrast, Morison's view shows a more
   enlightened acceptance of the secular political world.
   Ascham's statements show that Gentillet's attitude existed
   in England before the appearance of Discours . . . contre
   Nicolas Machiavel in 1576. See 1954.2 and 1974.2.

3 SMITH, JOHN HAZEL, ed. and trans. A Humanist's "Trew Imitation": Thomas Watson's "Absalom." A Critical Edition and
   Translation. Illinois Studies in Language and Literature,
   52. Urbana: University of Illinois Press, pp. 17-26,
   32-36 passim, 42-46.
      Detailed examination of Ascham's connections to Watson,
   useful for Ascham's Cambridge background in the years
   1534-44. The last passage examines Ascham's doctrine of
   imitation as a model for Watson's practice in Absalom.
   Appendix 3, pp. 272-73 details records of the presence of
   Ascham and Cheke at Cambridge from 1529-44. See 1914.1.

4 SMITH, JOHN HAZEL. Review of Roger Ascham, by Lawrence V.
   Ryan. JEGP 63, no. 3 (July): 488-91.
      Ryan's (1963.3) is the first "adequate" biography of
   Ascham in English, superseding both the "Life" in Giles's
   edition (1864.1) and Lee's DNB article (1908.2). The best
   previous biography, Katterfeld's (1879.1), "though sound
   for its time," is in German and eighty years out of date.
   Ryan corrects many of Giles's incompetent datings of letters. Smith himself clarifies some details and corrects
   minor errors (e.g. the length of Ascham's absence from
   Cambridge in the early 1540s and Ryan's confusion of two
   Thomas Watsons). He finds in Ryan a "tendency to senti-
   mentalize," but on the whole his flaws are offset by an

1964

"amazing amount of research." Thinks that Ryan should have used original editions rather than Giles's modernization, particularly for matters of style. Ryan's book "deserves" to become the standard study.

5   STATON, WALTER F., JR.   Review of Roger Ascham, by Lawrence V. Ryan.   MP 62, no. 2 (November): 160-61.
       Ryan (1963.3) made the correct decision to use Giles's edition, even though it meant using his modernized prose, because it is the only edition to contain letters, on which so much of Ryan's narrative rests. Evidence is thin for Ryan's claim that Ascham was Machiavelli's pupil as a history writer.

6   TEST, GEORGE A.   "Archers' Feathers in Chaucer and Ascham." American Notes and Queries 2, no. 5 (January): 67-68.
       Claims that Ascham's judgment in Toxophilus that peacock feathers are inferior is, according to the best modern authorities, wrong, and that Chaucer's "unerring eye for detail did not fail him" in the description of the Yeoman.

1965

1   British Museum General Catalogue of Printed Books. Photo-lithographic Edition to 1955. Vol. 7. London: Trustees of the British Museum, cols. 728-32.
       Cites fifty-three copies of Ascham's works, including Giles; Bennet's, Cochrane's, and Wright's English Works; letters in editions of 1576, 1578, 1581, 1590, 1607, 1610, 1611, 1703; Report of 1570; Scholemaster in editions of 1570, 1571, 1589, 1711, 1743, 1863, 1870, 1884, 1888, 1895, 1934, and a German translation of 1881; Toxophilus in editions of 1545, 1571, 1589, 1788, 1821, 1868, 1869, 1895.

2   CHARLTON, KENNETH.   Education in Renaissance England. London: Routledge & Kegan Paul; Toronto: University of Toronto Press, pp. 79, 84ff., 105, 109ff., 120, 122, 124, 137, 142, 161, 208ff., 213, 223ff., 233, 241ff.
       Although most of these merely cite or quote Ascham as authority, Charlton's history is a valuable complement to Simon (1966.7), approaching the subject with more emphasis on informal means of education, less on traditional institutions.

1966

3   McCONICA, JAMES KELSEY. English Humanists and Reformation
     Politics under Henry VIII and Edward VI. Oxford: Claren-
     don Press, pp. 2, 6-13, 260-63.
         Examines the writing and publication of Toxophilus as
     representing actions of the "new humanists," those of the
     generation following the death of Cranmer and associated
     with the circle of Catherine Parr. Considers the career
     of Ascham "typical" and calls him a "faithful bellwether"
     of "Erasmian court Protestantism" in the 1540s and 1550s.
     Sees the "breadth of Ascham's sponsorship at court" as
     "remarkable" and believes that this was the result of a
     "highly organized attempt to improve his fortunes."

4   ROBERTSON, JEAN. Review of Roger Ascham, by Lawrence V. Ryan.
     RES, n.s. 16 (February): 63-66.
         Finds Ryan (1963.3) "assiduous and fruitful" in his
     research, "right" in his defense of Ascham against gambling,
     and "successful" in dealing with the question of Ascham's
     time-serving during the Marian period (though she is not
     convinced that Ascham kept his Protestant faith under
     Mary); Ryan could have profited from reading Rosenberg's
     Leicester: Patron of Letters (1955.2).

                              1966

1   CROLL, MORRIS W[ILLIAM]. "The Sources of the Euphuistic
     Rhetoric," edited by J. Max Patrick and Richard J. Schoeck.
     In Style, Rhetoric, and Rhythm: Essays by Morris W. Croll.
     Edited by J. Max Patrick, and Robert O. Evans, with John M.
     Wallace and Richard J. Schoeck. Princeton: Princeton
     University Press, pp. 246-51, 276-79, 290-92.
         Reprint of the introduction to 1916.1, with notes and
     foreword by the two editors. See also 1961.2 and 1962.2.

2   JUSSERAND, [ADRIEN ANTOINE] J[EAN] J[ULES]. The English
     Novel in the Time of Shakespeare. Translated by Elizabeth
     Lee. New ed. with introduction by Philip Brockbank.
     London: Ernest Benn; New York: Barnes & Noble, pp. 71-75,
     87-88, 307-8.
         Finds Ascham's attitude to Italy ultimately ineffectual,
     as travellers "crowded" to the south. Points out Nashe's
     endorsement of Ascham's condemnation of romances. See
     1890.2.

*3   LEE, L. M. "Eloquence and Wisdom in Roger Ascham." Master's
     Thesis, University of Birmingham.
         Cited in Index, Vol. 17, p. 15.

                              141

1966

4 NEWKIRK, GLEN ALTON. "The Public and Private Ideal of the
Sixteenth Century Gentleman: A Representative Analysis."
Ph.D. dissertation, University of Denver, 345 pp.
  Traces the classical concept of the virtuous man
trained to serve his state and analyzes the "gentlemanly
ideal," which was undeveloped in England before the arrival of the humanists in Oxford but which in the course
of the century developed and was assimilated into "the
more imaginative literature," where it "received a more
valid representation."

5 RYDÉN, MATS. Relative Construction in Early Sixteenth Century
English, with Special Reference to Sir Thomas Elyot. Acta
Universitatis Upsaliensis. Studia Anglistica Upsaliensia
3. Uppsala: Almqvist & Wiksells, liv, 384 pp., with 24
unpaginated tables of frequency surveys.
  This descriptive-analytic study of all Elyot's works
also examines Ascham's Toxophilus, Report, and Scholemaster
in the Wright edition (1904.1). As there is no index, one
must glean the examples from Ascham by laboriously pouring
over the densely packed though well-organized pages. The
tables provided at the end will be of most immediate value
to Ascham students. Rydén reaches few conclusions with
specific reference to Ascham; most noteworthy is that he
uses double prepositions more frequently than his contemporaries and is "idiosyncratic" in his use of "anticipatory
that which."

6 SCHOECK, R[ICHARD] J. Introduction to his edition of The
Scholemaster. Don Mills, Ont.: J. M. Dent & Sons (Canada),
pp. vii-xxiv.
  Discusses Ascham's "world," chiefly the intellectual
milieu of St John's, Cambridge in the forties; provides a
brief introduction to "the man," though with the misleading implication that Ascham and Sturm had met; analyzes
Scholemaster, with particular attention to its two-book
structure and its style, the "full heritage" of which is
in Hooker's "judicious style"; includes selective annotated
bibliography and notes to the text.

7 SIMON, JOAN. Education and Society in Tudor England. Cambridge: Cambridge University Press, pp. 102-23 passim,
197-215 passim.
  Now the standard history of the subject. Although
there is no extended discussion of Ascham, nor anything
that could be called an original contribution to Ascham
scholarship, still valuable for placing Ascham's life and

thought in a larger educational framework, particularly
Chapters 3, "Erasmus and Vives on Education," and 7, "The
Reorientation of University Learning." See 1965.2.

8   SMITH, JOHN HAZEL. "Roger Ascham's Troubled Years." JEGP
    65, no. 1 (January): 36-46.
    Presents evidence for fixing the dates of Ascham's
    absence from Cambridge to period between 19 January 1541
    and May 1542 and for redating letters 13 and 18-21 to the
    months of March-April 1543. Suggests April 1543 as date
    of Ascham's parents' death. Calls in conclusion for a more
    thorough analysis of all the letters, which will demand a
    new edition, not only of letters but of the whole works.

1967

1   BROOKE, [C. F.] TUCKER. "The Renaissance." In A Literary
    History of England. Edited by Albert C. Baugh. 2d ed.
    New York and London: Appleton Century-Crofts, pp. 333-34.
    Text unchanged from the first edition (1948.2); bib-
    liography by Matthias A. Schaaber cites only 1963.3 and
    1959.6.

2   RYAN, LAWRENCE V. Introduction to his edition of The Schole-
    master. Ithaca, New York: Cornell University Press,
    pp. xi-xlii.
    A brief biography of Ascham, drawing upon Ryan's origi-
    nal researches; a discussion of Ascham's place in Renais-
    sance educational theory and practice and of the chief
    influences on them; an analysis of Scholemaster and of its
    significance for literary criticism and theory in England.
    Sees Scholemaster as the "first influential document of
    English neoclassicism." Ascham is the first English
    author acquainted with Aristotle's Poetics and is the
    "first authentic English critic of the stage." He is an
    important influence on Sidney. Although Scholemaster is
    "by no means a masterpiece of either humanistic thought
    or artistic prose" it is "a rich storehouse . . . of
    Elizabethan ideals."
    Ryan's edition modernizes spelling and punctuation and
    suppresses capital letters and italics to conform to cur-
    rent usage. Some of Ascham's longer periods are broken
    and some of his shorter, elliptical sentences are incor-
    porated into others. Leaves Ascham's quotations intact
    save to correct obvious misspellings; translates only in
    cases where Ascham himself does not translate or para-
    phrase in the text; provides the 1570 reading for all

emendations "where there is the slightest doubt about Ascham's meaning"; ignores marginal notes which are "mere indicators." Compare 1904.1.

3   TANNENBAUM, SAMUEL A., and TANNENBAUM, DOROTHY R. Elizabethan Bibliographies. Vol. 1, Roger Ascham, Beaumont and Fletcher, Nicholas Breton, George Chapman. Port Washington, New York: Kennikat Press, vii, 20 pp.
    Reprint of 1946.1.

1968

1   JOHNSON, ROBERT CARL, comp. "Roger Ascham, 1946–1966." In Elizabethan Bibliographies Supplements. Vol. 9. Minor Elizabethans: Roger Ascham, 1946–1966; George Gascoigne, 1941–1966; John Heywood, 1944–1966; Thomas Kyd, 1940–1966; Anthony Munday, 1941–1966. London: Nether Press, pp. 3–18.
    Continues 1946.1. Entries listed chronologically, then alphabetically; some omissions. Single index for all five authors contained in the volume. Compare Dees, 1980.1.

*2 PALUMBO, ROBERT M. "Roger Ascham: His Contribution to English Literature as Prose Writer and Literary Critic." Master's thesis, College of the Holy Names at Oakland, California.
    Cited in Patsy C. Howard, Theses in English Literature, 1894–1970 (Ann Arbor: Pierian Press, 1973), p. 6.

3   ROMANO, JOHN RIGOLETTO. "The Scholarly Archer: A Study of the Humanism of Ascham's Toxophilus." Ph.D. dissertation, Columbia University, 256 pp.
    Treats four generally overlooked facts about Toxophilus: first, Ascham's defense of archery is not personal, but is a marshalling of arguments from earlier works; second, Toxophilus is written in the tradition of "humanistic literature of wit" in its treatment of a "rarely treated subject"; third, Ascham is innovative in using the dialogue form for a sports treatise; fourth, in effectively creating a dialogue like those of the ancients, Ascham is mainly emulating Plato's Phaedrus and Cicero's De Oratore, aiming at "recreating the drama" of the first and the

"didactically effective organization" of the second.
Surveys the main sources of thinking on the subject of
imitatio.

4   ROTT, JEAN, and FAERBER, ROBERT. "Un Anglais à Strasbourg
    au milieu du XVIe siècle: John Hales, Roger Ascham, et
    Jean Sturm." EA 21, no. 4 (October-December): 381-94.
        Prints and annotates three letters from Hales to Ascham
    written in December and January 1551-52, prefixed by a
    brief essay providing biographical and historical matter
    necessary to appreciate their significance "comme témoignage
    du très vif intérêt que les humanistes anglais portaient
    à Sturm et à son oeuvre."

1969

1   GREENE, THOMAS M. "Roger Ascham: The Perfect End of Shoot-
    ing." ELH 36, no. 4 (December): 609-25.
        A fresh assessment of Ascham's writing. Although
    Ascham's pedagogy is narrow, lacking the "humane breadth"
    and "enlightened wisdom" of Vives, his literary criticism
    is "almost always good." The "thought and feeling" of his
    best prose "reach us with an admirable transparency."
    Argues against the judgments of Lewis (1954.1) that Ascham
    is a "narrow stylist"; on the contrary, style was "rather
    a discipline of beauty conceived almost as broadly as
    possible." At the deepest level all of Ascham's writings
    are about the same thing--a "facility, a skill," for which
    Ascham provides no name but which might be called "pre-
    cision," a skill "determined in operation, not in mere
    potentiality" and demonstrated by "hitting the mark." In
    this preoccupation with precision, Ascham "interrupts"
    the normal development of the English language into the
    rich symbolic capabilities of a Spenser or a Sidney, but
    at mid-sixteenth century in England, the language "required
    precisely the clarity and control which the Cambridge
    Humanists strove for."

2   The National Union Catalog, Pre-1956 Imprints. A Cummulative
    Author List Representing Library of Congress Printed Cards
    and Titles Reported by Other American Libraries. Vol. 23.
    Chicago and London: Mansell, pp. 245-53.
        Cites eighty-five separate imprints. Lists copies of
    all known editions of Ascham's works, including reissues
    of nineteenth-century editions such as Arber's (1888.1);

some selections (e.g. in G. Gregory Smith's Elizabethan
Critical Essays); and some MSS (e.g. a photocopy of British
Library MS. Royal 18.B xxiv. no. 2 of the first book of
Scholemaster.

1970

1   CAREY, JOHN. "Sixteenth and Seventeenth Century Prose, Part
     I, Prose before Elizabeth." In History of Literature in
     the English Language, vol. 2. English Poetry and Prose,
     1540-1674. Edited by Christopher Ricks. London: Barrie
     & Jenkins, pp. 353-56.
         Briefly assesses Report ("a step forward in English
     historiography":), Toxophilus (in which Ascham is evolving
     "familiarity, not rhetoric," by a "natural drift into
     simile and metaphor"), and Scholemaster (whereas in Toxo-
     philus Ascham had showed "enthusiasm" as a literary critic,
     in Scholemaster he shows more "discernment"). Scholemaster
     is a "model of expository prose" from which Bacon and
     Sidney were "the gainers."

2   FLEISCHAUER, JOHN FREDERICK. "A Plaine and Sensible Utter-
     ance: The Prose Style of Roger Ascham." Ph.D. disserta-
     tion, Ohio State University, 237 pp.
         Seeks to "isolate and define Ascham's literary intel-
     lect." Following a theory of stylistic analysis indebted
     to Leo Spitzer and Joan Webber, argues that Ascham's style
     changes significantly during his career. In Toxophilus he
     avoids reconciling apparent contradictions, and his syntax
     "moves correlatively, with incessant qualification." In
     Report the style is less conciliatory, but still refuses
     to accept simple extremes as truth, and Ascham retains "a
     remarkable informality" in syntax, use of colloquial de-
     tail, and "honesty of reaction." In Scholemaster Ascham
     is "less able than before to maintain an awareness of the
     complexity of truth" and instead emphasizes "the necessity
     for order." Yet he can, especially in passages written in
     1563, "reveal complexity in language" even while yielding
     to "absolutism in morality." Ascham sometimes "abuses"
     aphorism, leaving imperfectly defined generalizations open
     to misreading. "Ascham's style evolves through a search
     for practical truth toward the narrowness of absolute
     moral conviction. In this change and in the consistency
     of his honest and unpretentious colloquialism are the
     roots of his intellect and the clue to his contribution to
     English humanism." See 1971.3, 1974.6.

3   GIDDEY, ERNEST. "Note sur le style de Roger Ascham dans The
     Scholemaster (1570)." In Mélanges d'histoire du XVIe
     siècle offerts à Henri Meylan. Travaux d'humanisme et
     renaissance, 110. Geneva: Librairie Droz, pp. 153-57.
          A brief, general account of Ascham's style, stressing
     the sources of his metaphors and emphasizing a command of
     the concrete which enables him "to implant an oft-times
     subtle idea into fertilizing ground and thereby give it a
     new forcefulness." He concludes that "son style . . .
     loin de paraître artificiel, sans finesse ou ambivalent,
     témoignera de ce lent, modeste et généreux travail grâce
     auquel se crée, au sein d'une nation, une conscience
     linguistique."

4   HORNÁT, JAROSLAV. Anglická renesanční próza: eufuistická
     beletrie od Pettieho "Paláce Potěchy" do Greenova "Pandosta"
     [Renaissance Prose in England: Euphuistic Fiction from
     Petti's Palace of Pleasure to Grene's Pandosto.] Acta
     Universitatis Carolinae, Philologica, Monographia 33.
     Prague: Universita Karlova, pp. 42-69 passim, 156-57.
          Discusses influence of Ascham on Euphues: The Anatomy
     of Wit and Euphues and His England. The hero of the former
     "is undoubtedly derived" from Scholemaster, and The Anatomy
     of Wit "represents a serious pedagogical and edifying
     treatise written in Ascham's footsteps." In Euphues and
     His England "some leading ideas, views, predilections and
     even aversions" are also traceable to Scholemaster. Al
     though Lyly "is devoted to the seeking of ideal norms
     reflecting the presumed harmony of the world order," yet
     "the abstract reasoning of Ascham and other humanists . . .
     is instinct in his Euphues with more worldly and empirical
     thought. . . ." Includes English summary. See 1961.2.

5   LABRANCHE, ANTHONY. "Imitation: Getting in Touch." MLQ 31,
     no. 3 (September): 308-29.
          Although not specifically addressed to Ascham, provides
     a theoretical basis for reassessment of Ascham's doctrine
     of imitation. Complements Trousdale's essay (1976.2).
     Sees imitation as "the series of minute adjustments of
     one's external stylistic movements to some inner, imita-
     tive decorum--the sense of decorum which arises from an
     active inspection of the ways in which a classic model
     creates its effects and the contemporary ways which sug-
     gest themselves to the imitator." Asks "May not every
     imitation be . . . the imitation of a life-style perceived
     as extending outward from the model?"

1970

*6   STROZIER, ROBERT M., II. "Sixteenth Century Critical Theory
     in England: Ascham, Sidney, and Bacon." Ph.D. disserta-
     tion, University of Chicago.
         Cited in ADD, 1969-70, p. 213. See 1973.5.

                              1971

1   KINGHORN, A[LEXANDER] M[ANSON]. The Chorus of History:
     Literary-Historical Relations in Renaissance Britain,
     1485-1558. New York: Barnes & Noble, pp. 101-6, 143-46.
         Summarizes legal statutes regarding archery from 1503-
     58, and claims Toxophilus to be "in many ways more durable
     than the Scholemaster." In Scholemaster, Ascham's curri-
     culum "is an ideal one, though not of a kind likely to
     find much favour nowadays." Ascham "seems to have been
     hostile to poetry; . . . he was not a critic." Influenced
     generally by C. S. Lewis (1954.1).

*2   SALAMON, LINDA BRADLEY. "The Mirrors for The Scholemaster:
     Erasmus, Castiglione, Elyot, Ascham and the Humanistic
     'Speculum.'" Ph.D. dissertation, Bryn Mawr College.
         Cited in ADD, 1970-71, p. 220. See 1973.3-4.

*3   VOS, ALVIN. "The Prose Style of Roger Ascham." Ph.D. dis-
     sertation, University of Chicago.
         Cited in ADD, 1970-71, p. 221. See 1974.6, 1976.3-5.

                              1972

1   STROZIER, ROBERT M. "Roger Ascham and Cleanth Brooks: Ren-
     aissance and Modern Critical Thought." Essays in Criti-
     cism 22, no. 4 (October): 396-407.
         Argues that for Ascham and for the Renaissance generally,
     the critic "uses" a work "temporarily" to "resolve a prob-
     lem"; the same is true for a "New" or "Thematic" critic.
     For both Ascham and Brooks, the "work" is "indeterminate,"
     and the critic a "creator." The similarity between the
     two men suggests that sixteenth-century works may be val-
     uable to modern criticism "in promoting an awareness of
     underlying assumptions."

1973

1   COLE, HOWARD C. A Quest of Inquirie: Some Contexts of Tudor
    Literature. Pegasus Backgrounds in English Literature.
    Indianapolis and New York: Bobbs-Merrill Company, pp. 104-
    8, 146-49, 152-54, 226-28, 325-27.
        Discusses Ascham's views toward tragedy, toward rhymed
    verse, and toward imitation within the broader context of
    Elizabethan literary theory.

2   JOHNSTON, GEORGE BURKE. "William Camden's Elegy on Roger
    Ascham." SP 70, no. 2 (April): 160-71.
        Edits, with translation and introduction, the eighty-
    three line elegy appended by Camden to Grant's Disertis-
    simi Viri Rogeri Aschami (1581; Johnston uses this edition,
    not the 1576, because of minor corrections). The elegy
    is not personal, but of the public "enduring monument"
    type.

3   SALAMON, LINDA BRADLEY. "The Courtier and The Scholemaster."
    CL 25, no. 1 (Winter): 17-36.
        Studies the relation between the two works within the
    traditions of speculum principis and courtesy book; finds
    that after allowing for coincidental similarities "there
    remains a core of likeness between Castiglione and Ascham
    that is central to each." One common ground is their
    shared civic humanism. A second, "going beyond coincidence
    or contemporaneity," is their respective concepts of
    sprezzatura and comeliness: they both "imply a judgment
    of decorum based upon the appropriate and the unaffected,
    in rhetorical style and in courtly conduct."

4   _____. "The Imagery of Roger Ascham." Texas Studies in Lit-
    erature and Language 15, no. 1 (Spring): 5-23.
        Concerned with imagery which is "self-revelatory, of
    mind, of background, and of temperament." Finds three
    major classes of images; from classical literature, from
    Renaissance commonplaces, from personal life. The first
    two reveal "no distinct qualities of personality and few
    of mind," but the third class, containing his "character-
    istic" images, illuminates "with great singleness of pur-
    pose his single concern of learning." His figures are
    "people, not colors, jewels, flowers . . . busy, breathing
    human beings . . . specific Englishmen" who live "largely
    on the land or in town" and who are "not 'drab' but of the
    earth, earthy." His metaphors show him "a good and curious
    observer, genial and approachable, a man of simple tastes."

1973

5   STROZIER, ROBERT M.   "Theory and Structure in Roger Ascham's
    The Schoolmaster."   NM 74, no. 1: 144-62.
        Argues that Scholemaster is a "coherently structured
    work both in its underlying theoretical structure and in
    its overt organization," that the two are "intimately re-
    lated," and that "any discussion of the latter is useless
    unless the theoretical structure is made clear." As out-
    lined by Strozier, Ascham's theory assumes that form and
    content are distinct, that one cannot know things directly
    but only through expressions, that there are as many ex-
    pressions of a thing as there are experiences of it, that
    difference of expressions depends on the receiver and the
    situation from which he perceives, that all human action
    is a "process of particular problem solving," that imita-
    tion is a universal method of adapting to the relativity
    of these conditions, that man "must imitate in order to
    produce effective expressions." In light of this "theo-
    retical system" Ascham works "steadily" even if "uncriti-
    cally" toward "the specification of the learning situation
    for the young pupil."

6   WILSON, KENNETH JAY.   "The Early Tudor Dialogue." Ph.D. dis-
    sertation, Yale University, 308 pp.
        Compares themes and methods in Toxophilus, Elyot's
    Knowledge, and More's Dialogue of Comfort to define the
    "art" of the Tudor dialogue. A first chapter analyzing
    the mimetic art of Plato's and Cicero's dialogues, which
    are a "hybrid" form, between drama and dialectic, is fol-
    lowed by successive chapters on Elyot, Ascham, and More.
    Toxophilus is a "complex amalgam of Platonic and Ciceronian
    dialogue," in which Ascham's "primary business is measuring
    the mind." Shooting is "an art bearing affinities to the
    art of rhetoric, which the dialogue itself subtly epito-
    mizes." Concludes that "dialogues enlarge our insight into
    humanist ways of thought" and should be "ranked high among
    the achievements of humanist art."

1974

1   FIRESTINE, MARTHA WARN.   "The Doctrine of Imitation in the
    English Renaissance: Roger Ascham, Sir Philip Sidney, and
    Ben Jonson." Ph.D. dissertation, Indiana University, 295
    pp.
        Argues that all three men see imitation as valuable
    "because it develops a student's judgment," and if he em-
    ploys judgment comparable to the best authors, so that he

achieves equal excellence and effectiveness, he is engaged
in imitation, even though his work may depart significantly
from its predecessors in matter of style. In Scholemaster
"imitatio involves neither exclusive attention to Cicero nor
verbal reconstruction of his works." The imitator may
alter to suit his purposes, as Ascham himself does in re-
jecting a chronological arrangement for Report.

2   GASQUET, ÉMILE. Le courant machiavelien dans la pensée et la
littérature anglaise du XVIe siècle. Montreal, Paris,
and Brussels: Didier, pp. 35-36 and 110-11.
Observes that the "accents défavorables à Machiavelli"
in Report set the emotional tone for much later commentary
in England, but that at the same time Ascham is capable of
separating his morality from his role as a historiographer.
See 1963.3 and 1964.2.

3   M[cCONICA], J[AMES] K[ELSEY], comp. "Roger Ascham, 1515-68."
In The New Cambridge Bibliography of English Literature.
Vol. 1. 600-1660. Edited by George Watson. Cambridge:
Cambridge University Press, cols. 1822-23.
Cites thirty-one critical studies, beginning with Katterfeld's biography (1879.1), ending with Giddey's article
on Ascham's style (1970.3). Some unevenness: cites Parks'
article on "The First Italianate Englishman" (1961.3) but
omits his analysis of the MS of Scholemaster (1938.1). But
in the main a balanced representation of the scholarship on
Ascham between its inclusive dates. Omits significant
earlier criticism such as that of Johnson (1761.1) or
Coleridge (1852.1). See 1941.1.

4   MOREHEAD, ANN EDMONDSON. "A Critical Edition of Roger
Ascham's Toxophilus." Ph.D. dissertation, Ohio State University, 383 pp.
The "General Introduction," pp. 1-54, discusses the occasion and reception of Toxophilus; considers the appro-
priateness of archery as a suitable subject for a humanistic treatise; outlines the rhetorical structure; and analyzes its style, linguistically and rhetorically. The
"Historical Notes," pp. 296-371, identify Ascham's classical
sources, provide glosses for technical terms and for words
or phrases that might confuse the modern reader, and note
the more common aphorisms used by Ascham.

5   RICE, JUDITH ELAINE. "Decorum in the Prose Style of Roger
Ascham." Ph.D. dissertation, Indiana University, 249 pp.
Appeals to classical theories of decorum, chiefly the
three "characters of style," to explain Ascham's stylistic

1974

variety. Although Ascham uses all three, his basic style
is the middle. An increased use of Gorgianic schemes in
Report and Scholemaster does not indicate a development
toward euphuism, but reflects the stylistic tradition of
each genre. Purpose and genre are not the only factors
determining Ascham's variety, however; he also suits his
style to audience, time, place, and content. Perceives
"moral uncertainty" in the style of Report in contrast to
Fleischauer's perception of "moral complexity" (1970.2).
See also 1958.2.

6   VOS, ALVIN. "The Formation of Roger Ascham's Prose Style."
     SP 71, no. 3 (July): 344-70.
         Argues that modern critics who stress the Isocratean
     influence in the formation of Ascham's style wrongly dis-
     tinguish between Isocrates and Cicero in ways that a Ren-
     aissance writer would not. The basis of Ascham's style is
     an early Gorgianic Ciceronianism, discussed ambivalently
     by Cicero himself in Orator, but elevated by Sturm to be
     the very model of perfected style. Shows that for Sturm
     "Cicero's most mannered, most schematic periods . . . be-
     come the favored models of style." Demonstrates how
     closely Ascham follows Sturm's tastes. Concludes with
     general implications for the study of Renaissance prose
     style: scholars should revive the term concinnitas and
     should recognize that their conceptions of the development
     of prose style in the Renaissance "have readily been over-
     simplified."

1975

1   ANON. "Ascham, Roger." In The New Encyclopaedia Britannica
     in 30 Volumes. Micropaedia, Vol. 1. 15th ed. Chicago,
     London, Toronto, Geneva, Sydney, Tokyo, Manilla, Seoul,
     and Johannesburg: Encyclopaedia Britannica, Helen Heming-
     way Benton, Publisher, p. 571.
         Life shortened from earlier versions, with material
     dispersed in various Macropaedia articles. Scholemaster
     presents "an effective method of teaching Latin prose com-
     position," and Ascham is "one of the outstanding literary
     figures of the generation following that of Sir Thomas
     More. Compare 1929.1 and 1878.2.

2   MIGLIOR, GIORGIO. Roger Ascham: La dottrina umanistica
     inglese e la sperimentazione nelle prosa letteraria intorno
     alla metà del cinquencento. Biblioteca di studi inglesi,
     29. Bari: Adriatica Editrice, 301 pp.

The only modern book-length critical study apart from
Ryan's biography (see 1963.3). In seven chapters, Miglior
examines "the humanist on the margins of political power";
the three major English works; the 1551 "letter-diary" to
Edward Raven; the famous passage on "seeing the wind" in
Toxophilus; "Polemical Humanism in The Scholemaster";
varieties of "timbre" in Scholemaster; and Ascham's place
in the development of prose style in the sixteenth century.
By looking at issues which are still controversial (e.g.,
Ascham's place in euphuism, the roles of politics and religion in his thought, personal relations to important
historical figures, his anti-Italianism), the first chapter
raises questions to be considered at length in the remaining ones. Chapter 4 provides the fullest available aesthetic appraisal of the "wind" passage. Chapter 5 elabor-
ates the thesis that Scholemaster "esprime una fitta
polemica contro la società elisabettina tutta," and not
merely against educational inadequacies. Using the term
timbre in Chapter 6 to connote feelings and sensory perceptions rather than merely a phonic quality, Miglior
paints a picture of Ascham as "master of the graphic
particular." His examination of euphuism utilizes precise
comparisons of phrase length and rhetorical figures to
conclude that though the influence of Ascham on Lyly may
be inferred, it is difficult to define. Throughout,
Miglior places considerable stress on Ascham's independence
of thought, claiming that his originality reaches at times
a high level of artistry.

1976

1   LAWSON, SARAH. "An OED Oversight in Toxophilus: 'Lerdriving.'"
    NM 77, no. 1: 92.
        Ascham's use of the word seems to be a variant of sense
    11 of drive, but it deserves a cross reference and an entry
    under let-.

2   TROUSDALE, MARION. "Recurrence and Renaissance: Rhetorical
    Imitation in Ascham and Sturm." ELR 6, no. 2 (Spring):
    156-79.
        Suggests that for Elizabethans imitation meant "con-
    scious awareness of artistic method as a means of becoming
    accomplished in one's craft." For both Ascham and Sturm,
    what is imitated are abstract "patterns" which can "exist
    independent of the matter which they express [and] the
    words by which they are expressed." Examines examples of

1976

Renaissance drama to conclude that "there is a literal
sense in which by copying an earlier artist . . . the
sixteenth-century writer . . . made it possible for the
age of Augustus to be reborn." See 1970.5.

3   VOS, ALVIN. "Form and Function in Roger Ascham's Prose."
    PQ 55, no. 3 (Summer): 305-22.
       The questions that we have hiterto asked about Ascham's
    prose style have been generated by the debate over euphuism,
    and much of our ambivalence about his style has arisen from
    a consideration of form isolated from function. Shows that
    Ascham's "penchant" for Gorgianic periods is more than mere
    fashion; directed "chiefly to the mind," they "highlight
    distinctions of thought" and act to "reinforce [meaning]
    formally." Though Ascham's penchant for Gorgian style may
    lead on occasion "into affectation and even obscurity," it
    happens "infrequently." Ascham's occasional stylistic
    weaknesses result not from love of fanciful rhetoric, but
    from "an incomplete mastery of the art of writing well."
    See 1974.5-6.

4   _____. "The Humanism of Toxophilus: A New Source." ELR 6,
    no. 2 (Spring): 187-203.
       Peter Nanius' Dialogus de Milite Peregrine (Louvain,
    1543) is not only a source of information for Toxophilus,
    but also, and more importantly, a "model whose format and
    ideas are controlling principles in Ascham's writing of
    Toxophilus." Examines the influence of Nanius in the con-
    text of Ascham's "peculiar straits" in the four or five
    years preceding the publication of Toxophilus and finds
    the work providing "new inspiration" and teaching Ascham
    "how to give humanistic weight and dignity to a potentially
    chauvinistic and self-serving piece of propaganda." In
    part Toxophilus is a rebuttal of Nanius, mirroring the
    tensions in English-Imperial relations in the 1540s.

5   _____. "Humanistic Standards of Diction in the Inkhorn Con-
    troversy." SP 73, no. 4 (October): 376-96.
       Covers much the same ground as Hall (see Elyot, 1977.1),
    though with different emphases and conclusions. Argues
    that the positions of Wilson, Cheke, and Ascham regarding
    the inkhorn controversy were all "clearly informed by their
    study of the ancient rhetoricians." Classical conceptions
    of purity, propriety, and custom provided a means for these
    three to develop "moderate guidelines for remedying any in-
    adequacy in the English language," and to "delineate a
    firm, even-handed approach to diction based on hitherto
    unavailable concepts and principles."

6   WILSON, K[ENNETH] J[AY]. "Ascham's Toxophilus and the Rules
      of Art." RenQ 29, no. 1 (Spring): 30-51.
         Toxophilus is a genuine dialogue in which both inter-
      locutors learn from a common ground of assumptions, accept-
      ing each other's ideas and in turn using them. It is a
      serious, philosophical exploration of the relation between
      art and skill. It uses Plato's Phaedrus "subtly and com-
      plexly," as it puts forth and explores the idea that exer-
      cise of judgment transforms a man and that only by knowing
      the true standard of excellence can one perfect one's
      skill. Assuming as his reader someone already convinced of
      the value of archery, Ascham's "aesthetic" purpose is "to
      teach how judgments in shooting, and judgments generally,
      are made."

1977

1   SMITH, WILLIAM ELLSWORTH. "Roger Ascham's Toxophilus: The
      Rise and Fall of the Longbow." Ph.D. dissertation, Univer-
      sity of Utah, 213 pp.
         Provides historical background to Henry VIII's 1541
      archery statute. Argues that Toxophilus, written in the
      context of disobedience to the 1541 law, is "a patriotic
      archery handbook."

2   VAUGHAN, M. F. "An Unnoted Translation of Erasmus in Ascham's
      Scholemaster." MP 75, no. 2 (November): 184-86.
         The passage in Scholemaster on learning vs. experience
      is drawn directly from Erasmus's 1529 De pueris statim ac
      liberaliter instituendis. Suggests that a "closer analysis
      of Ascham's knowledge of Erasmus may help us "identify more
      clearly the distinctive aspects of Ascham's English prose."

1979

1   BARTLETT, KENNETH. "A Misdated Letter of Roger Ascham." N&Q,
      n.s. 26, no. 5 (October): 399-401.
         The letter in question is No. CXCIII in Giles's edition
      (1864.1), vol. I, part ii, pp. 449-50, from Ascham to the
      Doge of Venice on behalf of John, Lord Lumley. The correct
      date is that noted in Grant's 1578 edition (2 November
      1566) but erroneously altered in all subsequent editions
      to 2 November 1556.

1979

2   VOS, ALVIN. "'Good Matter and Good Utterance': The Character
    of English Ciceronianism." SEL 19, no. 1 (Winter): 3-18.
        Calling Ascham "the foremost English Ciceronian," dis-
    cusses the way he and Sturm subtly alter Cicero's formula-
    tion of the relation between rhetoric and philosophy:
    "the direction of both Sturm's and Ascham's thought is not
    first of all to adulate Cicero's style, but to revitalize
    his program." Ascham does, however, "find it very diffi-
    cult to avoid idolizing Cicero's style." Nevertheless, he
    does make distinctions about how Cicero is to be imitated
    "that are entirely foreign to the thought of servile
    Ciceronians." His primary concern "is not to parrot
    Cicero's speech, but to recover the process by which
    Cicero imitated others." In this respect his "second
    generation" Ciceronianism differs from that of Erasmus in
    the first or Harvey in the third.

1980

1   DEES, JEROME S[TEELE]. "Recent Studies in Ascham," ELR 10,
    no. 2 (Spring): 300-10.
        Provides descriptive analyses of significant critical
    studies and editions of Ascham between 1945 and 1978,
    categorized as follows: biographical studies; general
    critical studies; studies of style, criticism, and educa-
    tional theory; studies of individual works and of the
    Ascham canon. Assesses the state of criticism ("within
    the last five years . . . major reassessment has begun");
    offers a critique of the standard editions ("no critical
    edition . . . meeting the demands of today's textual
    scholars"); describes other editions. A section entitled
    "See also" lists additional studies in an attempt to pro-
    vide a "reasonably complete" bibliography for the period.

Addendum

1889

*1   L[EE,] [SIR] S[IDNEY]. "Elyot, Sir Thomas." In <u>Dictionary</u>
       <u>of</u> <u>National Biography</u>. Vol. 17. Edited by Leslie Stephen.
       London: Smith, Elder, & Co. <u>See</u> 1908.1.

1936

1   RAITH, JOSEF. Boccaccio in der englischen Literatur von
     Chaucer bis Painters "Palace of Pleasure": Ein Beitrag
     zur Geschichte der italienischen Novelle in England. Aus
     Schrifttum und Sprache der Angelsachsen, 3. Leipzig:
     Robert Noske, pp. 101-112.
       Examines in detail the similarities and differences
     between Elyot's, Boccaccio's, and Beroaldo's versions of
     "Titus and Gisyppus" in the broader intellectual contexts
     of Renaissance Platonism and Petrarchism. Elyot's story
     is "not a 'translation' in the ordinary sense of the term,
     but a new creation in the spirit of Platonic Love theory."
     Discusses Elyot's style.

Index to Elyot

"'Actors' and 'Play Acting' in the Morality Tradition," 1970.7

Ainger, Alfred, 1893.1

Amenities of Literature . . ., 1841.1; 1881.1, see also 1832.1

American Journal of Education, 1866.1

Ammann, Roman Ernst, 1961.1

Anglorum Speculum . . ., 1684.1

Anon, 1843.1; 1866.1; 1878.1; 1929.1; 1975.1

Arte of English Poesie, The, 1880.1

Articulate Citizen and the English Renaissance, The, 1965.3

Ascham, Roger, 1832.1; 1905.1; 1920.1; 1933.2; 1948.1; 1949.1; 1961.1; 1963.4; 1971.6; 1973.3

"Aspetti dell 'umanesimo in Inghilterra," 1939.2

Athenae Cantabrigienses, 1858.1

Athenae Oxonienses, 1691.1; 1813.1

Atkins, J[ohn] W[illiam] H[ey], 1947.1

Baker, Herschel, 1947.2; 1961.2

Barker, Sir Ernest, 1948.1

Barnes, Barnabe, 1936.1

Bateson, F[rederick] W[ilse], 1941.2

Baugh, Albert C., 1948.2; 1967.1

Baumer, Franklin le Van, 1940.1

Bayle, Pierre, 1750.1

"Before Euphues," 1948.3

Belvedere, The Garden of the Muses, 1933.6

Benndorf, Cornelie, 1905.1

Bennett, H[enry] S[tanley], 1952.1

Berdan, John M., 1920.1

Bibliographer's Manual of English Literature, The, 1834.1; 1871.1

Bibliography, 1824.1, 2; 1834.1; 1871.1; 1884.1; 1885.1; 1893.2; 1911.1; 1926.2; 1941.1; 1950.1; 1960.2; 1962.2; 1965.1; 1966.4; 1969.3; 1974.2; 1976.1

"Bibliography of Sir Thomas Elyot (1490?-1546)," 1962.2

Bibliotheca Britannica . . ., 1824.2

Biographica Britannica, 1750.1

Biographie universelle ancienne et moderne . . ., 1811.1; 1855.1

Biography, 1662.1; 1684.1; 1691.1; 1721.1; 1750.1; 1784.1; 1811.1; 1813.1; 1814.1; 1822.1; 1840.1; 1855.1; 1858.1; 1880.1; 1908.1; 1960.2; 1967.3

Bland, D. S., 1957.1. See also 1953.3

Boccaccio, Giovanni, 1922.1; 1937.3; 1948.3; 1950.3

Boccaccio in der englischen
Literatur von Chaucer bis
Painters "Palace of Pleas-
ure," 1936.1
Boccaccio nel Cinquecento inglese,
I1, 1974.1
Boccaccio nella culture inglese e
anglo-americana, I1, 1974.1
Boccaccio's Story of "Tito e
Gisippo" in European litera-
ture, 1937.3
Bohn, Henry G., 1871.1
Boke Named the Governour, The.
See Elyot, Sir Thomas, works
of (discussions)
Bossewell, John, 1957.4
Bouck, Constance, 1958.1
Brandl, Alois, 1896.1; 1915.1
"Breton, Elyot, and the Court of
Honour," 1938.2
Breton, Nicholas, 1938.2
Brink, Bernhard [Aegidius Kon-
rad] Ten, 1896.1
British Museum General Catalogue
of Printed Books, 1965.1
Brooke, [C. F.] Tucker, 1948.2;
1967.1
Brown, Marice Collins, 1968.1
Brydges, Sir [Samuel] Egerton,
1815.1
Buch vom Führer, Das, 1931.3
Bühler, Curt F., 1954.1
[Bullen, George], 1884.1
Bullough, Geoffrey, 1957.2;
1962.1; 1964.1
Burley, Walter, 1954.1
Bush, Douglas, 1937.1
Butt, John, 1947.3; 1951.1

Calepinus, Ambrosius, 1954.8
Cambridge Bibliography of English
Literature, 1941.2. See also
1974.2
Cambridge History of English Lit-
erature, The, 1909.1
Carey, John, 1970.1
Case, John, 1936.1
Caspari, Fritz, 1954.2

Castel of Helth, The. See Elyot,
Sir Thomas, works of (discus-
sions)
"Castel of Helth and its Author,
Sir Thomas Elyot, The" 1929.3
The Castel of Helthe (1541) by
Sir Thomas Elyot . . .,
1937.4
"Castle of Health, The," 1945.1
Castiglione, Baldasare, 1930.2;
1933.2; 1939.2-3; 1948.1,
1949.1; 1954.2; 1964.2;
1971.6; 1975.4
"Castiglione, Cicero, and English
Dialogues, 1533-1536," 1975.4
Castiglione und die englische
Renaissance, 1939.3
Catalogue general des livres im-
primés de la Bibliothèque
Nationale, 1911.1
Catalogue of Books in the Library
of the British Museum, 1884.1
Catalogue of Original and Early
Editions of Some of the Poet-
ical and Prose Works of Eng-
lish Writers . . ., 1893.2
Catalogue of the English Books
Printed before MDCI Now in
the Library of Trinity Col-
lege Cambridge, 1885.1
Censura Literaria, 1815.1
Chalmers, Alexander, 1814.1
Chambers, Raymond Wilson, 1932.1;
1935.1
Chambers's Cyclopaedia of English
Literature, 1901.2. See also
1843.1
Charles V (Holy Roman Emperor),
1880.1; 1930.4; 1932.1;
1935.1; 1951.2; 1960.2;
1967.3
Charlton, Kenneth, 1965.2
Cheke, Sir John, 1903.1
Chorus of History: Literary-
Historical Relations in Ren-
aissance Britain, 1485-1558,
The, 1971.3

Cicero, Marcus Tulliua, 1973.4; 1975.4; 1976.2
Cleland, James, 1957.4
Coogan, Robert, C.F.C., 1971.2
Conklin, Willet Titus, 1930.1
Conley, C[arey] H[erbert], 1927.1
Conniff, James Joseph, Jr., 1971.1
"Contributions of Plato, Cicero, and Quintilian to Sir Thomas Elyot's Theory of Language, The," 1976.2
Cooper, C[harles] H[enry], 1853.1; 1858.1
Cooper, Thomas, 1949.3; 1954.9
Cooper, Thompson, 1858.1
Copernicus, 1942.1
Court of Honour, The, 1938.2
Creeth, Edmund, 1969.1
"Critical Edition of Sir Thomas Elyot's The Boke Named the Governour, A," 1971.5
"Critical Edition of Sir Thomas Elyot's Pasquil the Playne, A," 1971.4
Croft, Henry Herbert Stephen, 1880.1. See also 1938.3, 4; 1950.4
Cromwell, Thomas, 1832.1; 1930.2; 1965.4
Cyclopaedia of English Litera ture . . ., 1843.1. See also 1901.2

Day, Angel, 1936.2
Dees, Jerome Steele, 1976.1
Defence of Good Women, The. See Elyot, Sir Thomas, works of (discussion)
"Descriptive Grammar of the Early Sixteenth Century as Ascertained from the Corpus, The Castel of Helth by Sir Thomas Elyot, A", 1968.1
Dialogue between Lucian and Diogenes, A. See Elyot, Sir Thomas, works of (discussions)
Dibdin, Thomas Frognall, 1824.1
Dictionary of National Biography, 1889.1; 1908.1

Dictionary of Sir Thomas Elyot, The. See Elyot, Sir Thomas, works of (discussions)
Dignity of Man: Studies in the Persistence of an Idea, The, 1947.2. See also 1961.2
"Diogenes and The Boke Named the Governour," 1954.1
Disraeli, Isaac, 1832.1; 1841.1; 1881.1
Doctrinal of Princes, The. See Elyot, Sir Thomas, works of (discussions)
Doctrine of the English Gentleman in the Sixteenth Century . . ., The, 1929.2
Donner, H. W., 1951.2
Dressler, Bruno, 1928.1

"Early Medical Humanists: Leonicenus, Linacre and Thomas Elyot," 1931.1
Early Tudor Criticism: Linguistic and Literary, 1940.5
"Early Tudor Dialogue, The," 1973.3
Early Tudor Poetry, 1485-1547, 1920.1
Early Tudor Theory of Kingship, The, 1940.1
Ecclesiastical Memorials, 1721.1; 1822.1
Editions, 1880.1; 1912.1; 1915.1; 1926.1; 1931.3; 1937.4; 1940.2; 1946.1; 1962.3; 1964.3; 1966.3; 1967.2; 1969.1-2; 1970.5; 1971.4-5; 1975.3; 1976.4. See also Elyot, Sir Thomas, works of (editions)
Edmonds, C[ecil] K[ay], 1933.1
Education and Society in Tudor England, 1966.5
Education in Renaissance England, 1965.2
"Education of the Aristocracy in the Renaissance, The," 1950.2
Education or Bringing Up of Children, The. See Elyot, Sir Thomas, works of (discussion)
Einflus des Erasmus auf die englische Bildungsidee, Der, 1939.1

Elyot, Richard, 1853.1
"Elyot and the 'Boke Called Cor-
    tigiano in Ytalion,'" 1930.2
"Elyot's Governour and Peacham's
    Compleat Gentleman," 1927.2
"Elyot's Governour-Ideal,"
    1933.2
Elyot, Sir Thomas
-sources, 1880.1; 1920.2; 1922.1;
    1930.2; 1936.1; 1938.3-4;
    1939.1, 3; 1946.1; 1948.4;
    1951.3; 1954.2, 8; 1960.2;
    1964.2; 1967.3; 1970.8;
    19731.; 1976.2
-style, 1933.3; 1948.5; 1961.1,
    3; 1965.5; 1966.4; 1971.5;
    1977.1
-works of (discussions)
--Bankette of Sapience, The,
    1960.2; 1967.2, 3
--Bibliotheca Eliotae, 1949.3;
    1951.5; 1954.7-9; 1967.3;
    1975.2
--Boke Named the Governour, The,
    1832.1; 1880.1; 1881.1; 1891.1;
    1896.1; 1905.2; 1906.2; 1907.1;
    1930.2; 1931.3; 1935.2; 1938.3;
    1950.4; 1954.2; 1958.2; 1960.2;
    1961.1, 3; 1962.3; 1963.3;
    1967.3; 1969.2; 1964.2; 1971.3,
    5; 1973.1
--Castel of Helth, The, 1832.1;
    1891.1; 1929.3; 1931.1; 1937.4;
    1945.1; 1960.2; 1964.2; 1967.3;
    1968.1; 1970.5
--Defence of Good Women, The,
    1912.1; 1915.1; 1940.2;
    1960.2; 1964.2; 1967.3
--Dialogue betweene Luciane and
    Diogenes, A, 1967.3
--Dictionary of Syr Thomas Elyot,
    The, 1954.7-8; 1960.2; 1967.3
--Doctrinal of Princes, The,
    1933.2; 1948.5; 1967.2-3
--Education or Bringinge up of
    Children, The, 1960.2; 1966.3;
    1967.3; 1977.2
--How one may take Profit of his
    Enemyes (attributed to Elyot),
    1967.3

--Image of Governance, The,
    1896.1; 1926.1; 1951.3;
    1960.2; 1964.2-3; 1967.2-3;
    1970.8
--Of the Knowledeg [sic] which
    Maketh a Wise Man, 1920.2;
    1946.1; 1958.3; 1960.2;
    1964.2; 1967.3; 1969.1;
    1973.3
--Pasquil the Playne, 1960.2;
    1964.2; 1967.2-3; 1970.2;
    1971.4
--P. Gemini Eleatis Hermathena
    (attributed to Elyot),
    1958.1; 1967.3
--Preservative agaynste Deth, A,
    1960.2; 1964.2; 1967.3
--Rule of a Christen Life made by
    Picus Erle of Mirandula, The,
    1960.2; 1964.2; 1967.3;
    1976.3
--Swete and Devoute Sermon of
    Sayngt Ciprian, A, 1960.2;
    1964.2; 1967.3
--"The Tale of Titus and Gysip-
    pus," 1922.1; 1936.1; 1937.3;
    1948.3; 1950.3; 1952.2
-works of (editions)
--Bankette of Sapience, The,
    1967.2
--Bibliotheca Eliotae, 1975.3
--Boke Named the Governour, The,
    1907.1; 1931.3; 1962.3;
    1969.2; 1971.5
--Castel of Helth, The, 1937.4;
    1970.5
--Defence of Good Women, The,
    1912.1; 1915.1; 1940.2
--Doctrinal of Princes, The,
    1967.2
--Image of Governance, The,
    1926.1; 1964.3; 1967.2
--Letters of Sir Thomas Elyot,
    The, 1976.4
--Of the Knowledeg [sic] which
    Maketh a Wise Man, 1946.1;
    1969.1
--Pasquil the Playne, 1967.2;
    1971.4
--Preservative agaynste Deth, A,
    1915.1

"Elyot, Sir Thomas," 1878.1;
1889.1; 1908.1; 1929.1; 1975.1
"Elyot's The Boke Named the Gov-
ernour and the Vernacular,"
1973.1
Emkes, Max Adolf, 1904.1
"Emperor and Sir Thomas Elyot,
The," 1951.2
Emsley, Bert, 1928.2
Encyclopaedia and Dictionary of
Education, The, 1921.1
Encyclopaedia Britannica, The,
1878.1; 1929.1. See also
1975.1
England im Zeitalter von Humanis-
mus, Renaissance, und Refor-
mation, 1952.3
Englische Pädagogic im 16.
Jahrhundert . . ., Die,
1905.1
English Books and Readers, 1457-
1557. . . ., 1952.1
"English Courtesy Literature
before 1557," 1919.1
English Grammar Schools to 1660,
The, 1908.2
"English Humanism and the New
Tudor Aristocracy," 1952.4
English Humanists and Reformation
Politics under Henry VIII and
Edward VI, 1965.4
English Literary Criticism: The
Renascence, 1947.1
English Literature: An Illus-
trated Record, 1906.1
English Literature in the Six-
teenth Century, Excluding
Drama, 1954.3
English Naturalists from Neckam
to Ray, 1947.4
English Prose: Selections with
Critical Introductions by
Various Writers . . ., 1893.1
English Renaissance Prose Fiction,
1500-1600: An Annotated Bib-
liography of Criticism,
1978.2

English Writers: An Attempt to-
wards a History of English
Literature, 1891.1
Erasmus, Desiderius, 1930.2;
1933.5; 1939.1; 1954.2;
1959.1; 1964.2; 1965.4; 1971.6
Erziehungsideal bei Sir Thomas
More, Sir Thomas Elyot, und
John Lyly, Das, 1904.1
Exner, Helmuth, 1939.1

Fall of the Monasteries and the
Social Changes in Eng-
land . . ., The, 1924.1
Falstaff, 1910.3
Ferguson, Arthur B., 1960.1;
1965.3
"First Edition of Sir Thomas
Elyot's Castell of Helthe,
with Introduction and Criti-
cal Notes, The," 1970.5
First English Translators of the
Classics, The, 1927.1
Floyd, Thomas, 1931.2
"Footnote on the Inkhorn Contro-
versy, A," 1949.2
Foreman, Joel Edward, 1975.2;
1976.2
Forrest, Thomas, 1957.4
Four Political Treatises . . . by
Sir Thomas Elyot, 1967.2
Four Tudor Books on Education,
1966.3
Freeman, Eric J., 1962.2
Fuller, Thomas, 1662.1; 1684.1;
1840.1. See also 1901.1
Fulton, John F., 1931.1

Galigani, Giuseppe, 1974.1
Garnett, Richard, 1903.1; 1906.1
The General Biographical Dic-
tionary . . ., 1814.1
Gentlefolk in the Making: Stud-
ies in the History of English
Courtesy Literature, 1935.2
Gentleman-Ideal und Gentleman
Erziehung . . ., 1933.2

Geschichte der englischen Erziehung . . ., 1928.1

Geschichte der englischen und amerikanischen Literatur . . . ., 1937.2; 1954.5

"Gloss on 'Daunsinge': Sir Thomas Elyot and T. S. Eliot's Four Quartets, A," 1973.2

Goode, Clement Tyson, 1922.1

Gordon, Ian, 1966.1

Gottesman, Lillian, 1963.2, 1967.2, 1975.3

Governour, The. See Elyot, Sir Thomas, works of (discussions)

Graesse, Jean George Théodore [Johann Georg Theodor], 1859.1; 1950.1

Green, A. Wigfall, 1952.2

Grether, Emil, 1938.1

Guevara, Antonio, 1896.1; 1951.3

Hale, David, 1978.1

Hale, Edward E., Jr., 1903.2

Hall, Anne Drury, 1977.1

Hallam, Henry, 1837.1; 1855.2

Harner, James L[owell], 1978.2

Harpsfield, Nicholas, 1932.1

Hebel, J[ohn] William, 1952.2

Heltzel, Virgil B., 1938.2

Hermathena. See Elyot, Sir Thomas, works of (discussions)

Hexter, J. H., 1950.2

Histoire de l'éducation en Angleterre, 1896.3

History of English Literature (from the Fourteenth Century to the Death of Surrey), 1896.1

History of the Worthies of England, The, 1662.1; 1840.1

Hitchcock, Elsie Vaughan, 1932.1

Hogrefe, Pearl, 1930.2; 1959.1; 1963.3; 1967.3

Holmes, Elisabeth, 1961.3

Homer, 1978.1

Horace, 1926.3

Howard, Edwin Johnston, 1940.2-3; 1942.1; 1943.1; 1946.1

Howe One May Take Profit of His Enemies (attributed to Elyot). See Elyot, Sir Thomas, works of (discussions)

Hoyler, August, 1933.2

Hudson, Hoyt H., 1952.2

"Humanism and Reform in Tudor England," 1971.1

Humanism and the Social Order in Tudor England, 1954.2

"Humanistic Doctrines of the Prince from Petrarch to Sir Thomas Elyot," 1938.4

"Humanistic Theory of Education, The," 1930.3

"Humanitas in Tudor Literature," 1949.1

"Ideal Conduct in Venus and Adonis," 1975.5

"Ideas on Rhetoric in the Sixteenth Century," 1903.2

Image of Governance, The. See Elyot, Sir Thomas, works of (discussions)

Image of Man: A Study of the Idea of Human Dignity . . ., 1961.2

Indian Summer of English Chivalry . . ., 1960.1

inkhorn terms, 1949.2; 1966.1; 1977.1

Introduction to the Literature of Europe . . ., 1837.1; 1855.2

Isocrates, 1933.3; 1948.5

Ist Thomas Elyot ein Vorgänger John Lockes in der Erziehungslehre?, 1896.2

Johnson, Francis R., 1952.2

Jones, Richard Foster, 1953.1

Joyce, Hewlett E., 1926.1

"Julius Caesar and Elyot's Governour," 1937.1; 1956.1

Jusserand, [Adrien Antoine] J[ean] J[ules], 1910.1

Kahin, Helen Andrews, 1940.3

Kelso, Ruth, 1929.2

Kinghorn, A[lexander] M[anson], 1971.3

Knowles, Dom David, 1959.2

"Language and Linguistic Interests of Sir Thomas Elyot, The," 1933.4

Lascelles, Mary, 1951.3

Lathrop, Henry Burrowes, 1933.3

"Latin Language Study as a Renaissance Puberty Rite," 1959.3

Laurie, Simon Somerville, 1903.3; 1905.2

Lee, Sir Sidney L., 1889.1: 1908.1

Lehmberg, Stanford E., 1957.3; 1960.2; 1962.3. See also 1961.4

Leonicenus, Nicolaus, 1931.1

"Letters of Sir Thomas Elyot, The," 1976.4

Lewis, C[live] S[taples], 1954.3

Lepzien, A[ugust Martin Johann], 1896.2

Library Companion . . ., The, 1824.1

Library of Literary Criticism of English and American Authors, The, 1901.1

Life and Death of Sir Thomas More, Knight . . ., The, 1932.1

Life and Times of Sir Thomas Elyot, Englishman, The, 1967.3

Liljegren, Sten Bodvar, 1924.1

Linacre, Thomas, 1931.1

Lindsay, T. M., 1909.1

Literary Bypaths of the Renaissance, 1924.2

Literary History of England, A, 1948.2; 1967.1

Literary History of the English People, A, 1910.1

Livre du Trésor, Le, 1880.1; 1948.4

Locke, John, 1896.2

Lowndes, Thomas, 1834.1; 1871.1

Lyly, John, 1904.1

McConica, James Kelsey, 1965.4; 1974.2

McCoy, Samuel Jesse, 1933.4

MacDonald, Michael Joseph, 1970.2; 1973.1

McKnight, George H., 1928.2

McLean, Andrew M., 1975.4

Major, John M., 1954.4; 1958.2; 1964.2; 1969.2

Mason, John E., 1935.2

Maxwell, J[ames] C[loutts], 1956.1

Meissner, Paul, 1952.3

Miller, Florence Graves, 1930.3

Millet, Fred B., 1919.1

Mirandola, Pico, 1964.2; 1976.3

Mirror for Magistrates, The, 1927.3

"Mirrors for 'The Scholemaster': Erasmus, Castiglione, Elyot, Ascham, and the Humanistic 'Speculum,' The," 1971.6

Modern English in the Making, 1928.2

Mohl, Ruth, 1933.5

Moore, John Lowry, 1910.2

"Moralization of the Dance in Elyot's Governour, The," 1958.2

"More About the Prince Hal Legend," 1936.2

More, Sir Thomas, 1832.1; 1880.1; 1904.1; 1930.4; 1932.1; 1935.1; 1954.2; 1959.1; 1960.2; 1964.2; 1973.3

Morley, Henry, 1878.2; 1891.1

Morris, Christopher, 1953.2

Moulton, Charles Wells, 1901.1

Movement of English Prose, The, 1966.1

Mulcaster, Richard, 1896.3; 1905.1

Narrative and Dramatic Sources of Shakespeare, 1957.2; 1962.1; 1964.1

Nashe, Thomas, 1903.2

National Union Catalogue, Pre-
    1956 Imprints . . ., The,
    1969.3
neologisms, 1933.4; 1953.1
Neoplatonism, 1920.2
New and General Biographical
    Dictionary, A, 1784.1
New Cambridge Bibliography of
    English Literature, The,
    1974.2
New Encyclopaedia Britannica,
    The, 1975.1. See also
    1878.1; 1929.1
Newkirk, Glen Alton, 1966.2
Northbrook, John, 1927.3
"Notes on Elyot's The Governour
    (1531)," 1927.3
"Notes on Thomas Elyot's View of
    Virtues," 1979.1
"Nowell's Vocabularium Saxonicum
    and the Elyot-Cooper Tradi-
    tion," 1954.6
Nugent, John Richard, 1932.2
Nuttall, P. Austin, 1840.1

Of the Knowledge Which Maketh a
    Wise Man. See Elyot, Sir
    Thomas, works of (discussions)
"Of the Three Earliest Authors in
    Our Vernacular Literature,"
    1832.1
"Old Honor and the New Courtesy:
    I Henry IV, The," 1978.3
O'Malley, C[harles] D[onald],
    1968.2
Ong, Walter J., S.J., 1959.3;
    1965.5
"On the Date of Sir Thomas Elyot's
    The Education or bringinge up
    of children," 1977.2
"On the Identity of Papyrius
    Geminus Eleates," 1958.1
"Oral Residue in Tudor Prose
    Style," 1965.5

Pace, George B., 1941.1
Painter, William, 1936.1
Parks, George B., 1948.3; 1976.3
Parmentier, Jacques, 1896.3

Partee, Morriss Henry, 1970.3
Pasquil the Playne. See Elyot,
    Sir Thomas, works of (dis-
    cussions)
Patrick, David, 1901.2
Patrizi, Francesco, 1880.1;
    1938.3; 1950.4; 1964.2
"Patrizi's De Regno et Regis
    Institutione and the Plan of
    Elyot's The Boke Named the
    Governour," 1950.4
Peacham, Henry, 1927.2
Peery, William, 1948.4
Pepper, Robert D., 1966.3
Perfit Commonwealth, A, 1933.6
Petrarch, Francesco, 1971.2
"Petrarch's Latin Prose and the
    English Renaissance," 1971.2
Petrus Alphonsus, 1922.1
P. Gemini Eleatis Hermathena.
    See Elyot, Sir Thomas, works
    of (discussions)
Phialas, Peter G., 1965.6
Phillips, Elias H., 1949.1
Phillips, James Emerson, 1940.4
Pico della Mirandola, 1920.2;
    1976.3
"Pico della Mirandola in Tudor
    Translation," 1976.3
"Picture of a Perfit Commonwealth,
    The," 1931.2
Pinckert, Robert Carl, 1964.3
Plato, 1920.2; 1946.1; 1954.2;
    1964.2; 1970.3-4; 1973.3;
    1976.2
Platonismus in der englischen
    Renaissance vor und bei Thom-
    as Elyot . . ., 1920.2
"Plea for More English Diction-
    aries, A," 1951.1
Pollard, A[lbert] F[rederick],
    1930.4
Pollard, Alfred William, 1926.2
Political Thought in England:
    Tyndale to Hooker, 1953.2
Preservative Against Death, A.
    See Elyot, Sir Thomas, works
    of (discussions)
Principles for Young Princes
    (1611), 1957.4

Princiss, G. M., 1978.3

"Profitable Studies: Humanists and Government in Early Tudor England," 1970.6

Prose of the English Renaissance: Selected from Early Editions and Manuscripts, 1952.2

"Public and Private Ideal of the Sixteenth Century Gentleman, The," 1966.2

Puttenham, George, 1880.1; 1903.2; 1926.4; 1927.3; 1960.2; 1967.3

Quintilian, 1964.2; 1976.2

Raith, Josef, 1936.1

Raven, Charles E., 1947.4

Rebora, Piero, 1939.2

"Recent Studies in Elyot," 1976.1

Redmond, James Patrick, 1971.4

Redgrave, Gilbert Richard, 1926.2

Reed, A. W., 1941.2

Relative Constructions in Early Sixteenth Century English, with Special Reference to Sir Thomas Elyot, 1966.4

Religious Orders in England, The, 1959.2

Renaissance Dictionaries; English-Latin and Latin-English, 1954.7-9

Renaissance Idea of Wisdom, The, 1958.3

Review of Sir Thomas Elyot's Of the Knowledge Which Maketh a Wise Man, 1947.3

"Rhetoric and Law in Sixteenth-Century England," 1953.3. See also 1957.1

"Rhetoric and the Law Student in Sixteenth-Century England," 1957.1. See also 1953.3

Rice, Eugene, 1958.3

Richards, Gertrude R. B., 1945.1

Rierdan, Richard Cotter, 1970.4

Robertson, W. G. Aitchison, 1929.3

Roger Ascham, 1963.4

Roper, William, 1932.1; 1951.2; 1960.2; 1967.3

Rude, Donald Warren, 1971.5; 1977.2

Rule of a Christian Life . . ., The. See Elyot, Sir Thomas, works of (discussions)

Ryan, Lawrence V., 1963.4

Rydén, Mats, 1966.4

Saintsbury, George, 1898.1. See also 1901.1

Salamon, Linda Bradley, 1971.6; 1973.2

Sandys, George, 1684.1

Sargent, Ralph M., 1950.3

Sasaki, Kuniya, 1979.1

S., C., 1894.1

Schirmer, Walter Franz, 1937.2; 1954.5

Schlotter, Josef, 1938.3. See also 1880.1; 1950.4

Schmitz, L. Dora, 1896.1

Schoeck, Richard J., 1953.3. See also 1957.1

Schrinner, Walter, 1939.3

Schroeder, Kurt, 1920.2

"Shakespeare and Elyot's Covernour," 1927.4

"Shakespeare and The Governour, Bk. II, ch. xiii. Parallels with Richard II and the More Addition," 1963.1

"Shakespeare's Henry V and the Second Tetralogy," 1965.6

Shakespeare, William (works of)

-Antony and Cleopatra, 1940.4

-Coriolanus, 1927.4; 1930.1

-Henry V, 1927.4; 1930.1; 1938.1; 1965.6

-Henry IV, Part I, 1978.3

-Henry IV, Part II, 1901.2; 1927.4; 1936.2

-Julius Caesar, 1937.1; 1940.4; 1964.1

-Richard II, 1963.1

-Troilus and Cressida, 1927.4

-Two Gentleman of Verona, 1950.3; 1957.2

-Venus and Adonis, 1975.4

Short History of English Literature, A, 1898.1

Short-title Catalogue of Books
  Printed in England . . ., A,
  1926.2
Sidney, Sir Philip, 1926.4
Siegel, Paul N., 1952.4
"Significance of Elyot's Revi-
  sions of The Governour, The,"
  1961.3
Simon, Joan, 1966.5
Sinker, Robert, 1885.1
"Sir Thomas Elyot," 1843.1;
  1853.1; 1866.1
"Sir Thomas Elyot Against Poetry,"
  1941.1
"Sir Thomas Elyot and 'Noble
  Homere,'" 1978.1
Sir Thomas Elyot and Renaissance
  Humanism, 1964.2
"Sir Thomas Elyot and the 'Ars
  Poetica,'" 1926.3
"Sir Thomas Elyot and the English
  Reformation," 1957.3
"Sir Thomas Elyot and the Inte-
  grity of the Two Gentlemen of
  Verona," 1950.3
"Sir Thomas Elyot and the Lan-
  quet-Cooper Chronicle,"
  1955.1
"Sir Thomas Elyot and the Legend
  of Alexander Severus," 1951.3
"Sir Thomas Elyot and the 'Say-
  ings of the Philosophers,'"
  1933.6
"Sir Thomas Elyot and the Trans-
  lation of Prose," 1948.5
"Sir Thomas Elyot: A Theory and
  Practice of Written Communi-
  cation in the Early Sixteenth
  Century," 1970.4
"Sir Thomas Elyot, Educator,"
  1963.2
"Sir Thomas Elyot on Plato's
  Aesthetics," 1970.3
"Sir Thomas Elyot on the Turning
  of the Earth," 1942.1
"Sir Thomas Elyot Redivivus,"
  1957.4
"Sir Thomas Elyot's Armorial
  Quarterings," 1894.1

"Sir Thomas Elyot's Defense of
  the Poets," 1926.4
"Sir Thomas Elyot's Intention in
  the Opening Chapter of The
  Governour," 1963.3
Sir Thomas Elyot's "The Book
  Named the Governor," 1969.2
Sir Thomas Elyot's "The Defence
  of Good Women," 1940.2-3
"Sir Thomas Elyot's The Image of
  Governance," 1926.1
"Sir Thomas Elyot's The Image of
  Governance: Its Sources and
  Political Significance,"
  1970.8
"Sir Thomas Elyot's The Image of
  Governance (1541): A Criti-
  cal Edition," 1964.3
"Sir Thomas Elyot's Titus and
  Gyssipus," 1922.1
"Sir Thomas Elyot: Studies in
  Early Tudor Humanism," 1954.4
Sir Thomas Elyot: Tudor Humanist,
  1960.2. See also 1961.4
"Sir Thomas More and Sir Thomas
  Elyot," 1930.4
Sir Thomas More Circle: A Pro-
  gram of Ideas . . ., The,
  1959.1
"Sixteenth and Seventeenth Cen-
  tury Prose, Part I: Prose
  Before Elizabeth," 1970.1
Sketches of Longer Works in Eng-
  lish Verse and Prose . . .,
  1878.2
Skov, John Villads, 1970.5
Slavin, Arthur J., 1970.6
Sledd, James, 1949.2; 1954.6
"Some Sources of Wits Theatre of
  the Little World (1599) and
  Bodenham's Belvedere (1600),"
  1951.4
"Some Words in Sir Thomas Elyot's
  Of the Knowledge Which Maketh
  a Wise Man," 1943.1
Sorieri, Louis, 1937.3
Spenser, Edmund, 1891.1
Starkey, Thomas, 1948.1; 1971.1;
  1975.4

Starnes, DeWitt Talmage, 1927.2-
4; 1931.2; 1933.6; 1936.2;
1949.3; 1951.4-5; 1954.7-9;
1955.1; 1957.4
State in Shakespeare's Greek and
Roman Plays, The, 1940.4
Stenberg, Theodore, 1926.3-4
Stephanus, Robert, 1951.5;
1954.7-8
Streitberger, W. R., 1975.5
Strozier, Robert M., 1972.1
Strype, John, 1721.1; 1822.1
Studies in Education during the
Age of the Renaissance,
1400-1600, 1906.2
Studies in the History of Educa-
tional Opinion from the Ren-
aissance, 1905.2
Studniczka, Hans, 1931.3
"Study of Sir Thomas Elyot's
Pasquil the Playne, A,"
1970.2
Sturm, Johann, 1896.3
"Supplement to the Short-Title
Catalogue," 1933.1
Sweet and Devout Sermon of Saint
Cyprian, A. See Elyot, Sir
Thomas, works of (discussions)
Sweeting, Elizabeth J., 1940.5
Sylvester, Richard S., 1961.4.
See also 1960.2

Tannenbaum, Samuel A., 1937.4
"Thomas Cooper and the Biblio-
theca Eliotae," 1951.5;
1954.8
"Thomas Cooper's Thesaurus: A
Chapter in Renaissance Lexi-
cography," 1949.3; 1954.9
"Thomas Elyot Redivivus," 1957.4
Thomas Elyots "Governour" in
seinem Verhältnis zu Francesco
Patrici, 1938.3
"Thomas Elyot's 'Schutzmittel
gegen den Tod' (1545),"
1915.1
"Thomas Elyot's 'Verteidigung
guter Frauen' (1545) . . .,"
1915.1
Thomas More, 1935.1

Thompson, Elbert N[evius]
S[ebring], 1924.2
Three Estates in Medieval and
Renaissance Literature, The,
1933.5
"Three Souls Again, The," 1948.4
"Titus and Gisyppus." See Elyot,
Sir Thomas, works of (dis-
cussions)
Traditions of Civility: Eight
Essays, 1948.1
Translations from the Classics
into English from Caxton to
Chapman, 1477-1620, 1933.3
Treatise of Morall Philosophy, A,
1933.6
Trésor des livres rares et
precieux . . ., 1859.1;
1950.1
Triumph of the English Lan-
guage . . ., The, 1953.1
"Tudor Medicine and Biology,"
1968.2
Tudor Prose, 1513-1570, 1969.1
"Tudor Prose Style: English
Humanists and the Problem of
a Standard," 1977.1
Tudor-Stuart Views on the Growth,
Status, and Destiny of the
English Language, 1910.2
Turner, William, 1947.4; 1951.5
"Two Further Notes on Shake-
speare's Use of Elyot's
Governour," 1930.1
"Two Sir John Fastolfs, The,"
1910.3

Udall, Nicholas, 1951.5; 1954.7
"Unacknowledged Use of the Cratylus by Thomas Elyot, An,"
1975.2
"Utopian Ideals in English Prose
of the Renaissance, The,"
1932.2

"Varro." See Disraeli, Isaac
Verbalsyntax in Sir Thomas Elyots
"Governour" . . ., Die,
1961.1

Verhältnis von Shakespeares
    "Heinrich V" zu Sir Thomas
    Elyots "Governour," Das,
    1938.1
Vernon Harcourt, L[evenson]
    W[illiam], 1910.3
Vertues Commonwealth, 1933.6
Vives, Juan Luis, 1912.1; 1920.1;
    1930.2; 1959.1; 1964.2
Vives and the Renascence Educa-
    tion of Women, 1912.1; 1940.3

Waller, A[lfred] R[aney], 1909.1
Ward, A[dolphus] W[illiam], 1909.1
Warren, Leslie C., 1938.4;
    1950.4
Watson, Foster, 1907.1; 1908.2;
    1912.1; 1921.1
Watson, George, 1974.2
Watt, Robert, 1824.2
Webbe, William, 1926.4; 1927.3
Wierum, Ann, 1970.7
Wilson, Kenneth Jay, 1973.3;
    1976.4
Wilson, Knox, 1945.2
Wilson, Thomas, 1903.2
Wits Commonwealth, 1933.6
Wits Theater of the Little World,
    1933.6
Wolff, S. L., 1922.1
Wood, Anthony à, 1691.1; 1813.1
Woodward, William Harrison,
    1906.2
Woolger, M. N., 1970.8
Wortham, James, 1948.5

"Xenophon in the English Renais-
    sance from Elyot to Holland,"
    1945.2

Index to Ascham

Ackerman, W. A., 1898.1

Ad Adolescentulos Latinae Linguae Studiosus, E. G. Oratio de Vita et Obitu Rogeri Aschami . . ., 1576.1. See also 1864.1

Adams, W[illiam] H[enry] Davenport, 1875.1; 1883.1; 1884.1

Addison, Joseph, 1910.1

Aeschylus & Sophocles: Their Work and Influence, 1927.2

Age of Transition: 1400-1580, The, 1905.7

Ainsworth, Oliver Morley, 1928.1

Ainsworth, William Harrison, 1840.1

Allibone, S[amuel] Austin, 1858.1; 1878.1

Amenities of Literature, Consisting of Sketches and Characters of English Literature, 1841.1; 1881.4

Ammann, Roman Ernst, 1961.1

Anderson, J. J., 1934.1

Anderson, Elizabeth K[yrsten], 1935.1

"Anglais à Strasbourg au milieu de XVIe siècle, Un," 1968.4

Anglická renesanční próza . . ., 1970.4

Anglorum Speculum: Or the Worthies of England in Church and State . . ., 1684.1

Annual Report of the Department of the Interior . . ., 1903.4

Anon., 1822.1; 1835.1; 1857.1-3; 1863.1; 1867.1; 1878.2; 1901.1; 1905.1; 1915.1; 1920.1; 1929.1; 1975.1

Antike, Renaissance und Puritanismus: Ein Studie zur englischen Literaturgeschichte des 16. und 17. Jahrhunderts, 1933.3

Arber, Edward, 1868.1; 1870.1; 1888.1

[Archer, William], 1905.2

"Archers' Feathers in Chaucer and Ascham," 1964.6

Aristotle, 1922.1; 1963.3; 1967.2

Arnstadt, Fr[iedrich] Aug[ust], 1881.1

"Art and Practice of Archery, Including a Comment upon the Toxophilus of Ascham, The," 1801.1

"Ascham and Brinsley," 1908.7

"Ascham and Colet," 1905.2

"Ascham and His Scholemaster," 1862.2

"Ascham and Lady Jane Grey," 1882.1; 1883.4

"Ascham and the Schools of the Renaissance," 1900.2

"Ascham Borrowing from Erasmus, An," 1955.1

Ascham Letters. An Annotated Translation of the Latin Correspondence in the Giles Edition of Ascham's Works, The, 1948.4

Ascham, Roger
-sources, 1863.4; 1879.1; 1900.3;
   1915.2; 1920.3; 1937.1;
   1940.1; 1963.3; 1968.3;
   1974.4; 1976.4; 1977.2
-style, 1887.1; 1893.2; 1894.1;
   1905.8; 1914.3; 1915.2-3;
   1916.1, 3; 1933.4; 1935.3;
   1954.1; 1958.2; 1961.1;
   1963.3; 1966.5; 1969.1;
   1970.2-3; 1971.3; 1974.5-6;
   1975.2; 1976.3
-works of (discussions),
--Apologia . . . pro caena Domi-
   nica, 1963.3
--Dissertissimi Viri Rogeri
   Aschami Angli, Regiae Olim
   Maiestati a Latinis Epistolis . . ., 1859.2; 1864.1;
   1963.3
--Oecumenius' Commantaries on
   Paul's Epistles to Philemon
   and Titus (in manuscript
   translation. See Ryan,
   1963.3, p. 301, n. 23);
   1963.3
--Report and Discourse written
   by Roger Ascham, of the Af-
   fairs and State of Germany
   . . ., A, 1761.1; 1879.1;
   1959.6; 1963.3; 1966.5;
   1970.2; 1975.2
--Scholemaster, Or Plaine and
   Perfite Way of Teachyng
   Children to Understand,
   Write, and Speake, the Latin
   Tong . . ., The, 1836.1;
   1864.1; 1875.1; 1879.1;
   1883.2; 1888.1; 1889.3;
   1900.3; 1908.8; 1938.1;
   1944.1; 1954.1; 1961.1;
   1963.3; 1966.5; 1967.2;
   1970.2; 1973.3, 5; 1975.2
--Themata Theologica, 1963.3
--Toxophilus, The Schoole of
   Shootinge Conteyned in Two
   Bookes, 1761.1; 1801.1;
   1822.1; 1879.1; 1889.3;
   1897.1; 1954.1; 1963.3;
   1966.5; 1968.2; 1970.2;
   1973.6; 1974.3; 1975.2;
   1976.4, 6; 1977.1

-works of (editions)
--Epistolarum, 1703.1; 1859.2;
   1864.1
--Report and Discourse . . . of
   Germany, 1761.1; 1815.1;
   1864.1; 1904.1
--Scholemaster, 1761.1; 1815.1;
   1863.4; 1864.1; 1870.1;
   1888.1; 1904.1; 1934.3;
   1966.6; 1967.2
--Toxophilus, 1761.1; 1815.1;
   1864.1; 1868.1; 1904.1;
   1974.4
"Ascham, Roger," 1878.1; 1929.1;
   1975.1
"Ascham's Scholemaster," 1863.1
"Ascham's Scholemaster and Spen-
   ser's February Eclogue,"
   1940.2
"Ascham's Toxophilus and the Rules
   of Art," 1976.6
Athenae Cantabrigienses, 1858.2
Athenaeum, The, 1886.1-4
Atkins, J[ohn] W[illiam] H[ey],
   1947.1
Atkinson, B[asil] F[erris]
   C[ampbell], 1931.1
Atkinson, Ernest G., 1886.1-2.
   See also 1886.3-4
Ayscough, Samuel, 1782.1

Baldwin, James, 1881.2
Baldwin, T[homas] W[hitfield],
   1944.1
Bandello, Matteo, 1898.2
Barker, Ernest, 1948.1
Barnard, Henry, 1862.1
Bartlett, David W., [1853].1
Bartlett, Kenneth, 1979.1
Bateson, F[rederick] W[ilse],
   1941.1
Baugh, Albert C., 1948.2; 1967.1
Bayle, Pierre, 1735.1; 1747.1;
   1750.1
Bayne, Thomas, 1913.1
Benndorf, Cornelie, 1905.3.
   See also 1908.5
Bennet, James, 1761.1
Berdan, John M., 1920.2
The Bibliographer's Manual of
   English Literature . . .,
   1834.1; 1871.1

Bibliography, 1782.1; 1819.1;
1824.2; 1871.1; 1884.2;
1885.2; 1888.3; 1889.1;
1893.1; 1899.1; 1900.1;
1901.2-3; 1904.2; 1916.2;
1918.1; 1926.4; 1933.1;
1941.1; 1950.1; 1965.1;
1966.6; 1967.3; 1968.1;
1969.2; 1974.3; 1980.1
Bibliomania; or Book Madness: A
Bibliographical Romance,
1809.1; 1876.1
Bibliotheca Britannica; or a
General Index to British and
Foreign Literature, 1824.2
Biographia Borealis . . .,
1833.1. See also 1852.1
Biographia Britannica: Or,
Lives of the Most Eminent
Persons Who Have Flourished
in Great Britain and Ire-
land . . ., 1747.1
Biographie universelle ancienne
et moderne . . ., 1811.1;
1854.1
Biography, 1576.1; 1684.1;
1735.1; 1747.1; 1750.1;
1761.1; 1784.1; 1812.1;
1815.1-2; 1840.2; 1848.1;
1851.1; 1852.1; 1854.1;
1857.1; 1858.2; 1864.1;
1878.1; 1879.1; 1890.1;
1908.2; 1929.1-2; 1955.2;
1957.2; 1963.3; 1966.8;
1967.2
"Biography of Roger Ascham,"
1857.1. See also 1826.1
Black, J[ohn] B[ennet], 1936.1;
1959.1
Blundeville, Thomas, 1955.2
Boas, Frederick S., 1914.1
Boccaccio, Giovanni, 1929.1
Bohn, Henry G., 1871.1
Book of Authors: A Collection
of Criticism, Ana, Mots,
Personal Descriptions,
Etc. . . ., The, 1871.2
Book of Earnest Lives, A, 1884.1
"Bradgate Park, the Residence of
Jane Grey," 1822.2

Brief Course in the History of
Education, A, 1907.1
Brinsley, John, 1908.7
British Museum General Catalogue
of Printed Books . . .,
1965.1
British Plutarch, The, 1816.1
Braham, Lionel, 1956.1-2
Brooke, [C. F.] Tucker, 1948.2;
1967.1
Browning, Oscar, 1881.3; 1905.4
[Bullen, George], 1884.2
Burghers, Michael, 1908.1
Burnett, George, 1807.1
Bush, Douglas, 1939.1

Cambridge Bibliography of Eng-
lish Literature, 1941.1. See
also 1974.3
Cambridge History of English
Literature, The, 1909.3
Campbell, Lily B[ess], 1947.2;
1964.1
Carey, John, 1970.1
Carlisle, James H., 1890.1
Castiglione, Baldasare, 1935.5;
1939.2; 1963.3; 1971.2;
1973.3; 1975.2
Castiglione und die englische
Renaissance, 1939.2
Catalogue général des livres
imprimés de la Bibliothèque
Nationale, 1900.1
Catalogue of Additions to the
Manuscripts in the British
Museum in the Years 1882-
1887, 1889.1
Catalogue of Additions to the
Manuscripts in the British
Museum in the Years 1894-
1899, 1901.2
Catalogue of Books in the Library
of the British Museum Printed
in England, Scotland, and
Ireland . . ., 1884.2
Catalogue of Engraved British
Portraits Preserved in the
Department of Prints and
Drawings in the British Mu-
seum, 1908.1

Catalogue of Manuscripts Preserved in the British Museum Hitherto Undescribed, A, 1782.1

Catalogue of Original and Early Editions of Some of the Poetical and Prose Works of English Writers . . ., 1893.1

Catalogue of the English Books Printed before MDCI Now in the Library of Trinity College Cambridge, 1885.2

Catalogue of the Lansdowne Manuscripts in the British Museum, 1819.1

Catalogue of the Printed Books and Manuscripts in the John Rylands Library, 1899.1

Catalogue of the Printed Books in the Library of the University of Edinburgh, 1918.1

Cazamian, Louis [Francis], 1926.1; 1935.3

Certain Tragical Discourses of Bandello, 1898.2

Chalmers, Alexander, 1812.1

Chambers's Cyclopaedia of English Literature, 1901.1. See also 1843.1

"Characters of Style in Elizabethan Prose, The," 1958.2

Charlton, Kenneth, 1965.2

Chaucer, Geoffrey, 1892.2; 1964.6

Chauffepié, Jacques George de, 1750.1

Cheke, John, 1821.1; 1928.2-3; 1976.5

Chorus of History: Literary-Historical Relations in Renaissance Britain, 1485-1558, The, 1971.1

Cicero, Marcus Tullius, 1908.4; 1922.1; 1963.3; 1968.3; 1973.6; 1974.1, 6; 1979.2

Clark, Donald Lemen, 1922.1; 1948.3

classical meters, 1908.3; 8; 1921.1; 1934.1; 1941.2

"Classical Metres in England from Roger Ascham to Samuel Daniel," 1934.1

Clemons, Harry, 1916.1

Cleveland, Charles D., 1892.7

Cobb, Carl W., 1963.1

[Cochrane, J. G.], 1815.1

Cole, Howard C., 1973.1

Coleridge, Hartley, 1833.1; 1852.1

Columbia University Library Bulletins, No. 2: Books on Education in The Libraries of Columbia University, 1901.3

Conley, C[arey] H[erbert], 1927.1

Connolly, P. P., 1949.1

Cooper, Charles Henry, 1858.2

Cooper, Thompson, 1858.2

Courant Machiavelien dans la pensée et la littérature anglaises du XVIe siècle, Le, 1974.2

Course of English Classicism from the Tudor to the Victorian Age, The, 1930.3

"The Courtier and The Scholemaster," 1973.3

Craik, Henry, 1893.2

Critical Dictionary of English Literature and British and American Authors . . ., A, 1858.1; 1878.1

"Critical Edition of Roger Ascham's Toxophilus, A," 1974.4

criticism, 1891.1; 1902.5; 1903.3; 1913.4; 1914.4; 1940.3; 1947.1; 1957.1; 1963.3; 1969.1; 1970.6; 1972.1; 1975.2

Croll, Morris William, 1916.1; 1966.1,

Cubberley, Ellwood P., 1902.1; 1904.2

Cunningham, George Godfrey, 1837.1; 1863.2

Curry, John T., 1904.3; 1911.1

Cyclopaedia of English Literature: Consisting of a Series
of Specimens of British
Writers, 1843.1. See also
1901.1

Dalgleish, W. Scott, 1862.2
Daltenheym, Gabrielle, 1844.1
Damon, Karl, 1873.1
Daniel, Samuel, 1934.1
Dargaud, J[ean] M[arie], 1863.3
Davey, Richard, 1909.1
Débuts de la critique dramatique
en Angleterre jusqu'à la
mort de Shakespeare, Les,
1903.3
"Decorum in the Prose Style of
Roger Ascham," 1974.5
Dees, Jerome S[teele], 1980.1
Denham, John, 1873.2
Dibdin, Thomas Frognall, 1809.1;
1876.1
Dickono, Bruce, 1962.1
Dictionary of National Biography,
1908.2
Disraeli, Isaac, 1832.1; 1841.1;
1842.1; 1001.4
"Doctrine of Imitation in the
English Renaissance: Roger
Ascham, Sir Philip Sidney,
and Ben Jonson, The," 1974.1
Doctrine of the English Gentle
man in the Sixteenth Centu
ry . . ., The, 1929.3
double translation, 1761.1;
1852.1; 1862.1; 1883.2;
1892.3; 1900.3; 1902.5;
1905.3; 1944.1; 1948.3;
1963.2
"Double Translation in English
Humanistic Education,"
1963.2
Douce, Francis, 1819.1
Douglas, Robert Langton, 1898.2
Drei Studien zur englischen
Literaturgeschichte, 1892.1
Dudley, Robert, 1955.2
D'Urfey, Thomas, 1959.5

Earlier, Renaissance, The, 1901.5
Early Tudor Criticism: Linguis-
tic and Literary, 1940.3
"Early Tudor Dialogue, The,"
1973.6
Early Tudor Poetry, 1485-1547,
1920.2
Editions, 1761.1; 1815.1; 1863.4;
1864.1; 1865.1; 1868.1;
1881.5; 1888.1; 1904.1;
1934.2-3; 1948.4; 1966.6;
1967.2. See also Ascham,
Roger, works of (editions)
Edmonds, C[ecil] K[ay], 1933.1
E[dward] G[rant] Oratio de Vita
& Obitu Rogeri Aschami . . .,
1576.1. See also 1865.1
"Éducateurs: Roger Ascham, Les,"
1914.3
Educational Aims and Methods,
1900.2
Education and Society in Tudor
England, 1966.7
Education in Renaissance England,
1965.2
"Education of the Aristocracy in
the Renaissance, The," 1950.2
Education, the School, and the
Teacher, in English Litera-
ture, 1862.1
Einige Gedanken aus Roger Aschams
"The Scholemaster" über
Erziehung, besonders über
behandlung der Schüler,
1873.1
Elizabethan Bibliographies,
1967.3
Elizabethan Bibliographies Sup-
plements, 1968.1
Elizabethan Criticism of Poetry
. . ., 1914.4
Ellis, Henry, 1819.1
"Eloquence and Wisdom in Roger
Ascham," 1966.3
Elyot, Sir Thomas, 1904.4;
1905.3; 1920.2-3, 1948.1;
1971.2; 1973.6

Emkes, Max Adolf, 1904.4
Emsley, Bert, 1928.2
Encyclopaedia Britannica, The,
   1878.2; 1929.1. See also
   1975.1
Encyclopedia italiana di scienze,
   lettere ed arte, 1929.2
England im Zeitalter von Human-
   ismus, Renaissance, und Re-
   formation, 1952.2
England Under the Reigns of
   Edward VI and Mary, with the
   Contemporary History of
   Europe . . ., 1839.1
Englische Pädagogik im 16.
   Jahrhundert . . ., Die,
   1905.3
"English Anti-Machiavellianism
   before Gentillet," 1954.2
English Bowman, or Tracts on
   Archery . . ., The, 1801.1
English Face of Machiavelli, The,
   1964.2
English Grammar Schools to 1660:
   Their Curriculum and Practice,
   The, 1908.7
English Humanists and Reformation
   Politics under Henry VIII and
   Edward VI, 1965.3
"English Letters of Roger Asch-
   am, The," 1934.2
English Literary Autographs,
   1550-1650, 1932.1
English Literary Criticism: The
   Renascence, 1947.1
English Literature: An Illus-
   trated Record, 1906.1
English Literature in the Six-
   teenth Century, Excluding
   Drama, 1954.1
English Metrists: Being a Sketch
   of English Prosodical Criti-
   cism . . ., 1921.1
English Nation; Or a History of
   England in the Lives of Eng-
   lishmen, The, 1863.2
English Novel in the Time of
   Shakespeare, The, 1890.2;
   1966.2

English Ode to 1660 . . ., The,
   1918.3
English Poetry and Prose, 1540-
   1674, 1970.1
English Prose: Selections with
   Critical Introductions by
   Various Writers . . ., 1893.2
English Works of Roger Ascham,
   1761.1
English Works of Roger Ascham,
   The, 1815.1
English Works: "Toxophilus," "Re-
   port of the Affaires and
   State of Germany," "The
   Scholemaster," 1904.1
English Writers: An Attempt
   towards a History of English
   Literature, 1892.4
Erasmus, Desiderius, 1955.1;
   1959.2; 1965.3; 1971.2;
   1977.2
Erziehungsideal bei Sir Thomas
   More, Sir Thomas Elyot,
   Roger Ascham und John Lyly,
   Das, 1904.4
Essays on Educational Reformers,
   1868.2; 1902.4
Essay toward a History of Educa-
   tion, An, 1935.2
Ethical Teachings in Old English
   Literature, 1892.2
Euphues: The Anatomy of Wit,
   Euphues & His England, by
   John Lyly, 1916.1
euphuism, 1905.8; 1913.2;
   1916.1, 3; 1961.2; 1963.3;
   1975.2
Evans, Robert O., 1966.1
"Extension of Educational Activ-
   ity," 1902.2

Faerber, Robert, 1968.4
Fairbank, Alfred, 1960.1; 1962.1
Famous Books: Sketches in the
   Highways and Byeways of Eng-
   lish Literature, 1875.1
Fasti Oxoniensis, 1721.1; 1815.2

Fenton, Geoffrey, 1898.2
Firestine, Martha Warn, 1974.1
"First Draft of Ascham's Schole-
    master, The," 1938.1
"First English Essay: Toxophil-
    us by Roger Ascham, The,"
    1924.1
First English Translators of the
    Classics, The, 1927.1
"First Italianate Englishmen,
    The," 1961.3
First Sketch of English Litera-
    ture, A, 1883.3
Fischer, Thomas A., 1892.1
Fisher, John, 1912.1
Fitch, Sir Joshua [Girling],
    1900.2, See also 1905.2
Fleischauer, John Frederick,
    1970.2
Forbes, Clarence A., 1945.1
"Form and Function in Roger
    Ascham's Prose," 1976.3
"Formation of Roger Ascham's
    Prose Style, The," 1974.6
"Foundations of English Poetics,
    1570-1575," 1957.1
"From Troilus to Euphues," 1913.2
Fuller, Thomas, 1662.1; 1684.1;
    1840.2

Gabriel Harvey's "Ciceronianus,"
    1945.1
Garnett, Richard, 1903.1; 1906.1
Gascoigne, George, 1957.1
Gasquet, Émile, 1974.2
General and Biographical Dic-
    tionary, A, 1851.1
General Biographical Dictionary:
    Containing an Historical and
    Critical Account of the Lives
    and Writings of the Most
    Eminent Persons . . ., The,
    1812.1
General Dictionary, Historical
    and Critical: in Which a
    New and Accurate Translation
    of That of the Celebrated
    Mr. Bayle . . . Is Included
    . . ., A, 1735.1

Gentleman-Ideal und Gentleman
    Erziehung: mit besonderer
    Beruchsichtigung der Renais-
    sance . . ., 1933.2
Geschichte der Erziehung von
    Anfang an bis auf unsere
    Zeit . . ., 1892.6
Geschichte und Kritik des eng-
    lischen Hexameters, 1908.8
Giddey, Ernest, 1970.3
Giles, J[ohn] A[llen], 1864.1
Gill, John, 1889.2; 1899.2
"'Good Matter and Good Utterance':
    The Character of English
    Ciceronianism," 1979.2
Good Samaritans; Or Biographical
    Illustrations of the Law of
    Human Kindness, 1883.1
Gorton, John, 1826.1; 1851.1
Graesse, Jean George Théodore
    [Johann George Theodor],
    1859.1; 1950.1
Grange, John, 1913.2
Grant, Edward, 1576.1; 1865.1
"Grant's Oration on the Life and
    Death of Roger Ascham,"
    1865.1
"Great Tutor, A," 1915.1
Green, A. Wigfall, 1952.1
Greene, Thomas M., 1969.1
Greg, W[alter] W[ilson], 1932.1
Grey, Lady Jane, 1809.2; 1822.2-
    3; 1826.2; 1844.1; [1853].1;
    1863.3; 1883.4; 1908.6;
    1909.1; 1926.3

Hafner, Charles Yates, 1957.1
Hafner, Mamie, 1953.1
Hales, John, 1968.4
Hallam, George W., 1955.1
Hallam, Henry, 1837.2; 1855.1
Hall, Roger Schultz, 1940.1
handwriting, 1932.1; 1960.1;
    1962.1
Hatch, Maurice Addison, 1948.4
Hayes, Albert McHarg, 1934.2
Hazlit, W[illiam] Carew, 1888.2
H., E., 1822.2
Hebel, J[ohn] William, 1952.1

Hettler, Albert, 1915.2
Hexter, J. H., 1950.2
Higgins, Rachael Jennings, 1924.1
Histoire de Jane Grey, 1863.3
Histoire de l'éducation en Angle-
    terre . . ., 1896.1
Historical Point of View in Eng-
    lish Literary Criticism from
    1570-1770, The, 1913.4
History of Christian Education,
    1926.2
History of Classical Scholarship,
    A, 1908.4
History of Criticism and Liter-
    ary Taste in Europe . . ., A,
    1902.5
History of Education, 1899.3;
    1902.2
History of Elizabethan Litera-
    ture, A, 1887.1
History of English Literature, A,
    1902.3; 1918.2; 1926.1;
    1935.3
History of English Literature
    from "Beowulf" to Swinburne,
    1914.2
History of English Prose Rhythm,
    A, 1912.1
History of English Prosody from
    the Twelfth Century to the
    Present Day, 1908.3
History of the English Paragraph,
    The, 1894.1
History of the Worthies of Eng-
    land, The, 1840.2
Hoby, Thomas, 1948.1
Hodgson, Francis, 1809.2
Hoffman, C. Fenno, Jr., 1953.2
Hogrefe, Pearl, 1959.2
Holzamer, Josef, 1881.5
Hooker, Richard, 1912.1
Hornát, Jaroslav, 1961.2; 1970.4
Horsley, J. C., 1867.1
Howard, George, 1822.3
Hoyler, August, 1933.2
H., R., 1873.2
Hudson, Hoyt, H., 1952.1
"Humanism of Roger Ascham: A
    Quantitative Study of Clas-
    sical References in Ascham's
    Scholemaster, The," 1915.4

"Humanism of Toxophilus: a New
    Source, The," 1976.4
"Humanistic and Modern Educa-
    tional Theory in The Schole-
    master," 1935.4
"Humanistic Standards of Diction
    in the Inkhorn Controversy,"
    1976.5
"Humanistic Theory of Education,
    The," 1930.1
Humanist's "Trew Imitation":
    Thomas Watson's "Absalom"
    . . ., A, 1964.3
"Humanitas in Tudor Literature,"
    1949.2
Hunter, G. K., 1962.2
Hunt, Theodore, W., 1892.2
Hurd, Richard, 1871.2

imagery, 1973.4
"Imagery of Roger Ascham, The,"
    1973.4
Imaginary Conversations of Lit-
    erary Men and Statesmen,
    1824.1; 1826.2
imitation, 1935.5; 1968.3;
    1970.5; 1974.1; 1976.2
"Imitation: Getting in Touch,"
    1970.5
"Influence of Xenophon and Plato
    upon the Educational Princi-
    ples of Roger Ascham, As
    Shown in Toxophilus and The
    Scholemaster, The," 1940.1
inkhorn controversy, 1976.5
"Introduction," 1868.1; 1870.1;
    1888.1; 1898.2; 1934.3;
    1945.1; 1948.4; 1966.6;
    1967.2
Introduction to the History of
    Educational Theories, An,
    1881.3; 1905.4. See also
    1842.1
Introduction to the Literature
    of Europe in the Fifteenth,
    Sixteenth, and Seventeenth
    Centuries, 1837.2; 1855.1
Irvine, Helen Douglas, 1935.3
Isocrates, 1915.2-3; 1916.3;
    1974.5-6

"'Italianate' Englishman, The,"
1954.3
Italic Hand in Tudor Cambridge,
The, 1962.1

"Jane Grey, Tragédie en cinq
actes et en vers," 1844.1
John Lyly, 1905.8
John Lyly: The Humanist as
Courtier, 1962.2
John Milton at St. Paul's
School . . ., 1948.3
Johnson, Francis R., 1952.1
Johnson, Robert Carl, 1968.1
Johnson, Samuel, 1761.1; 1815.1;
1890.1; 1956.1
"Johnson's Edition of Roger
Ascham," 1956.1
Johnston, George Burke, 1973.2
"'Joncy,'" 1913.5
Jonson, Ben, 1974.1
Jusserand, [Adrien Antoine]
J[ean] J[ules], 1890.2;
1910.1; 1966.2

Kane, W[illiam Terrence], S.J.,
1935.2
Katterfeld, Alfred, 1879.1;
1883.2; 1900.3
Kelso, Ruth, 1929.3
Kemp, Ellwood L., 1902.2
Kinghorn, A[lexander] M[anson],
1971.1
Kingsley, Rose G., 1884.3
Kirsten, 1857.4
Krapp, George Philip, 1915.3

Labranche, Anthony, 1970.5
Lady Jane Grey [tragedy in ten
scenes], 1926.3
Lady Jane Grey, and Her Times,
1822.3
Lady Jane Grey, A Tale, in Two
Books, 1809.2
[Laird, Francis Charles]. See
Howard, George
Landor, Walter Savage, 1824.1;
1826.2. See also 1857.1
Lang, Andrew, 1914.2

Latimer, Hugh, 1912.1
"Latin Language Study as a Ren-
aissance Puberty Rite,"
1959.4
Laurie, Simon Somerville, 1892.3;
1903.2; 1905.5
Lawson, Sarah, 1976.1
Lectures on the History of Edu-
cation, 1892.5
Lee, L. M., 1966.3
Lee, Sidney L., 1885.1; 1886.3-4;
1908.2. See also 1886.1, 3
Legouis, Emile [Hyacinthe],
1914.3; 1926.1; 1935.3
Leicester, Earl of. See Dudley,
Robert
Leicester, Patron of Letters,
1955.2
"Lethrediensis," 1857.5
Letter Book . . ., A, 1922.2
"Letters of Roger Ascham, Com-
municated by John E. B.
Mayor . . .," 1859.2
Let Youth But Know; A Plea for
Reason in Education, 1905.2
Lewis, C[live] S[taple], 1954.1
Lewis, Edwin Herbert, 1894.1
Library of Literary Criticism of
English and American Authors,
The, 1901.4
"Life of Ascham," 1761.1
"Life of Ascham, The," 1864.1
Life of Lady Jane Grey, The,
[1853].1
Life of the Learned Sir John
Cheke, Kt. . . ., The,
1705.1; 1821.1
Literary Bypaths of the Renais-
sance, 1924.2
Literary History of England, A,
1948.2; 1967.1
Literary History of the English
People, A, 1910.1
Lives of Eminent and Illustri-
ous Englishmen, from Alfred
the Great to the Latest
Times, 1837.1
Lives of Northern Worthies,
1852.1

Locke, John, 1828.1; 1883.2;
1900.3; 1962.3
London University Press; Or
Remarks upon a Late Publication . . . "A Popular System
of Classical Instruction .
. .," The, 1828.1
Long, Percy Waldron, 1913.2
Lovett, Robert Morss, 1902.3;
1918.2
Lowndes, William Thomas, 1834.1;
1871.1
Lucky, George Washington Andrew,
1916.2
Lyly, John, 1904.4; 1905.8,
1913.2; 1916.1, 3; 1930.1;
1961.2; 1962.2; 1970.4;
1975.2
"Lyly's Anatomy of Wit and Asch-
cham's Scholemaster," 1961.2

McConica, James Kelsey, 1965.3;
1974.3
McCue, George Sutherland,
1935.4
Machiavelli, Niccolo, 1954.2;
1964.2; 1974.2
MacInnes, W. D., 1935.3
McKnight, George H., 1928.2
McShane, Mother Edith E., 1950.3
Manual of English Literature, A,
1879.2
Marique, Pierre J[oseph], 1926.2
Maxwell, J[ames] C[loutts],
1954.2
Mayor, J[ohn] E. B., 1854.2-3;
1859.2; 1862.3; 1863.4
Mead, Edwin D., 1884.3
Meissner, Paul, 1952.2
Memorials of the Most Reverend
Father in God Thomas Cran-
mer, 1694.1; 1840.3
Miglior, Giorgio, 1975.2
Miller, Edwin Haviland, 1959.3
Miller, Erma Esther, 1913.3
Miller, Florence Graves, 1930.1
Miller G[eorge] M[orey], 1913.4
Miller, William E., 1963.2

Milton, John, 1828.1; 1892.2;
1928.1; 1963.1
"Milton and Blank Verse in
Spain," 1963.1
Milton on Education: The Trac-
tate "Of Education" . . .,
1928.1
Mirror, The, 1842.1
"Mirrors for 'The Scholemaster':
Erasmus, Castiglione, Elyot,
Ascham, and the Humanistic
'Speculum,' The," 1971.2
"Misdated Letter of Roger Ascham,
A," 1979.1
Mitchell, Mary, 1926.3
Modern English in the Making,
1928.2
Monroe, Paul, 1907.1
Montaigne, Michel de, 1886.5;
1907.1. See also 1902.4
Moody, William Vaughan, 1902.3;
1918.2
Moore, J[ohn] L[owry], 1909.2;
1910.2
Moore Smith, G[eorge] C[harles],
1913.5
"Morals and Ethics in the Works
of Roger Ascham," 1953.1
Morehead, Ann Edmondson, 1974.4
More, Sir Thomas, 1904.4; 1959.2
Morison, Richard, 1879.1; 1963.4
Morley, Henry, 1878.3-4; 1879.2;
1883.3; 1892.4
[Morley, John], 1861.1
Moulton, Charles Wells, 1901.4
Mulcaster and Ascham: Two Eng-
lish Schoolmasters, 1899.2
Mulcaster, Richard, 1899.2;
1905.3
Mullinger, James Bass, 1884.4

Nannius, Peter, 1976.4
Nathan, Walter Ludwig, 1928.3
National Union Catalogue, Pre-
1956 Imprints, The, 1969.2
New and General Biographical
Dictionary, A, 1848.1

New and General Biographical
Dictionary; Containing an
Historical Account of the
Lives and Writings of the
Most Eminent Persons in
Every Nation . . ., A,
1751.1; 1784.1
New Cambridge Bibliography of
English Literature, The,
1974.3. See also 1941.1
New Encyclopaedia Britannica in
30 Volumes, The, 1975.1.
See also 1878.2; 1929.1
Newkirk, Glen Alton, 1966.4
Nine Days' Queen: Lady Jane
Grey and Her Times, The,
1909.1
"Note sur le style de Roger
Ascham dans The Scholemas-
ter," 1970.3
"Notices of some Early English
Writers on Education--Part
II," 1903.4
Nouveau Dictionnaire historique
et critique . . ., 1750.1
Nowell, Alexander, 1871.2
Noyes, Gertrude Elizabeth, 1937.1
Nugent, John Richard, 1932.2

"OED Oversight in Toxophilus,
An," 1976.1
Officina, vel Naturae Historiae
per Locos, 1911.1
"Of the Three Earliest Authors
in Our Vernacular Litera-
ture," 1832.1
"Old School-Master, An," 1881.2
Omond, T[homas] S[tewart],
1921.1
Ong, Walter J., S.J., 1959.4
Oration on the Life and Death of
Roger Ascham, 1576.1. See
also 1865.1
Orthographie in Roger Ascham's
"Toxophilus" und "Schole-
master" mit besonderer
Berüchsichtigung der für den
Volksismus sich ergebenden
Resultate, Die, 1889.3
Outlines of the History of Edu-
cation, 1916.2

Palumbo, Roberta, 1968.2
Parmentier, Jacques, 1896.1
Parks, George B., 1938.1; 1961.3
Parr, Catherine, 1963.3; 1965.3
Patrick, David, 1901.1
Patrick, J. Max, 1966.1
Patterson, Herbert, 1915.4
Paulus Aemilius, 1959.6
Payne, Joseph, 1892.5
Phelps, William Franklin, 1879.3
Phillips, Elias H., 1949.2
Pindar, 1918.3
Plagiarism and Imitation During
the English Renaissance,
1935.5
"Plaine and Sensible Utterance:
The Prose Style of Roger
Ascham, A," 1970.2
Plato, 1920.3; 1940.1; 1963.3;
1968.3; 1973.6; 1976.6
Platonismus in der englischen
Renaissance vor und bei
Thomas Elyot, 1920.3
Platt, James, Jr., 1905.6
Pliny the Second, 1900.3
Poetic and Verse Criticism of
the Reign of Elizabeth,
1891.1
Poetic Diction in the English
Renaissance from Skelton
through Spenser, 1941.2
Pollard, A[lfred] W[illiam],
1926.4
Polydore Vergil, 1959.6
Porter, H[arry] C[ulverwell],
1958.1
"Portrait of Ascham," 1857.5
Professional Writer in Eliza-
bethan England . . ., The,
1959.3
"Proposed Emendation in Ascham,"
1913.1, 6
Prose of the English Renaissance:
Selected from Early Editions
and Manuscripts, 1952.1
"Prose Style of Roger Ascham,
The," 1971.3
"Public and Private Ideal of the
Sixteenth Century Gentleman,
The," 1966.4

Quarterly Review, The, 1861.1;
1931.2
Queen Elizabeth's Schoolmaster,"
1884.3
Quest of Inquirie: Some Con-
texts of Tudor Literature,
A, 1973.1
Quick, Robert Herbert, 1868.2;
1886.5; 1902.4
Quintilian, 1908.4; 1963.3
"Quotations in Roger Ascham's
Scholemaster," 1862.3

Raab, Felix, 1964.2
Radford, Lewis B., 1931.2
Raven, Edward, 1922.2; 1975.2
Reaney, P[ercy] H[ide], 1957.2
"Recent Studies in Ascham,"
1980.1
"Recurrence and Renaissance:
Rhetorical Imitation in
Ascham and Sturm," 1976.2
Redgrave, G[ilbert] R[ichard],
1926.4
R[eed], A. W., 1941.1
Reformation and Reaction in
Tudor Cambridge, 1958.1
Reign of Elizabeth, 1558-1603,
The, 1936.1; 1959.1
Relative Constructions in Early
Sixteenth Century English .
. ., 1966.5
"Renaissance, The," 1967.1
Renaissance and English Human-
ism, The, 1939.1
Renaissance Hand-Writing: An
Anthology of Italic Scripts,
1960.1
Renaissance Prose in England .
. ., 1970.4
Report of . . . Germany. See
Ascham, Roger, works of
(discussions)
Review of Roger Ascham by Law-
rence V. Ryan, 1964.4-5;
1965.4
Review of The English Works of
Roger Ascham, edited by
William Aldis Wright, 1908.5
Review of The Dramatic Works of
John Lilly (The Euphuist)
. . ., 1861.1

Review of The Worthies of York-
shire and Lancanshire . . .
by Hartley Coleridge, 1835.1
Rhetoric and Poetry in the Ren-
aissance . . ., 1922.1
Rice, Judith Elaine, 1974.5
Rimbault, Edward F., 1861.2
Rise of English Literary Prose,
The, 1915.3
Roberts, T[homas], 1801.1
Robertson, Jean, 1965.4
Robinson, F. N., 1913.2
"Roger Ascham," 1842.1; 1861.2;
1886.1-4; 1905.1; 1920.1;
1931.2; 1949.1
Roger Ascham, 1880.1; 1963.3
Roger Ascham: A Concise Bibliog-
raphy, 1946.1. See also
1967.3
Roger Ascham als Pädagoge, 1900.3
"Roger Ascham and Cleanth Brooks:
Renaissance and Modern Criti-
cal Thought," 1972.1
"Roger Ascham and His Letters,"
1854.2
"Roger Ascham and His Relation
to Education," 1898.1
"Roger Ascham and Humanist Educa-
tion in Sixteenth Century
England," 1953.2
"Roger Ascham and Ioannes Ravis-
ius Textor," 1911.1
Roger Ascham and John Sturm,
1879.3
"Roger Ascham and Princess Eliza-
beth" [Plate], 1908.1
"Roger Ascham and Sir John Den-
ham," 1873.2
"Roger Ascham and the Regius
Professorships," 1956.2
"Roger Ascham as a Literary Fig-
ure in the Sixteenth Cen-
tury," 1913.3
Roger Ascham: ein englischer
Pädagog des XVI Jahrhun-
derts . . ., 1881.1
"Roger Ascham: ein Studie aus
dem Zeitalter der Königen
Elisabeth," 1892.1
"Roger Ascham--English Old and
New," 1892.2

"Roger Ascham: Father of School
    Method," 1899.2
"Roger Ascham: His Contribution
    to English Literature as
    Prose Writer and Literary
    Critic," 1968.2
Roger Ascham: la dottrina
    umanistica inglese e la
    sperimentazione nelle prosa
    letteraria intorno allo metá
    del cinquecento, 1975.2
"Roger Ascham, Margaret Rampston,
    and Salisbury Hall," 1957.2
"Roger Ascham, 1515-68," 1974.3
"Roger Ascham, 1946-1966,"
    1968.1
"Roger Ascham: 'Schedule,'"
    1905.6
Roger Ascham: sein Leben und
    seine Werke . . ., 1879.1
Roger Ascham: sein Stil und
    seine Beziehung zur Antike
    . . ., 1915.2
"Roger Ascham's Letters," 1854.3
"Roger Ascham's pädagogische
    Ansichten," 1883.2
Roger Ascham's Schulmeister,
    Einleitung, Übersetzung,
    und Commentar von Josef
    Holzamer, 1881.5
"Roger Ascham's Theory of His-
    tory Writing," 1959.6
"Roger Ascham's Toxophilus in
    Heroic Verse," 1959.5
"Roger Ascham's Toxophilus: The
    Rise and Fall of the Long-
    bow," 1977.1
"Roger Ascham's Troubled Years,"
    1966.8
"Roger Ascham, the Humanist,"
    1892.3
"Roger Ascham: The Perfect End
    of Shooting," 1969.1
Romano, John Rigoletto, 1968.3
Rope, H[enry] E[dward] G[eorge],
    1954.3
Rose, Hugh James, 1848.1
Rosenberg, Eleanor, 1955.2
Rosenzweig, Sidney, 1940.2

Rott, Jean, 1968.4
Rousseau, Jean, 1883.2
Rubel, Veré L[aura], 1941.2
Rushton, William Lowes, 1897.1
Russell, W[illiam] Clark, 1871.2
Ryan, Lawrence V., 1959.5;
    1963.3; 1967.2. See also
    1964.4-5; 1965.4
Rydén, Mats, 1966.5

Saintsbury, George, 1887.1;
    1898.3; 1901.5; 1902.5;
    1908.3; 1912.1; 1922.2
Salamon, Linda Bradley, 1971.2;
    1973.3-4
Salmon, David, 1905.6
Sandys, George, 1684.1
Sandys, John Edwin, 1908.4
Schelling, Felix E., 1891.1
Schirmer, Walter F., 1933.3
Schmid, Georg, 1892.6
Schmid, K[arl] A[dolf], 1892.6
Schoeck, Richard J., 1966.1, 6
"Scholarly Archer: A Study of
    the Humanism of Ascham's
    Toxophilus, The," 1968.3
Scholemaster, The. See Ascham,
    Roger, works of (discussions)
Scholz, A., 1872.1
"Schoolmaster: An Analytical
    Account of Ascham's School-
    master, The," 1836.1
Schoolmaster: Essays on Practi-
    cal Education, The, 1836.1
Schoolmaster in Comedy and
    Satire, The, 1894.2
Schoolmaster in Literature, The,
    1892.7
"Schoolmaster, or a Plain and
    Perfect Way of Teaching
    Children to Understand,
    Write and Speak the Latin
    Tongue, The," 1857.2
Schools of the Jesuits: Ascham,
    Montaigne, Rattich, Milton,
    1886.5. See also 1902.2
Schools, School-books, and
    School-masters . . ., 1888.2

Schott, Wilhelm, 1908.5
Schrinner, Walter, 1939.2
Schroeder, Kurt, 1920.3
Seeley, Levi, 1899.3
"Selected Pictures. From the
    Picture in the Collection of
    John Hick, Esq., Bolton.
    Lady Jane Grey and Roger
    Ascham," 1867.1
Shafer, Robert, 1918.3
Shakespeare an Archer, 1897.1
Shakespeare's "Histories": Mir-
    rors of Elizabethan Policy,
    1947.2 ; 1964.1
Shakespeare, William, 1897.1;
    1947.2; 1964.1
Sheppard, J[ohn] T[ressider],
    1927.2
Shorter Works in English Prose,
    1878.4
Short History of English Litera-
    ture, A, 1898.3
Short-title Catalogue of Books
    Printed in England, Scotland,
    & Ireland . . ., A, 1926.4
Shottrell, Robert, 1959.5
Sidney, Sir Philip, 1963.3;
    1970.6; 1974.1
Simon, Joan, 1966.7
Sinker, Robert, 1885.2
Sir John Cheke und der englische
    Humanismus, 1928.3
Sir Thomas More Circle: A Pro-
    gram of Ideas . . ., The,
    1959.2
"Sixteenth and Seventeenth Cen-
    tury Prose, Part I, Prose
    Before Elizabeth," 1970.1
"Sixteenth Century Critical
    Theory in England: Ascham,
    Sidney, and Bacon," 1970.6
Sketches of Longer Works in Eng-
    lish Verse and Prose . . .,
    1878.3
Skinner, Herbert Marshall,
    1892.7; 1894.2
Smith, Constance I., 1962.3
Smith, John Hazel, 1964.3-4;
    1966.8

Smith, William Ellsworth, 1977.1
Snell, F[rederick] J[ohn], 1905.7
"Some Ideas on Education Before
    Locke," 1962.3
Sophocles, 1927.2; 1963.3
Soumet, Alexandre, 1844.1
sources. See Ascham, Roger,
    sources
"Sources of the Euphuistic Rhet-
    oric, The," 1966.1
Specimens of English Prose
    Writers, from the Earliest
    Times to the Close of the
    Seventeenth Century, 1807.1
Spectator, The, 1905.1
Starkey, Thomas, 1948.1
Staton, Walter F., Jr., 1958.2;
    1959.6; 1964.5
Strachan, L[ionel] R[ichard]
    M[ortimer], 1913.6
Strozier, Robert M., II, 1970.6;
    1972.1; 1973.5
structure, 1973.5
Strype, John, 1694.1; 1705.1;
    1821.1; 1840.3
Studies in the History of Educa-
    tional Opinion from the
    Renaissance, 1903.2; 1905.5
"Study of Roger Ascham's Literary
    Citations with Particular
    Reference to His Knowledge
    of the Classics, A," 1937.1
"Study of the Vocabulary of Roger
    Ascham, A," 1935.1
Sturm, John, 1879.2; 1881.1;
    1963.3; 1968.4; 1974.6; 1976.2
style. See Ascham, Roger, style
"Style of Roger Ascham's Prose
    in The Scholemaster, The,"
    1933.4
Style, Rhetoric, and Rhythm:
    Essays by Morris W. Croll,
    1966.1
"Supplement to the Short Title
    Catalogue," 1933.1
Sweeting, Elizabeth J., 1940.3
Syllabus of Lectures on the His-
    tory of Education . . .,
    1902.1; 1904.2

Symmes, Harold S., 1903.3
Systems of Education: A History
    and Criticism . . ., 1889.2

Tannenbaum, Dorothy R., 1946.1;
    1967.3
Tannenbaum, Samuel A., 1946.1;
    1967.3
Taylor, I[da] A[shworth], 1908.6
    1930.2
Taylor, Ida Ashworth, 1908.6
Teachers' Guild Addresses and
    the Registration of Teachers,
    1892.3. See also 1905.5
Terry, F. C. Birkbeck, 1883.4
Test, George A., 1964.6
Textor, Ioannes Ravisius. See
    Tixier, Jean
Theoretische Stellungnahme der
    englischen Schriftsteller,
    Die, 1909.2
"Theory and Structure in Roger
    Ascham's The Schoolmaster,"
    1973.5
Thompson, Elbert N[evius] S[eb-
    ring], 1924.2
Thompson, Guy Andrew, 1914.4
Thought and Expression in the
    Sixteenth Century, 1920.4;
    1930.2
"'Three Guns,'" 1904.3
Times Educational Supplement,
    The, 1920.1
Tixier, Jean, Seigneur de Ravisi,
    1911.1
Tower of London: A Historical
    Romance, The, 1840.1
Toxophilus. See Ascham, Roger,
    works of (discussions)
"Toxophilus; The Schole of Shoot-
    inge," 1857.3
"Toxophilus, the Schole or Parti-
    tions of Shooting . . . by
    Thomas Marsh," 1822.1
Traditions of Civility: Eight
    Essays, 1948.1
Trésor des livres rares et
    précieux . . ., 1859.1;
    1950.1
Trousdale, Marion, 1976.2

Tudor Opinions of the Chivalric
    Romance . . ., 1950.3
Tudor-Stuart Views on the Growth,
    Status, and Destiny of the
    English Language, 1910.2
Turner, J[oseph] Horsfall, 1888.3
Two Great Teachers: Johnson's
    Memoir of Roger Ascham . . .,
    1890.1
Tyler, Moses Coit, 1879.2
Tytler, Patrick Fraser, 1839.1

Ueber Ascham's Leben und Schrift-
    en, 1857.4
Ueber Roger Ascham's Schoolmaster,
    1872.1
University Drama in the Tudor
    Age, 1914.1
University of Cambridge from the
    Royal Injunctions of 1535 to
    the Accession of Charles the
    First, The, 1884.4
"Unnoted Translation of Erasmus
    in Ascham's Scholemaster,
    An," 1977.2
"Utopian Ideals in English Prose
    of the Renaissance, The,"
    1932.2

"Varro," 1832.1
Vaughan, M. F., 1977.2
Verbalsyntax in Sir Thomas Elyots
    "Governour" mit vergleich-
    enden Beispielen aus Roger
    Aschams "Scholemaster," Die,
    1961.1
Vines, Sherard, 1930.3
Vives, Juan Luis, 1920.2; 1959.2
vocabulary, 1935.1
Vos, Alvin, 1971.3; 1974.6;
    1976.3-5; 1979.2

Wallace, John M., 1966.1
Wallenfels, A., 1880.1
Waller, A[lfred] R[aney], 1909.3
Walton, Isaac, 1906.1; 1929.1
Ward, A[dolphus] W[illiam],
    1909.3
Washingtons' English Home and
    Other Stories of Biography,
    The, 1884.3

Watson, Foster, 1903.4; 1908.7
Watson, George, 1974.3
Watson, Thomas, 1914.1; 1964.3
Watt, Robert, 1824.2
Weidemann, Gerhard, 1900.3
Whole Works of Roger Ascham,
    Now First Collected and Re-
    vised, 1864.1; 1865.1
Whimster, D[onald] C[ameron],
    1934.3
Whipple, T. K., 1916.3
White, Harold Ogden, 1935.5
"Whittlesford Rectory and the
    Ascham Family," 1931.1
Wille, Justus, 1889.3
"William Camden's Elegy on Roger
    Ascham," 1973.2
William Shakspere's Small Latine
    & Lesse Greeke, 1944.1
Wills, Richard, 1957.1
Wilson, Harold S., 1945.1
Wilson, John Dover, 1905.8
Wilson, Kenneth Jay, 1973.6;
    1976.6
Wilson, Thomas, 1976.5
Wodhoms, J. R., 1882.1
Woelk, Georg Konrad, 1908.8
Wolpe, Berthold, 1960.1
Wood, Anthony à, 1721.1; 1815.2
Wrangham, Francis, 1816.1
Wright, William Aldis, 1904.1;
    1905.1. See also 1908.5

Xenophon, 1940.1

Yorkshire Bibliographer, 1888.3
Youel, Donald Bruce, 1933.4